Debating Immigration

Debating Immigration presents 18 original essays, written by some of the world's leading experts and preeminent scholars, that explore the nuances of contemporary immigration and citizenship affecting the United States and Europe. The volume is organized around the following themes: philosophy and religion, law and policy, economics and demographics, race, and cosmopolitanism. Critical questions addressed include: What accounts for the disconnect between public attitudes about immigration and the policies produced by elected officials? Why has the United States not developed a well-articulated public philosophy of immigration? What does the Christian Bible have to say about immigration policy? What are our moral and social obligations to our fellow citizens, and do these trump our obligations to the world's poor? What accounts for the tendency to frame the immigration debate in the dichotomous terms of legal versus illegal and citizen versus noncitizen when our most pressing problems result from immigration itself and not from its legality or lack thereof? How does the European experience differ from the American situation? Given its past failures to integrate earlier waves of migrants, can Europe ensure the socioeconomic integration of new migrants?

Carol M. Swain is a professor of political science and a professor of law at Vanderbilt University. Before joining Vanderbilt in 1999, Professor Swain was a tenured associate professor of politics and public policy at Princeton University. Her highly acclaimed book, *Black Faces, Black Interests: The Representation of African Americans in Congress*, was named one of the seven outstanding academic books of 1994 by *Library Choice Journal*. It received the 1994 Woodrow Wilson Prize for the best book published in the United States on government, politics, or international affairs and the Hardeman Prize for best scholarly work on Congress during 1994–1995 and was the co-winner of the Key Award for the best book published on Southern politics. *Black Faces, Black Interests* has received three U.S. Supreme Court citations. Swain's more recent books are *The New White Nationalism in America: Its Challenge to Integration* and *Contemporary Voices of White Nationalism* (co-authored with Russ Nieli). Professor Swain's work on representation and race relations has earned her national and international accolades. She has appeared on numerous radio and television shows, including C-Span's *Washington Journal*, PBS's *News Hour with Jim Lehrer*, ABC *News, Fox News Live*, CNBC, *Tavis Smiley Show*, National Public Radio's *Morning Edition, Here and Now*, and *The Connection*.

Debating Immigration

Edited by

CAROL M. SWAIN
Vanderbilt University

CAMBRIDGE
UNIVERSITY PRESS

CAMBRIDGE UNIVERSITY PRESS
Cambridge, New York, Melbourne, Madrid, Cape Town, Singapore, São Paulo, Delhi

Cambridge University Press
32 Avenue of the Americas, New York, NY 10013-2473, USA

www.cambridge.org
Information on this title: www.cambridge.org/9780521875608

First published 2007
Reprinted 2007

Printed in the United States of America

A catalog record for this publication is available from the British Library.

Library of Congress Cataloging in Publication Data

Debating immigration / [edited by] Carol M. Swain.
    p. cm.
Includes bibliographical references and index.
ISBN-13: 978-0-521-87560-8 (hardback)
ISBN-13: 978-0-521-69866-5 (pbk.)
1. United States – Emigration and immigration. 2. European Union countries –
Emigration and immigration. 3. United States – Emigration and immigration –
Government policy. 4. European Union countries – Emigration and immigration –
Government policy. 5. Immigrants – United States. 6. Immigrants – European
Union countries. I. Swain, Carol M. (Carol Miller) II. Title.
JV6483.D423 2007
325.4–dc22   2006034143

ISBN 978-0-521-87560-8 hardback
ISBN 978-0-521-69866-5 paperback

Contents

About the Contributors

Linda Bosniak, professor of law at Rutgers University

Peter Brimelow, editor of VDARE.com, senior Fellow at the Pacific Research Institute, and columnist for CBS MarketWatch

Steven A. Camarota, PhD, research director for the Center for Immigration Studies

Elizabeth F. Cohen, assistant professor of political science at the Maxwell School of Citizenship and Public Affairs at Syracuse University

James R. Edwards, Jr., PhD, adjunct Fellow with the Hudson Institute

Amitai Etzioni, University Professor and director of the Institute for Communitarian Policy Studies at The George Washington University

Nathan Glazer, professor emeritus of sociology and education at Harvard University

Randall Hansen, associate professor of political science and Canada Research Chair in Immigration and Governance at the University of Toronto

Marc Morjé Howard, associate professor of government at Georgetown University

Stephen Macedo, Laurence S. Rockefeller Professor of Politics and director of the Center for Human Values at Princeton University

Douglas S. Massey, Henry G. Bryant Professor of Sociology and Public Affairs at the Woodrow Wilson School of Public and International Affairs at Princeton University

Noah Pickus, associate director of the Kenan Institute for Ethics and adjunct associate professor of public policy at the Sanford Institute of Public Policy at Duke University

Peter H. Schuck, Simeon E. Baldwin Professor of Law at Yale University

Peter Skerry, professor of political science at Boston College and nonresident senior Fellow at the Brookings Institution

Rogers M. Smith, Christopher H. Browne Distinguished Professor of Political Science at the University of Pennsylvania

Carol M. Swain, professor of political science and professor of law at Vanderbilt University and founding director of Veritas Institute

Jonathan Tilove, reporter, Newhouse News Service

Charles F. Westoff, professor of demographic studies and sociology, emeritus, at Princeton University

Preface

The origins of this volume lie in a conference I organized at Princeton University in January 2005 on the theme "Contemporary Politics of Immigration in the United States." With the sponsorship of the James Madison Program and the close assistance of program manager Reggie Feiner, we convened a diverse group of well-known activists, scholars, and journalists, most of whom had taken highly visible public positions on various aspects of immigration policy. Conference participants included Tamar Jacoby of the Manhattan Institute; Peter Brimelow of VDARE; Amitai Etzioni of George Washington University; Stephen Camarota of the Center for Immigration Studies; Stephen Macedo of Princeton University; Philip Kasinitz of the City University of New York; Jane Junn of Rutgers University; Ken Masugi of Claremont University; Rogers Smith of the University of Pennsylvania; Linda Bosniak of Rutgers University Law School; Elizabeth Cohen of the Maxwell School at Syracuse University; Lina Newton of Hunter College; Noah Pickus of Duke University; Peter Skerry of Boston College; and Charles Westoff of Princeton University.

Our group spent two days together grappling with some of the more troubling aspects of the current immigration situation in the United States. At the top of the list was the issue of the nation's estimated 11 million–14 million illegal aliens. Other topics treated included the history of American attitudes toward newcomers and the impact of large-scale immigration on current U.S. citizens, especially poor minorities. A major goal of the conference was to bring together people who rarely converse with each other and create a place where they could have a vigorous conversation that might allow them to find common ground on certain aspects of these issues. To their credit, the participants were cordial and civil to one another, even though they often had quite divergent viewpoints. What emerged from that conference forms the core of the following anthology, which examines from a variety of ideological perspectives the current realities and projections about immigration in the United States.

Some of our participants were unable to contribute chapters to the volume. In order to achieve balance and to ensure coverage of a number of issues not specifically addressed by the conference, including the biblical perspective on immigration and immigration's impact on certain historically disenfranchised groups, we invited Nathan Glazer of Harvard University; Randall Hansen of the University of Toronto; Marc M. Howard of Georgetown University; Peter Schuck of Yale University; James R. Edwards, Jr., of the Hudson Institute; and Jonathan Tilove of Newhouse News Service to contribute additional chapters. One of my own essays also appears here. The resulting volume is a timely, multifaceted interrogation of a highly visible and pertinent issue in contemporary America and one that includes the viewpoints of some of the most distinguished thinkers and activists in the world.

Acknowledgments

This book is a collaborative enterprise made possible through the support of several organizations and a number of good people. In particular, I want to thank Vanderbilt University for granting me a sabbatical leave and Princeton University for awarding me a research fellowship that made it possible for me to pursue the research and writing that have resulted in this publication. I am also indebted for the inspiration provided by the Veritas Institute, an organization I founded in 2003 to provide a forum for discussion of prominent public-policy issues by persons holding a broad diversity of views. During the spring of 2006, I was a Copenhaver Scholar at Roanoke College, and I want to thank the president, Sabine O'Hara, and the faculty for the opportunity to present my views on immigration. I am also grateful to Wheaton College for providing me with a similar opportunity to discuss immigration issues in a series of lectures.

Those who nurtured this venture are numerous. Foremost among those to whom I am especially grateful is Lew Bateman, my friend and editor at Cambridge University Press. Lew's unflagging support and his wise and steady guidance saw this project through to completion. Equally indispensable to the completion of this project has been the generous support of Robert P. George, director of the James Madison Program in American Ideals and Institutions at Princeton University. I want to thank Vanderbilt University Law School dean Ed Rubin, arts and sciences dean Richard McCarty, and my chair, Neal Tate, who were instrumental in granting my leave. I am also indebted for the timely and generous help provided by James F. Reische and for his magnanimous support at a critical stage in this project. My colleague Bill Keech, former Vanderbilt Law School dean

Kent Syverud, and Jane Delung, president of the Population Resource Center, are also thanked for their support.

I especially want to express my deep gratitude to the chapter contributors, who produced work of the highest quality and substance. Helpful comments and advice were provided at various stages by readers, including Julia Mitchell and Andrew Houchins at Vanderbilt Law School, Natalie Rink and Alexander LeRoy at the University of Utrecht, and Russ Nieli at Princeton University. Staff at Vanderbilt University who provided invaluable assistance include Emily Walker, Amy Nickens, Suzanne Wilson, Dorothy Kuchinski, and Renee Hawkins. I also want to thank the staff at Cambridge University Press for all their excellent work. Duanyi Wang, at Princeton University, has been with this project since its inception, and I am deeply grateful to her for notable oversight of the entire enterprise, her meticulous attention to every detail, and her patient and generous, collaborative good nature. Cyril Ghosh, at Syracuse University, consulted on the volume, providing invaluable editorial and research assistance. Lastly, I thank Reggie Feiner, my Jewish mother and co-conspirator in this and other adventures.

I

Introduction

Carol M. Swain

> [W]e are divided on the question of what principles should govern our efforts to control immigration. No policy set by Congress, or the Executive, or even the courts – though their interventions have affected policy deeply – now truly controls 'whom we shall welcome.'[1]

Harvard University professor Nathan Glazer wrote the statement above in the mid-1980s. It is as applicable today as it was back then. For more than 25 years, our nation has struggled with its immigration policy.[2] Whom should we admit? What rights and benefits do we wish to confer on them? What, if anything, do immigrants owe us in return? Often our best efforts to address the immigration issue have worsened matters.[3] One noted example of this occurred in 1964, when Congress ended the controversial Bracero farmworker program that it had established in 1942 to allow temporary workers from Mexico and a few other countries to live and work in the United States. This bold action was followed a year later by the passage of the Immigration and Nationality Amendments, which removed racial quotas for certain nations and increased the percentage of legal immigrants the nation would take in and the weight given to family reunification. Soon after these changes, illegal migration surged.

Figure 1.1 depicts the growth of legal immigration since 1965 and lists major legislative efforts. Congress has repeatedly tried to address the immigration problem, with mixed results. In 1986, Congress passed the Immigration and Reform Control Act (IRCA),[4] and four years later it passed the 1990 Immigration Act.[5] Next came the Illegal Immigration Reform and Immigrant Responsibility Act of 1996 (IIRIRA).[6] Each congressional act has brought negative unintended consequences, causing

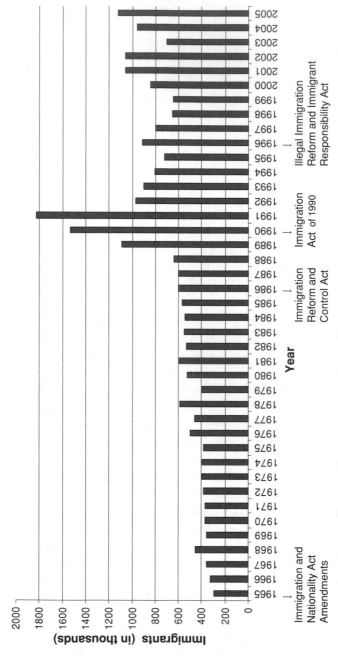

FIGURE 1.1. Legal immigration and congressional reform efforts. Includes July 1, 1975, to September 30, 1976, because the end date of fiscal years was changed from June 30 to September 30. *Source: 2005 Yearbook of Immigration Statistics,* available at http://www.uscis.gov/graphics/shared/statistics/yearbook/LPR05.htm.

what was once a regionally confined problem to spread across the nation and create major social and economic upheavals. Much of the illegal immigration is from Mexico. According to Douglas Massey, U.S. policy since 1986 has been a policy of contradictions (see Chapter 9, this volume). Rather than reducing illegal immigration, U.S. policies have made it less likely that illegal migrants from Mexico will return home of their own accord.[7]

The situation is dire. More than 11 million illegals live in the United States, and an estimated nearly 1,400 new illegals sneak across the border or overstay their visas each year. Illegals constitute 5 percent of the workforce. Many of the newest immigrants have entered the country with low skills and low levels of education during an era when federal resources for fighting poverty are shrinking. In many areas of the country, the sheer volume of new immigrants has created enormous drains on educational institutions, hospitals and clinics, jails and prisons, and the supply of low-income housing.

This collection presents original essays, written by some of the world's leading experts and preeminent scholars, that collectively explore the nuances of contemporary immigration and citizenship affecting the United States and Europe. Its contributors have taken widely differing approaches to the host of issues confronting policymakers and citizens on both sides of the Atlantic. This has led some of the writers to tackle issues rarely discussed in scholarly debates on immigration. The volume is organized around the following themes: philosophy and religion, law and policy, economics and demographics, race, and cosmopolitanism.

Many critical questions are addressed here: What accounts for the disconnect between public attitudes about immigration and the policies produced by elected officials? Why has the United States not developed a well-articulated public philosophy of immigration? What does the Christian Bible have to say about immigration policy? What are our moral and social obligations to our fellow citizens, and do these trump our obligations to the world's poor?

Additionally, what contending policy approaches should guide our discussions on immigrants and alienage? What accounts for the tendency to frame the immigration debate in the dichotomous terms of legal versus illegal and citizen versus noncitizen when our most pressing problems result from immigration itself and not from its legality or lack thereof? How have the terrorist attacks of September 11, 2001, affected the treatment of immigrants and the rights of American citizens? Why have our best efforts to control the border with Mexico failed?

What are the costs and benefits of mass immigration? Do immigrants take jobs from American workers? How does immigration affect projected population growth? Furthermore, what about race and ethnicity? Who, if anyone, represents the interests of African Americans in the immigration debate? Will Hispanic and Asian immigrants do more to help reshape American values and social structures than blacks ever did? What accounts for the unusual alliances that black politicians have forged that have caused some of them to turn a deaf ear to the plight of African Americans?

Finally, what is happening with citizenship and immigration issues in European nations – is there a democratic deficit around immigration policymaking in the United States as there is alleged to be in Europe? How does the European experience differ from the American situation? Given its past failures to integrate earlier waves of migrants, can Europe ensure the socioeconomic integration of new migrants? What can be done to ensure that the new migrants embrace the liberal democratic values presently institutionalized in European nations?

These are among some of the central questions addressed by contributors to this volume. These essays were written in the mid-2000s and are informed by the mass immigrant demonstrations of 2006, legislative debates in Congress, the enforcement efforts of the Department of Homeland Security, the national emphasis on border control and national security, and the war in Iraq. We include Europe because, on both sides of the Atlantic, wealthy nations share borders with poorer nations and find themselves endlessly battling illegal migration and unassimilated foreigners who reject the culture and values of the host nation. Dissatisfaction ensues. France has recently experienced violent rioting and destruction of property by angry Arab and African immigrants frustrated with their ghettos, substandard living conditions, and limited job opportunities. In Morocco, government officials have complained about a different kind of problem: leaders have accused nearby Algeria of promoting the illegal migration of Africans south of the Sahara Desert who use their country as a shortcut to more desirable European destinations. In the United States, 2006 brought large-scale public demonstrations in cities and towns across the nation.

A major strength of this volume lies in the willingness of its contributors to tackle such controversial issues as race and religion and the diversity of viewpoints and backgrounds they bring, as well as the breadth of approaches regarding the issues involved – approaches that range from economics, to demographics, to moral and religious perspectives.

Given the many anthologies on immigration, it is appropriate to explain why such a volume is needed. Race and religion have been neglected aspects of immigration debates, despite their centrality in the thoughts and policy preferences of many Americans. The impact of immigration on African Americans particularly is usually neglected in public debates and scholarly treatises. Similarly, most discussions of religion focus on the Catholic Church's more universal approach, while ignoring or belittling as racist any restrictionist viewpoints emanating from mainstream Protestants. This volume is a wholehearted effort to address these voids in public debate as well as in the scholarly literature and the popular press. It should be noted, however, that the contributors to this volume have widely differing views on a range of issues. We do not pretend to have definitive answers to the questions we raise; rather, it is our desire to stimulate an open and vigorous debate on the subject of immigration and citizenship, and we would like to see more public forums where opponents can get together and share their views as we have done here.

How did this volume come to be? My interest in the subject of immigration was piqued several years ago as I conducted research on the white nationalist movement in the United States. On the basis of that research, I published a book titled *The New White Nationalism in America: Its Challenge to Integration.* As one component of the study, I commissioned interviews with some key figures in what has variously been styled as the white nationalist, white protest, and white civil rights movement in America. I was interested in finding out about the background of these individuals, how they came to hold their views, and their positions on key race-related issues of the day. Repeatedly, the interviewees offered harsh commentary on the high level of legal and illegal immigration flowing into the United States from "third world nations" and the failure of the U.S. government to stem this tide – a development the interviewees perceived as a threat to Euro-American values and culture. Although many of the views expressed were openly racist, the respondents did not seem to care how critics might perceive them.

After listening to their arguments and watching events unfold in border states as the Minute Men and other militia groups formed, it became increasingly clear that a situation was developing in America in which the racist Right was framing the debate on serious and potent issues regarding immigration and naturalization. Although these issues are of great concern to many Americans, they have been largely ignored, and an open debate was suppressed by many people in the mainstream who feared being dismissed as racist. Accordingly, a very limited public discussion was being monopolized by a small minority on the racist Right. This was effectively silencing legitimate conversations that ought to be taking place in the public realm among more mainstream thinkers about the changing demographics of the nation and the continued existence and embrace of public immigration policies that many Americans believed placed the needs and concerns of new immigrants above those of the native-born.

My instincts about these issues were perhaps confirmed in November 2005, when I received an e-mail from a stranger whom I will here call Martha. Martha described herself as a 65-year-old white woman who had recently joined the California Minute Men, a group of citizens organized to help stem what Martha described as an invasion of her beloved country. Martha wrote me to lament the fact that a 15-year friendship with a black neighbor ended on the day that she asked her black friend to join her at the border. With horror, disdain, and anger, the black friend exclaimed, "I don't do anything to help white people." Martha was crushed. She is not a racist, she explained to me in her e-mail. She does not hate Mexicans – her husband of 23 years is Mexican American. Rather, her e-mail expressed rage at illegal immigration and at the failure of blacks to join the fight against it. After all, she argued, it is their country, too, that is being invaded.

Martha's frustration has risen to the point that she is willing to stay up all night patrolling the border in the belief, or hope, that her lone act, multiplied by the acts of several hundred others, might actually reduce illegal immigration. Her e-mail expressed fear about not wanting her children and grandchildren to be forced to learn Spanish in order to live and work in their own country. She decries the 14th Amendment's guarantee of citizenship by birth for those who entered the country illegally, and she laments the drain on local goods and services that she claims has even led hospital emergency rooms in Los Angeles to close. She ended her e-mail with the capitalized words GOD BLESS AMERICA.

Martha's fears might appear extreme, but they are not without foundation. Immigration is a growing and increasingly public concern in the United States today. The following review of immigration trends, including the contemporary immigrant protests and proposed legislative reforms, will illustrate the heightened significance of this topic.

THE IMMIGRANT PROTESTS OF THE 2000S

In the United States, hundreds of thousands of legal and illegal immigrants and their supporters engaged in mass protests during the spring of 2006.

These organized rallies have politicized other immigrants, brought about a greater sense of solidarity, and raised the national consciousness about illegal immigration and the enormous financial burden it imposes on many cities and towns around the nation. Breathtakingly large public demonstrations first occurred in April 2006, and then again on May 1, 2006, when organizers ratcheted up the stakes by arranging a national boycott called "A Day Without Immigrants," which was intended to bring the U.S. economy to a crawl. The impact of the boycott was minimal, but the new assertiveness made the issue one that members of Congress could no longer ignore, particularly after media images of angry protesters, many waving homeland flags, reached into the homes of formerly indifferent Americans. What was seen was an image of illegals that stood in direct contradiction to an earlier portrait of them as a frightened, docile people, cowering behind locked doors, never knowing if the next knock would bring deportation.

The initial politicization of illegal immigrants came with the Freedom Rides of October 2003 that mimicked the black Freedom Rides of the 1960s. Thousands of protesters traveled to Washington, D.C., to press their demands for better treatment. Many immigrants were upset about the perceived foot-dragging and promise-reneging on the part of President George W. Bush in his interactions with Mexican President Vicente Fox. What was once an auspicious climate for immigration reform changed overnight in the wake of the terrorist attacks of September 11, 2001. The attacks halted the momentum for creating a new guestworker program with Mexico and caused the nation to turn its attention to border control and national security.[8] The Department of Homeland Security was created to absorb various units of the Immigration and Naturalization Service (INS). Since October 2003, the increased visibility and assertiveness of illegals have caused a once-sleeping public to press their elected officials for action. Greater enforcement of existing laws has been demanded by the public, and in 2005 Congress passed the Real ID Act of 2005, which created restrictions on political asylum, increased enforcement mechanisms, restricted some due process rights, and imposed federal restrictions on state driver's licenses for immigrants, making it more difficult for illegals to procure and use certain types of documents for official purposes.

The protests have led to a backlash. Instead of making Americans more sympathetic to the immigrant cause, the mass protests may have had the unfortunate and unintended consequence of directing public attention to negative economic and social spillover effects such as the displacement

of American workers, drains on public services, and overcrowded housing. Within days of the April 2006 protest, the Department of Homeland
Security made headlines when it announced the arrest of 1,100 illegal
workers in a Texas pallet supply shop in Houston.[9] Since then, crack-
downs, arrests, and mass deportations have garnered regular headlines.

A March 2006 national survey, taken before the mass demonstrations
of April and May, showed Americans conflicted over the immigration
issue.[10] Fifty-two percent of Americans agreed that "immigrants today
are a burden on our country because they take our jobs, housing, and
healthcare." A majority of the public (also 52 percent) said that illegals
should be made to go home, and 40 percent of this group said they would
support a program that would allow illegals to stay temporarily in a
legal status. Almost half of all Americans would like to see increased
border patrols and tougher penalties for employers who violate the law
by hiring illegals. The least amount of enthusiasm (9 percent) was shown
for building walls along the border, and the most (76 percent) was shown
for a proposal to create a national database that employers could use to
check for employment verification and eligibility. Perhaps in recognition of
Congress's past failures to improve the situation, 56 percent of Americans
have expressed more confidence in local government's ability to reform
immigration than they have that President Bush (42 percent) and the major
political parties will do so. The Republican and Democratic parties earn
ratings of 45 percent and 53 percent, respectively, in answer to the question
of who is best suited to reform immigration.

Since the mass demonstrations, Hispanics are reporting a greater fre-
quency of ethnic discrimination. More than half of all Hispanics sur-
veyed (54 percent) by the Pew Hispanic Center said that they have seen
an increase in discrimination as a result of the policy debate. While there
may have been some backlash from the public, 63 percent of Hispanics
thought that the pro-immigration marches signaled the beginning of a new
social movement that would politically energize Hispanics and spur higher
Hispanic voter turnout.[11] Although some immigrants speak of the protests
with pride and believe they have helped their cause, public-opinion polls
and the passage of numerous restrictive laws and ordinances in cities and
states across the nation suggest otherwise. Moreover, the Southern Poverty
Law Center has reported a 33 percent rise in hate groups over the past
five years, citing Hispanic immigration as the single most important issue
driving the growth of racial hate groups.[12] This hostility was evident and
growing long before the protests.

It is interesting to note that as with other social movements, such as the women's and gay rights movements, the organizers of the immigrant rallies have borrowed heavily from the strategies and moral claims of the black civil rights movement and have used these in an attempt to silence critics. But the parallels are actually weak. Most illegal immigrants have willingly left their homelands to seek their fortunes in a more prosperous nation. They were not brought here in chains. They made a decision to enter another country without a formal invitation or entry visa. A significant proportion of blacks in the United States are the descendants of former slaves, whose civil rights movement was a struggle over the issue of basic human rights and human dignity, which were accorded to only a select few in the land of their birth. When illegal residents and their supporters demand more rights and privileges, in most cases they are not risking life and limb. Moreover, they benefit from lingering tensions between blacks and whites, and this enhances their status as a more favored group in the minds of mainstream, white, America.

IMMIGRATION PROPOSALS DEBATED BY THE 109TH CONGRESS

It has been more than 10 years since any major immigration legislation has emerged from Congress. Instead, the issue has been addressed piecemeal. However, bills that could radically restructure immigration are looming. In December 2005, the House of Representatives passed a restrictionist immigration bill (H.R. 4437) that many people see as punitive, although it seems to be in harmony with public wishes. The bill would have criminalized being in the country illegally, required the deportation of illegals, and imposed new penalties on employers and service providers who offered assistance to illegals. Bill H.R. 4437 is focused primarily on border security and employer sanctions. It provides no provisions for guestworkers or guidelines on what to do about the millions of illegals already working in the country and insisting on their right to remain. A hue and cry ensued following the passage of the bill. A few months later, the Senate passed a much more immigrant-friendly bill (S. 2611) that offered a tiered path to citizenship, a guestworker program, and a provision for more legal entrants. It also included a controversial provision that would require private and public employers to pay the prevailing wage to guestworkers on all construction projects. Opponents have argued that the latter provision would guarantee higher wages for immigrants than American workers receive for doing the same job.

As of August 2006, the House and Senate had made no efforts to reconcile differences between the two versions of the bill. House members and senators who were passionate about the issue took their respective cases directly to the public in a series of public hearings and forums scattered throughout the nation. Meanwhile, as Congress was haggling over the specifics of immigration reform, the states were actively passing legislation and ordinances. By July 2006, 30 states had passed 57 laws that dealt with some aspect of immigration reform. Although a few of these laws expanded benefits for noncitizens, the vast majority made it more difficult for illegal immigrants to receive government benefits such as unemployment, driver's licenses, employment in government-funded projects, and gun permits.[13] Aggressive actions by state and local governments are likely to continue until Congress offers some real leadership on the issue.

There are slight differences here in the approaches of Democrats and Republicans. Both groups would like to gain the votes of the new immigrants, but Republicans have an additional incentive: to continue to provide cheap, docile labor for big business and for middle-class families who can now afford nannies, gardeners, and cooks. Democrats would like to see a liberal bill passed that includes a guestworker program and a path to citizenship because they believe the immigrants will eventually support their political party.

Congress has not been much of a leader on this issue. In the heat of the 2006 fall elections, Congress passed and President Bush signed into law a new immigration bill authorizing the construction of a fence along parts of the Mexican border.[14] Of course, this new fence is a mostly symbolic gesture that will not solve the problem of illegal migration. It is a band-aid remedy consistent with the piecemeal approaches of the past. The magnitude of the problem and the changing demographics of the nation cause one to wonder when legislators and Supreme Court justices will finally get around to removing obvious sources of ethnic and racial conflict, such as race-based affirmative action, which makes little sense in a nation as diverse as the United States. It seems more appropriate to make affirmative action contingent on demonstrated need, with benefits limited to native-born Americans. Much discrimination still exists in the United States. However, one can argue that other legislative measures, including vigorous enforcement of Titles VI, VII, and IX of the civil rights legislation of the 1960s, can be used to address the ongoing discrimination related to race, alienage, and gender.

A part of our problem comes from the failure of our national leaders to articulate a clear public philosophy of immigration. Elizabeth

Cohen argues in Chapter 3 of this volume that this is mainly because our understanding of citizenship has been focused inward. According to Cohen, a philosophy of citizenship for native-born minorities and immigrants is conceptually distinct. Immigration has not received the systematic scrutiny accorded to other elements of citizenship, such as race. In our focus on racial issues, we have missed forms of discrimination connected with nationality and foreignness. Moreover, policymakers have not been courageous enough to acknowledge the truth pointed out by Noah Pickus and Peter Skerry (see Chapter 7, this volume) that the major issue confronting the nation is much bigger than what to do about illegal immigration. The major issue is immigration, period. These authors decry the muted conversations taking place around the issue of immigration and the reluctance of scholars and policymakers to acknowledge both the problem and the mounting and increasingly visible public outrage.

CONCLUSION

The American public deserves better representation on immigration than it has received from Washington and from other elites in positions of power and decision-making roles. Whatever reforms are initiated must take into account the needs and desires of native-born Americans. Presently, elites in both major political parties have largely ignored the concerns of the people. But federalism appears to be working. Since 2006, there have been a spate of immigration laws and ordinances passed in states and cities around the country. It has become increasingly clear that many ordinary people, like my e-mail correspondent Martha, do not trust the government in Washington to do right by them.

The Christian leadership is torn over the issue, with Catholic bishops and cardinals typically expressing a universal approach that leans heavily toward open borders for the world's poor – many of whom are Catholic. Perhaps more common is the Protestant view, passionately delineated by James R. Edwards, Jr. (see Chapter 4, this volume), which uses scripture from the Old and New Testaments to make the case for civil authorities to legitimately act to protect the interests of citizens from threats to their well-being that might emanate from unrestricted immigration.

A number of important policy issues related to immigration are not being considered because too many individuals in positions of power and influence have allowed themselves to be silenced by the threat of name-calling. These issues include birthright citizenship to the children of illegals, racial and ethnic preferences for the foreign-born and their offspring, blatant selective enforcement of immigration laws, and outright discrimination against immigrants from disfavored parts of the world. Moreover, immigrant-supporters do themselves and their country a disservice when they fail to consider all aspects of the problem and the national obligations to historically disadvantaged groups such as Native Americans, African Americans, poor whites, and legal Hispanics and Asians who struggle to get ahead in sometimes adverse circumstances. Further disservice emerges when groups are encouraged to cling to group identities, old-world languages, and cultural practices condemned by "civilized" society. A better tactic would include encouraging immigrants to become fully American by learning the language and the history of the host nation, where most will be embraced with open arms.

OVERVIEW OF THE BOOK

This volume is divided into five parts. Part I focuses on philosophy and religion. Here, Peter Schuck argues that there is a "political disconnect" between public attitudes and policy on immigration, which is reflected in restrictionist public attitudes but expansive public policies toward immigration. Elizabeth Cohen addresses why the United States, despite having a history as an immigrant-receiving nation, has failed to produce a well-articulated public philosophy of immigration. And James Edwards, Jr., draws upon his perspective as a Christian congressional staffer to outline the principles that he believes should guide immigration policy. According to him, the Bible and Judeo-Christian ideology place emphasis on the authority of civil government to preserve the rule of law and defend nations against invasion. Stephen Macedo discusses the moral issues surrounding immigration in the United States and elsewhere. After discussing the debate between a "cosmopolitan" viewpoint that promotes shared citizenship and a universal obligation of distributive justice and a "civic obligations" viewpoint that argues for the existence of special obligations among citizens, Macedo rejects the cosmopolitan view and argues that Americans have special obligations as members in a self-governing political community to prioritize the needs of the poorest Americans rather than the global impoverished.

Part II addresses law and policy. Linda Bosniak outlines contending policy approaches and observes that current policy debates about the status of undocumented immigrants concern both immigration and alienage. Noah Pickus and Peter Skerry argue that dichotomous terms such as legal–illegal and citizenship–noncitizenship, in which the immigration debate has been framed, are misleading and inhibit creative public policy. Rogers Smith observes that in the wake of 9/11 and national security concerns, there has been a renewed legitimacy for discriminatory policies toward immigrants and reductions in immigrant legal rights. The focus on security has reduced due process rights for immigrants and endangered the rights of American citizens.

Part III presents essays related to demographic and economic issues. Douglas Massey argues that the United States has followed a politics of contradiction in its relations with Mexico. This policy has backfired. Rather than reducing illegal immigration, U.S. immigration policies have transformed what was once a circular pattern of itinerant male workers affecting 3 states into a settled population of families in 50 states. Steve Camarota uses census data to show immigrant employment gains and native losses between 2000 and 2004. Camarota shows a direct relationship between unemployment of native-born workers and increases in the immigrant population. Peter Brimelow challenges the notion that immigration provides widespread benefits to the U.S. economy. According to Brimelow, immigration has had some impact on increasing the U.S. output in terms of sheer population size and an increase in the workforce, but this increase has not led to any actual benefit to the economy. Charles Westoff focuses on the magnitude and numerical implications of current rates of immigration on population growth and demographics of the U.S. population. Despite slowdowns in the U.S. economy and increasing unemployment of immigrants, immigration in recent years has continued to increase. There has been a shift from immigrants of European origin to those from Latin America and Asia. There is also an increasing trend toward more female immigrants, which increases the likelihood of permanent settlement.

Part IV deals with issues of race and ethnicity. Carol Swain examines the Congressional Black Caucus's record on immigration, raising the question of who best represents the interests of African Americans. Amitai Etzioni contends that Hispanic and Asian immigrants may rehabilitate American society by restoring a communitarian balance by fostering stronger commitment to family, community, and moral values. These groups are industrious and are less inclined than blacks to view themselves as victims. Jonathan Tilove argues that immigration is transforming America in terms of race and that, at the leadership level, black civil rights leaders have been aligned with leaders of immigrant communities, which seems odd because Hispanic and Asian immigrants may have helped to further marginalize blacks.

Part V turns its attention to how European nations are dealing with immigration under some of the same constraints as the United States. Marc Morjé Howard addresses the new reality facing European Union countries that now include significant minority populations with the legal right to remain in the country. After discussing citizenship, Howard develops a defense for national citizenship, even in an age of globalization. Finally, Randall Hansen explores the impact of welfare, work, and migration in Europe and the United States. Here, he shows us how integration into the host country might be contingent upon such factors as welfare policies of the country and common identity and common values. In some European countries, unlike in the United States, immigrants find it more lucrative not to find jobs and to live off welfare provisions – thus impeding the process of integration.

The volume concludes with some observations from Nathan Glazer, who has spent many decades studying issues related to immigration and ethnic politics. Glazer points out the significance of the volume in its treatment of the ethical and moral bases for immigration policy and also the importance of paying attention to history, race relations, and the disconnect between elite policy and public wants in the study of immigration policy.

PART I

PHILOSOPHY AND RELIGION

2

The Disconnect between Public Attitudes and Policy Outcomes in Immigration

Peter H. Schuck

Immigration law and policy exhibit a deep structure that shapes them at every turn and that catches my attention every time I teach about immigration or discuss it with my friends and with other scholars in the field. The structure is this: the political economy of immigration is far more one-sided and expansionist than the public attitudes toward immigration, and this is even more true of immigration law scholarship. That is, almost all of the significant political interest groups in the United States with an interest in immigration policy, and almost all immigration law scholars, advocate very strongly in the direction of maintaining an expansive immigration policy – and the policy outcomes testify to their success. Finally, and perhaps needless to say, the principal lawyers' organizations in this field – the American Bar Association and the American Immigration Lawyers Association – also favor expansion.

In contrast, the general public evidently favors – and has always favored, as far as one can tell from opinion surveys[1] – either more restrictive immigration policies or at least no further expansion of immigration. As a shorthand, I call this discrepancy between restrictive or status quo public attitudes and expansive policy outcomes a "political disconnect." In this chapter, I shall describe this disconnect and the immigration-specific political economy that I believe largely explains it, concluding with some brief reflections on the phenomenon.

Let me define my terms. By an expansive immigration policy, I mean both (1) a law that admits a number of legal permanent residents (more than 1.12 million in 2005) and temporary visitors or "nonimmigrants" (3.8 million on a typical day in 2004) that is relatively large in world- and American-historical terms, and (2) a policy that tolerates (for want of a better word) the long-term presence, if not de facto permanent residence, of a number of undocumented immigrants (an estimated 11 million–12 million in 2006) that is also very large in historical terms. For example, most estimates for the mid-1980s, when the last general amnesty was enacted, placed the number of the undocumented in the 5 million–6 million range. Note that I use the word "policy" here in a special sense, referring not to official pronouncements about the government's expressed goals, which of course firmly oppose illegal immigration, but rather to its actual behavior in deciding how to deploy its limited enforcement resources, which in fact inevitably results in a certain (high) level of such immigration.[2]

The political economy of almost any issue of significant public concern consists of interests that are starkly opposed to one another, and usually opposed from more than two directions. In the last few decades, many factors have combined to increase and diversify the number of interests affected (and affected *differently*) by public policies – factors such as rapid technological change, increased foreign trade and global competition, the decline of private-sector labor unions, a better-educated and more diverse population, the differentiation of product and service markets, the proliferation of the nonprofit sector, and many others. The classic struggles between warring interests – for example, capital versus labor, rural versus urban, importers versus exporters, agriculture versus industry, producers versus consumers, military versus civilian, national versus local, ethnoracial majorities versus minorities – have largely gone the way of carbon paper and Studebakers. Those traditional dualisms no longer capture (indeed, they usually conceal) the actual dynamics of today's far more complicated political pluralism.

Immigration politics is, of course, complicated. What strikes me as unusual and important, however, is the extent to which almost all of the many vectors of immigration politics, except unorganized public opinion, converge to press for more expansionist policies – that is, more legal immigrants and less systematic removal of undocumented ones. But before I discuss this political disconnect – restrictionist public attitudes coupled with expansive public policies – let me be clear about what I am *not* saying.

First, I am not asserting that this kind of disconnect is unique to immigration policy. Indeed, every public-policy domain I can think of exhibits some tendency toward disconnection. This primarily reflects the political inertia that tends to buttress even an undesirable status quo. The difficulty of altering any policy once it is in place is especially true of those policies embedded in legislation or court rulings (particularly constitutional ones). I am also not saying that a political disconnect is always socially undesirable. Indeed, the contrary is often true. As one who supports an expansive immigration policy, I believe that the political disconnect in this area has benefited American society by fostering more – and more wealth-enhancing – immigration than our people say they want at any particular point in time.

To cite another example, it has been said that if the American people were to vote today on the Bill of Rights, they would reject much of it, including some of our most precious liberties. In any case, these examples remind us that the public in a democracy is not always wise and that there is an important role for leadership by political elites or others who may possess a larger, longer-term, better-informed, or more penetrating view of the public interest. George Washington famously praised the Senate as the saucer that cools the coffee; he recognized that a sound democratic polity needs some institutions that use deliberation, temporizing, compromise, and other techniques to help regulate and moderate spasmodic public passions.

Furthermore, I am not saying that just because a political disconnect – such as immigration policy – has led to some policy outcomes in the past that I and many others favor, this will necessarily continue to be so. I shall return to this point in my conclusion.

PUBLIC ATTITUDES ABOUT IMMIGRATION

With these preliminaries out of the way, I now turn to a discussion of the distinctive political disconnect in immigration policy. Writing in 1997, I summarized the then existing survey evidence on public attitudes toward immigration as follows:

Americans like immigrants more than they like immigration, favor past immigration more than recent immigration, prefer legal immigrants to illegal ones, prefer refugees to other immigrants, support immigrants' access to educational and health benefits but not to welfare or Social Security, and feel that immigrants' distinctive cultures have contributed positively to American life and that diversity continues to strengthen American society today. At the same time, they overwhelmingly resist any conception of multiculturalism that discourages immigrants from learning and using the English language.

... Americans treasure their immigrant roots yet believe that current immigration levels are too high. Anxiety about immigration, it seems, is aroused by the newer immigrant groups, a bias that a 1982 Gallup poll places in a revealing historical light. When asked about its views on the contributions of particular immigrant groups, the public gave the highest scores to precisely the groups that had been widely reviled in the nineteenth and early twentieth centuries; the lowest scoring groups were the newer arrivals (in 1982 Cubans and Haitians). Professor Rita Simon has captured this ambivalence in an arresting metaphor: "We view immigrants with rose-colored glasses turned backwards."

... When viewed over time, however, the polling evidence suggests that in attitudes toward immigration as in so many other areas, the more things change, the more they stay the same. The public, it appears, has *always* thought that the immigration levels of their day were too high. Over the course of the past fifty years, Americans asked (in slightly different formulations) whether immigration levels should be increased, reduced, or kept the same have responded in remarkably similar ways. During that period, only 4–13 percent have favored an increase, while 33–66 percent have favored a decrease, and 27 percent preferred no change. The trend in attitudes has been toward greater negativity. In 1965, the percentage favoring reduced immigration began rising steadily until the late 1970s, then rose more sharply until the mid-1980s, then declined somewhat for several years, fluctuating until the early 1990s when it again rose sharply. Since about 1980, this attitudinal trend has traced the trend in the unemployment rate very closely. Hence attitudes can and do change abruptly.

One might expect restrictionist attitudes to have increased in the nine years since I wrote this. After all, both legal and illegal immigration levels since 1997 increased dramatically even as unemployment levels rose and post–9/11 security anxieties prompted new, often indiscriminate concerns about immigration. Yet although restrictionism is still the most common public attitude by far, it has declined significantly since 1995. In June 2006, the Gallup organization reported that 39 percent of respondents wanted lower levels of legal immigration, 42 percent wanted it to stay at current levels, and 17 percent wanted it increased. Interestingly, Hispanic respondents seem to be more restrictionist with respect to Latin American immigrants than are Americans generally.[3] At the same time – and confirming the findings in my quoted excerpt – 67 percent thought that immigration was a good thing for the country.[4] For purposes of exploring the political disconnect in immigration policy, however, the relevant statistic is that 81 percent of Americans oppose higher immigration[5] – a level of opposition that contradicts the thrust of immigration's political economy, which is decidedly expansionist, as I shall show.

In thinking about and characterizing these public attitudes toward immigration, some distinctions are in order. I argued in 1997, and remain convinced, that *nativism* and *xenophobia* are not significant factors in American politics today. The vast majority of Americans are what I call *principled restrictionists* and *pragmatic restrictionists*. The main difference is that principled restrictionists (the group Federation for American

Immigration Reform, or FAIR, for example)[6] believe that immigration poses a threat to their goals or values that is inherent in the nature and fact of immigration, while pragmatic restrictionists (many social scientists, for example) view such conflicts as contingent and changing, not inevitable.

Pragmatic restrictionists tend to think, for example, that the actual effects of immigration on population, the environment, national unity, cultural consensus, and so forth are all empirical questions whose answers depend on the interaction of a variety of factors. They do not oppose immigration in principle or in general. They may even be prepared to support it if they can be persuaded, for example, that immigrants actually create jobs rather than take them away from native workers, that they are mastering the English language without undue delay, and that they do not exploit the welfare system, commit too many serious crimes, or otherwise threaten social cohesion. Although certain labor unions, taxpayer organizations, and other interest groups may have closed their minds on these factual questions, the pragmatist remains open – at least in theory – to persuasion by contrary evidence.

Most Americans, I suspect, are pragmatic restrictionists, although one cannot be certain. That is, their assumptions about immigration lead most Americans to favor lower levels, but they are open to argument and evidence about what those levels should be and about what immigration's actual effects are. Thus their views about the wisdom and level of restriction are amenable to change, although perhaps not easily.[7]

One more wrinkle in public attitudes toward immigration should be mentioned, one that surely contributes to the Janus-like quality of these attitudes. Migration that is illegal but that brings willing workers together with willing employers to produce shared wealth and no obvious, clearly identifiable victims can plausibly be seen by people as a kind of victimless crime. Presumably, many Americans and politicians do in fact think of illegal immigration in this way – even as they affirm the value of the rule of law and the need to control illegal migration. This way of thinking about undocumented workers is simply another aspect of the ambivalent attitudes described earlier. Such attitudes surely complicate how the public perceives both the illegal migration problem and the agency charged with solving it. In addition, these attitudes surely affect how enforcement officials perceive their role, which in turn might help to explain some of the immigration agency's notorious pathologies – its randomness, low morale, arbitrariness, inconsistency, incompetence, illegality, and political vulnerability.[8] More to my point here, this mix of attitudes may also help to explain why the public tolerates a more expansionist immigration policy than it says it wants.

POLITICAL ECONOMY AND POLICY OUTCOMES

Let us turn now to the political economy of immigration and the policy outcomes that it produces. The Immigration Act of 1990 was the most recent major effort to overhaul the basic structure of legal immigration.[9] In my study of the political history of the 1990 law, I documented a legislative dynamic in which expansionist forces overwhelmed those that favored either restriction or the status quo.[10] The triumph of immigration expansion in 1990, moreover, was doubly impressive in that it occurred during an economic recession (traditionally conducive to restriction) and at a time of strong opposition to even limited immigration in virtually all other democratic states.

The interest groups that pressed in the late 1980s both for more legal immigrants and for amnesties or other bars to removal of illegals continue to do so. Perhaps the most important of these groups is growers, whose demand for agricultural labor seems inexhaustible and whose prosperity is vital to the economies and political establishments in many of our states, including the most populous ones (e.g., California, Texas, Florida, and New York). These interests, of course, were the main impetus for the large (and fraud-ridden) legalization program for undocumented agricultural workers adopted in the Immigration Reform and Control Act of 1986 (IRCA), and they are the strongest supporters of the Bush administration's proposals for new amnesty and guestworker programs, particularly those targeting Mexican laborers.

Many other business and university-related groups depend increasingly, and in some cases almost entirely, on immigration for their workforces. At the high-skill end is the computer software industry and a large number of other high-tech employers who look abroad for programmers, engineers, researchers, and other specialists to augment the domestic workforce through the H-1B and other "temporary" visa programs, which in fact provide a majority of those who later qualify for green cards in the United States. (In 2005, 66 percent of all legal immigrants were already in the United States when they gained permanent legal residence.)[11] American hospitals chronically depend on foreign doctors and nurses to staff their wards, and many universities look to foreign graduate students to help conduct research and to teach undergraduates. At the lower end, foreign nannies help to free up American mothers to return to the paid workforce, and hotels and restaurants rely heavily on immigrants, often undocumented ones, to perform jobs that American workers are said (controversially) to be unwilling to do.

Ethnic groups are also major, and often effective, proponents of immigration. In the case of the Immigration Act of 1990, the Irish were particularly important advocates, possessing some uniquely valuable political advantages (including Senator Ted Kennedy and Congressman Bruce Morrison) and succeeding in getting the adoption of an Irish-friendly lottery awarding a large number of "diversity" visas.[12] But other groups, including Jewish, Hispanic, and Asian organizations, also lobbied effectively for more visas and lower admission barriers. Today, with immigrants filling the pews of Catholic, evangelical, and other churches and synagogues in the United States and reinvigorating religious communities in many urban areas, the ethnic coalition seeking to expand immigration has grown more powerful.

Another important lobby pushing the 1990 immigration expansion consisted of a variety of groups that sought to ease the standards for asylum seekers, ideological dissidents, and victims of human rights abuses. The influence of such organizations has only grown with time. The Bush administration has been particularly responsive to claims about the oppression of religious minorities in the third world. Tragically, there is no dearth of injustices that galvanize these groups to press for expanded protection of those minorities through migration to the United States today.

Against this politically influential army of expansionist interests, who and where are the restrictionists? Traditionally, opposition to immigration came primarily from nativist and xenophobic organizations, but today such groups are few and far between and, where they exist, they operate underground. Environmentalists, concerned about immigrants' relatively high fertility rates, have sometimes worried about the effect of immigration on natural resources, wildlife, and human ecology in the United States. Environmental groups, however, tend to be ideologically liberal and inclusive, which tends to neutralize whatever anti-immigration propensities they might otherwise harbor. Exemplifying this struggle are the periodic debates within the Sierra Club, the oldest and most iconic of environmental groups, over what its position on immigration should be. So far, the restrictionists have lost, thus limiting the organization's potential as a political counterforce to the dominant expansionists.

Black civil rights organizations, another traditional opponent of immigration, have also been neutralized by their political liberalism and by their tactical alliances with Hispanic and other pro-immigrant groups to secure their cooperation on other issues. As I show, this occurred during the political jockeying that led to the 1990 law, when black groups felt obliged to support the forces pressing for a broad amnesty for undocumented workers.[13]

Public officials in immigrant-receiving states and localities, which bear a disproportionate share of the costs of social services required by low-skilled immigrants, have sometimes called for restrictions on immigration, but their loudest complaints have tended to be about criminal aliens rather than about immigrants generally.[14] As to the latter, officials' opposition has usually been muted, focusing on the federal government's failure to control the borders and to defray the local costs of this failure. The principal reason for this has been the political difficulty of opposing immigration, even of the undocumented, without alienating the significant group of voters in high-immigration states or localities who for ethnic loyalty, economic dependence, or other reasons support immigrants' rights. The most prominent example of this dilemma was that California governor Pete Wilson's Pyrrhic victory in his campaign for Proposition 187 in 1994 turned out to be a political disaster both for him and for his party.[15]

Recently, however, some state and local governments have become quite aggressive in challenging the federal government's weak enforcement efforts. In the first half of 2006 alone, encouraged by the public's growing impatience with illegal migration and the debates in Congress over new legislation, more than 500 immigration-related bills were introduced in state legislatures, and 57 of them were enacted in 27 states. Many of these local initiatives, moreover, are occurring in small towns and suburbs far from the borders. One such effort, in Hazleton, Pennsylvania, received national press coverage. This initiative would revoke permits for businesses employing undocumented workers, fine landlords who rent to them, and make English the city's official language. Some of the new laws would bar public spending on social services for the undocumented, involve state and local police in immigration enforcement, and mandate other sanctions.[16] It is not clear, however, whether these laws are even constitutional – they seek to regulate in an area over which the federal government has long had plenary power[17] – much less how effective they will be. Nevertheless, they testify to the intensity of local concerns, which are likely to affect congressional politics surrounding these issues.

Up until very recently, the most important group opposing immigration was organized labor, which viewed immigrants as low-wage competitors for their members' jobs and a brake on wage growth. Even in the run-up to the 1990 law, however, the unions found themselves in a compromised position. Significantly, labor did not seek to limit family-oriented admissions; to the contrary, it sought to expand them despite the fact that those entering under family visas are more likely to compete for the jobs that the unions covet than those entering under employment visas, who are (especially after the 1990 act) more highly skilled workers. Indeed, workers admitted as family members need not even obtain labor certifications. "The unions fight over fewer than 200,000 worker slots," Congressman Bruce Morrison (who managed the legislation in the House) noted, "but they support the more than 500,000 slots for family members, refugees, and ethnic diversity."[18] Indeed, a decade later, the AFL-CIO reached a turning point in its position on immigration, voting to support legalization of the undocumented in the hopes that this would make them easier to organize, improve their economic well-being, and strengthen the government's enforcement of labor standards for all workers. The Service Employees International Union, a large group that broke away from the AFL-CIO in 2005, supports an amnesty for the undocumented.

The political economy of immigration policy, then, turns out to be decidedly expansive in both senses of the term described at the outset. Even the reckless and unfair provisions of the Illegal Immigration Reform and Immigrant Responsibility Act (IIRIRA) should not obscure a fundamental fact about immigration politics: challenges to the high levels of *legal* immigration set in the 1990 law, including the Jordan Commission's proposal to reduce legal admissions by more than one-third, have all failed. Tough on undocumented and criminal aliens, skeptical toward asylum seekers, and arbitrary and inflexible on deportation hardship cases, the IIRIRA had only one significant direct effect on other law-abiding immigrants: to raise their sponsors' income requirements. Indeed, in the years after IIRIRA, Congress greatly increased the quota for temporary high-skilled foreign workers, many of whom predictably will later adjust their status to that of permanent resident. Although it later reduced that quota by two-thirds, Congress is likely to amend the law to restore, or even exceed, those earlier high levels.

Perhaps the best evidence of the strength of today's pro-immigration political consensus lies in Congress's treatment of two categories of aliens: those who are undocumented and those who are in prison for nonimmigration crimes committed in the United States. Targeting these two groups, of course, is the moral, political, and policy equivalent of attacking motherhood and apple pie. Yet although the undocumented, whether surreptitious border crossers or out-of-status visa violators,[19] have broken our law and have no right to be in the United States, the powerful pro-immigration lobby has convinced Congress to let them remain. In addition to legalizing 2.7 million illegal immigrants in the late 1980s, Congress enacted new amnesties a decade later for hundreds of thousands of Central Americans and grandfathered in many more illegal aliens under a now-lapsed provision allowing otherwise-eligible immigrants to gain permanent residence by paying a $1,000 fee and filing for their green cards while being in the United States, relieving them even of the inconvenience of having to travel back home to apply for admission. (This provision was allowed to lapse.) As noted earlier, President Bush has proposed, and the Senate in 2006 supported, another very large amnesty (euphemistically called "earned legalization") and a guestworker program that will also require payment of back taxes and fees, among other things.[20]

Even convicted criminal aliens enjoy a perverse kind of de facto protection from removal. Unlike the undocumented, they have no political sponsors at all, yet they still remain in the United States in large numbers – even when they are already under lock and key and thus should be easy to remove. Criminal aliens constitute a substantial share of the federal, state, and local prison population. An estimated 600,000 alien defendants in criminal proceedings enter these facilities each year.[21] Yet even with a long-term, statutorily grounded, high-priority effort by the Bureau of Immigration and Customs Enforcement (ICE) to remove these criminals, the agency still managed to remove only 89,406 in 2005 (77 percent of these were Mexicans), an increase over the previous year but only a small percentage of the removable aliens in custody or under supervision.[22]

For the present purposes, the important point is that current and long-standing immigration patterns – high levels of legal and illegal migration and criminal alien activity, chronically weak enforcement, and high public anxiety and anger about these trends – present restrictionists with much political ammunition to advance their policy agenda. Yet despite these rich political opportunities, they have utterly failed to dislodge the expansionist status quo. Perhaps the most important cause and consequence of this political inertia is the emerging position of the Republican Party on immigration issues. Actively competing for votes among independents and traditionally Democratic blocs, many Republican leaders, most notably President Bush, are determined to increase their support among Hispanic voters. Accordingly, they strive to avoid being associated with any measure that can be depicted as being anti-immigrant, while supporting proposals, such as the president's amnesty and guestworker plan, that can be sold to the public as rewarding "good" illegal immigrants while cracking down on "bad" ones.[23]

All of this has produced a remarkably durable political economy of immigration – a political disconnect in which a vector of social forces sustains expansion even in the face of conditions that would seem conducive to restrictive policies that most voters claim to favor.

LEGAL SCHOLARS

In a polity in which only 17 percent of the public thinks that immigration levels should be higher and 39 percent thinks they should be lower, one would expect that at least *some* legal scholars who write about immigration issues would favor restriction. If so, one would be wrong. In over two decades of immersion in immigration scholarship, I have not encountered a single academic specialist on immigration law[24] who favors reducing the number of legal immigrants admitted each year. (I favor higher admissions, albeit with a greater emphasis on skills than in the existing system.) This virtual unanimity among academics in favor of expanded immigration constitutes a particularly striking element of the political disconnect under discussion here.

Recall that I defined restrictionism and expansionism in terms not only of attitudes about legal admissions but also attitudes about how rigorous enforcement against the undocumented should be. Here, too, immigration law scholars tend to be expansionist. While they acknowledge the large and steadily growing number of undocumented aliens in the United States – after all, only willful blindness could miss this gigantic elephant in the room – few if any favor either an intensive campaign to apprehend and remove the undocumented or an enhancement of ICE's effective power to do so. (This is not a question of legal authority, which is already ample.)

Apart from the few exceptions cited here, there appears to be no recent support among immigration law scholars for increasing workplace raids, beefing up the Border Patrol, encouraging public officials or private individuals to identify illegal immigrants to the ICE, penalizing those who provide sanctuary to them, using state and local police to augment the ICE,[25] limiting the procedural rights available to asylum claimants at the border or immigrants in enforcement proceedings,[26] increasing penalties for illegal entry or visa violations, sanctioning lawyers who seek to delay proceedings to remove their clients, extending the period of time during which aliens can be detained either before or after a final removal order is issued,[27] denying amnesty to undocumented workers, or limiting automatic birthright citizenship for their children. Many of these scholars, of course, do favor using ICE's existing authority and resources more effectively to reduce illegal migration. They correctly note, for example, that the ICE seldom imposes serious penalties on employers who rely on facially valid but frequently forged identification documents while hiring foreign workers; that its actual follow-up on final removal orders is notoriously haphazard and feckless; that its management and information systems remain obsolete and chaotic; and that it exhibits many other chronic deficiencies and injustices.

This is not the place to debate the merits of expansion, much less the numerous specific reform measures about which reasonable people can and do differ. Rather, my point here is simply that in sharp contrast to the American public generally, virtually all immigration law scholars, like all immigrant advocacy groups and all lawyers who represent immigrants, strongly support an immigration policy that is expansive in almost every sense. That is, they favor high and higher levels of legal admissions, generous amnesties for undocumented workers, reduced detention of the undocumented, more liberal grants of asylum, and more extensive procedural rights for the undocumented that make it harder for the government to remove them. I cannot recall a single academic presenter at any program in the more than 20 years of the Immigration Law Section of the American Association of Law Schools[28] who did not take these positions. More speculatively, but based on my participation in many academic conversations and conferences, I imagine that the vast majority of immigration law scholars also support substantive entitlements – economic and welfare rights and even some voting rights – to equalize the status of citizens and noncitizens. It is here, presumably, that the political disconnect over immigration policy becomes most stark.

EXPLAINING THE DISCONNECT

Discrepancies between public attitudes and policy outcomes are common in many areas of public policy, at least until some political convulsion or lesser adjustment narrows the gap. In this respect, the disconnect in immigration policy may be no different. Positive political theory would predict as much. Political economists such as James Buchanan and Gordon Tullock, and political scientists such as James Q. Wilson, have shown that the differential distribution of policy costs and benefits can explain many political outcomes of policy debates.[29]

Immigration policy lends itself to this kind of explanation. Although the precise magnitudes are certainly in dispute, policy experts generally agree that immigration, including at the level that the United States has experienced in recent decades, confers economic benefits on the society as a whole, while concentrating the costs primarily on the low-skilled workers, both native-born and immigrant, who compete with low-skilled immigrants for jobs.[30] As the earlier discussion of immigration's political economy shows, many politically influential lobbies – particularly growers and many other important industries – have a powerful economic stake in high levels of immigration, including illegal migration, while the groups that bear most of the costs of immigration tend to vote at lower levels and are not as well organized politically. In addition, a growing public recognition of the demographic and welfare state crises facing Western Europe and Japan in the absence of immigration there seems likely to increase Americans' appreciation of the long-term fiscal benefits of immigration.[31] Immigration, moreover, is not nearly as salient an issue to most Americans as it is to those of us who study it or as media coverage of illegal border crossings and other iconic images might suggest. Even during congressional and presidential election campaigns, when candidates might have political incentives to exploit restrictionist sentiment, immigration ranks pretty far down the priority list of voters' concerns. Indeed, a Pew Research Center survey published in the midst of the congressional debates over immigration enforcement in 2006 indicated that only 3 percent of Americans view immigration as the most important problem facing their community; even in Phoenix, the city evidencing the most concern, only 18 percent cited immigration.[32]

Buttressing (but also transcending) the material interests favoring immigration are ideological commitments. The immigration *mythos* is powerful among Americans generally and, as we have seen, among many opinion shapers. Pro-immigration attitudes are likely to increase, moreover, as the percentage of the foreign-born steadily grows, tending to blunt the nativist and xenophobic impulses so common and corrosive in other societies. Most of the mass media are decidedly pro-immigration; indeed, the influential editorial page of the *Wall Street Journal* favors not only more immigration but essentially open borders (security considerations aside), insisting that so long as immigrants do not receive welfare benefits, they will more than pay their own way economically and strengthen the nation socially.[33]

For all these reasons, even the large majority of voters who say they want less (or at least no more) immigration tend to be ambivalent about it,[34] and this ambivalence surely limits their inclination to join in political activism on the subject. The quietist equilibrium that ambivalence encourages and sustains, however, is a condition that will last only as long as the pressures on both sides remain in some rough balance. In that sense, it is always vulnerable to shifts in facts, values, and other aspects of the political and policy environment.[35]

Are we witnessing such a shift today, with the House having passed an "enforcement only" bill in December 2005 and aggressively resisting the more expansionist Senate and White House? My prediction is that when the legislative dust clears, we will have either a deadlock that leaves the expansive status quo in effect or a compromise that gives restrictionists some enhanced enforcement of the southern border and tougher employer sanctions, while giving expansionists a reformed agricultural guestworker program and an "earned legalization" (aka amnesty) program. Most significantly, the current high level of legal admissions is unlikely to be restricted, except perhaps for the small "diversity visas" program (which in my view lacks any good policy justification and should be transformed into something quite different).[36] In short, we are likely to have more of the same, which means an expansive immigration policy – and a continuation of the long-standing political disconnect that I have sought to demonstrate and explain.

CONCLUSION

If a policy does not adequately reflect the social values and facts that are politically relevant to its effectiveness and legitimacy, a political disconnect arises – by definition. If those values and facts change but the policy does not, the disconnect will widen. At some point, the gap between policy and political support may come to exceed a zone of public indifference or passivity, at which point the disconnect ceases to be politically sustainable. Viewed schematically, this is how much fundamental policy change occurs. A widening disconnect, then, should cause concern among the policy's supporters, as well as creating a ripe political opportunity for its opponents. In a democracy based on public accountability, government cannot straddle a significant disconnect indefinitely. Some reasonable relation between voter preferences and policy outcomes is not only prudent but essential for democratic legitimacy.

I use the phrase "reasonable relation" advisedly, in recognition of several realities. As is well known, any democratic process for translating voter preferences into policy outcomes is inevitably imperfect, violating even the most basic rules of logical consistency.[37] In a dynamic political environment, moreover, the shifting values of voters and changing facts on the ground mean that as a practical matter there must be, and as a normative matter probably should be, a certain amount of slippage between preferences and policies. But if the political modalities for mediating between preferences and policies are too rigid, any significant changes in one of them will trigger political tectonic shifts, unleashing hard-to-control and potentially transformative effects that may bear little resemblance to what any responsible reformer would want.

This widening of the political disconnect, I believe, is the best way to understand the immigration policy earthquakes that have occurred since the early 1990s: California's Proposition 187 in 1994, the IIRIRA of 1996, the immigration-related provisions of the 1996 welfare reform law, Arizona's Proposition 200 in 2004, and the House's "enforcement-only" bill. These are all examples of political backlash on the part of voters angered and frustrated by what they see as a recalcitrant, unresponsive, unrealistic political establishment. The new immigration policy equilibria established by these laws sometimes went far beyond what, in my view, the relevant changes in the underlying social facts and values warranted – in the case of Proposition 187, even violating the Constitution.[38] This fact, however, should be an important warning to those of us whose firm support for more expansive immigration policies sometimes blinds us to the need to find better political and policy responses to the legitimate public concerns generated by more than a quarter-century of scarcely acknowledged expansionism, and to the democratic impulses that it inevitably inspires.

3

Carved from the Inside Out

Immigration and America's Public Philosophy of Citizenship

Elizabeth F. Cohen

During the second session of the 109th Congress, bitter debate broke out about how many guestworker immigrants we should admit within our borders and under what conditions they may remain here. Should they receive permission to stay permanently? That immigration should be the topic of raging debate is unsurprising. What is surprising is that it is taking place only now, two and a half immigration-laden centuries after the founding of our nation. Immigration has shaped us as a country in manifold ways, and yet it can hardly be said that at any point in the United States' history we – as a nation-state, as a republic, or as a people – have shaped immigration. Why is it that subjects as basic as the status of children born on American soil to undocumented immigrants or the fairness of guestworker programs have received sustained national attention only recently?

Despite its lengthy history as an immigrant-receiving nation, the United States has as yet failed to produce a well-articulated public philosophy of immigration. Many European nations, most of which have been the recipients of large-scale immigration for less than half a century, seem as well or even better equipped than the United States to answer these questions through a coherent public philosophy of immigration.[1] This leaves 21st-century Americans in the position of trying to extract a reasoned set of policies to govern the border from a relatively shallow well of precedent and philosophy. If we are to come to conclusions regarding how much and what sort of immigration we ought to tolerate, it seems sensible to first ask ourselves why it is that the United States, of all nations, has not yet answered these questions. In this chapter, I will suggest that fundamental principles of American public law have contributed to an understanding of citizenship driven by concerns of difference, particularly racial difference, ascribed among native-born citizens. This internal differentiation[2] domestically produces foreignness that renders ostensible citizens (including, but not limited to, African Americans) foreign despite their native birth. The priority placed on managing racial distinctions through citizenship law has precluded a reconciliation of our relationship to immigrants, whose outsider or foreigner status cannot be reduced to or equated with that of the marginal native-born groups who have continually been deprived of full citizenship within the American polity.

If immigrants have not always been the most foreign people in our midst, then it makes sense that immigration has not been either central to or well attended to by existing definitions of citizenship. We have no public philosophy of immigration because our understanding of citizenship is focused inward, on differences that exist within the native-born population. In the first half of the chapter, I will describe the contours of the problem: how immigration has been understood in the context of citizenship, and how the dilemmas created by an absence of a public philosophy of immigration manifest themselves. In the second half, I will offer an explanation for these circumstances that looks to the common-law tradition we inherited from England, in particular the jurisprudence based on *Calvin's Case*. I will argue that this jurisprudence meshed effectively with our own commitment to racial and other internal classifications in order to produce an understanding of citizenship that was not attentive to questions of immigration.

CONTEMPORARY POLITICAL THEORIES OF IMMIGRATION AND CITIZENSHIP

Most nation-states publicly declare whether they consider themselves to be "countries of immigration." Patrick Weil notes that as countries begin to perceive themselves as countries of immigration, they tend to invoke rhetoric and policies that are geared toward absorbing and assimilating immigrants.[3] Thus not only can we expect to generate public philosophies of immigration, but there ought to be a direct relationship between a country's philosophy, or general approach to immigration, the mechanics of the immigration policy itself, and the treatment of the foreign-born, particularly but not exclusively through the alienage law that governs immigrants once they have arrived. In the United States, there is public consensus that we are a nation of immigration, and we have declared as much to the world. However, this has not put an end to disagreement about who ought to be able to immigrate, the rights they ought to enjoy, and the circumstances under which they should or should not be granted citizenship. In other words, while many among us view an abstract notion of immigration as integral to our politics, there still exists widespread ambivalence toward the foreigners who actually appear at our doorstep at any given point in time.

[In his recent and controversial book *Who Are We?*, Samuel Huntington makes the case that America's settlers never intended to create a nation that would be defined and continually redefined by an ever-changing cast (or caste) of immigrants.] This thesis flies in the face of a voluminous and well-grounded literature that regards open immigration as central to American identity.[4] For many, the quintessential national tale is the American Dream, which speaks more directly to immigrants than perhaps any other social group. While for Huntington immigration has been a process through which new members became Americanized, others view immigration itself as the defining American experience and attribute. It comes as no surprise, then, that we find ourselves so divided over the subject of our borders. We have never been entirely certain whether we were subjects of a state dedicated to accommodating the varying needs of successive generations of new members or sovereigns of an empire whose conquests are found within rather than outside of our borders.

Many would protest the claim that we lack a well-articulated approach to immigration, arguing that in fact American history has engendered an intense debate over the meaning of citizenship that is both public and self-conscious. Settlers arrived on our shores with the express purpose of founding a community in which they could enjoy freedoms they had not experienced in their homelands. The transition from colonial settlement to nation-state instigated a set of very public and deliberate debates over the content and right to membership in the newly formed republic. These debates have replayed themselves repeatedly as Americans have come to terms with internal conflicts over the meaning of citizenship. It could therefore hardly be said that we have no public philosophy of citizenship even though this philosophy has evolved significantly since it was first conceived.

Yet, what this implies for the politics of immigration remains unclear. Many historians of American political thought who study the nature and lineage of American philosophies of citizenship examine immigration through the lens of an overarching theory of American citizenship. Rogers Smith's *Civic Ideals* details the development of multiple traditions of liberalism, republicanism, and ascriptive exclusion through an analysis of public law from the colonial period through the end of the 19th century. Smith's is the most recent in a history of venerable tomes that includes Louis Hartz's[5] defense of liberalism as the defining American ideology and Gunnar Myrdal's[6] civic republican rejoinder. Each of these texts has presumed that we can infer a great deal regarding attitudes toward immigration based on approaches to citizenship.

However, a philosophy of citizenship need not make central, or even answer, important questions regarding immigration. Indeed, normative political philosophers have long noted that the theories of membership upon which practices of citizenship are founded tend to function very well when applied to bounded communities but fail the tests posed by immigration. Of the ancient theorists, only the Stoics envisioned cosmopolitanism, and even they did so in a limited fashion. Plato and Aristotle both set very narrow limits on the inclusion of foreigners, offering them at best the very form of second-class citizenship that Aristotle himself held. Modern liberal theory invites further conundrums of inclusion by espousing principles of universal worth while simultaneously recognizing that self-governance can occur only within well-bounded communities. Contemporary theorists, most famously John Rawls, have only replicated this internal contradiction of liberalism. Rawls qualified the entirety of *A Theory of Justice* with a statement that it only applies to nation-states. If the abstract world of normative theory cannot manage to produce theories of citizenship that accommodate immigration, then the much messier reality of public philosophy and the policies it informs can only be expected to engender further complications and contradictions.

A few scholars of citizenship explicitly acknowledge the challenges of trying to reconcile philosophies of citizenship and immigration. In her examination of the peculiar philosophies that have forged American citizenship, Judith Shklar makes an important distinction between her goal of elucidating the role of race in American citizenship and what she views as the important, but different, task of characterizing American approaches to immigration. Shklar writes, "The history of immigration and naturalization policies is not, however, my subject. It has its own ups and downs, but is not the same as the exclusion of native-born Americans from citizenship. The two histories have their parallels, since both involve inclusion and exclusion, but there is a vast difference between discriminatory immigration laws and the enslavement of a people."[7] In contrast, Smith, whose subject and spirit of inquiry is much the same as Shklar's, treats the application of the ascriptive principles, which he and Shklar indict for their effect on native-born racial minorities, to immigration laws as an extension of the same processes. He moves nearly seamlessly between discussions of the laws governing the citizenship of native-born racial minorities and women and laws governing immigration and the rights of the foreign-born.

As Shklar indicates, this is not an illogical move because the two sets of rules are, in her words, parallel. But it might not be entirely warranted, for as parallel, or at least distinct, processes, the forging of a philosophy of citizenship is not necessarily coextensive with that of a philosophy of immigration. Not only are the two conceptually distinct, but for a variety of reasons Americans did not produce a philosophy of immigration alongside their philosophy of citizenship. The ascriptive principles guiding the exclusion of some from full citizenship prove an uneasy fit with the realities of immigrant populations and, further, the role of immigrants in, and their relationship to, American society is also different from that of native-born minorities. One can observe moments in which awkward attempts were made to fuse racial ideologies with nativism, such as the cry that the Irish would never be white, yet the experiences of being an immigrant and a native-born minority in America are – and always have been – vastly different. Indeed, evidence drawn from American political thought, public law, and policy indicates that even today we have not yet fully articulated our understanding of the challenges of immigration, let alone our responses to them. A full examination of this phenomenon would consume more space than this essay permits. However, a few illustrations will indicate the degree to which immigration has managed to shape American identity without being subjected to the sort of systematic philosophical scrutiny accorded to other elements of citizenship.[8]

OBSERVING AMERICAN INATTENTION TO IMMIGRATION

Indications that immigration has not received systematic thought in the context of an otherwise well-articulated and self-conscious understanding of citizenship abound. Perhaps the most telling institutional evidence of American ambivalence toward immigration and border concerns is the fact that immigration has only relatively recently come to be governed nationally. For most of American history, immigration was regulated by the states. Aristide Zolberg notes that the Passenger Act (1819) indicates early interest on the part of the national government in limiting immigration, but a federal apparatus for regulating immigration only began to emerge in a very nascent form following anti-Chinese immigration measures passed in the 1870s.[9] A full federal bureaucracy only came to pass in 1929, as a means of implementing the 1924 National Origins Quota

Act. The reasons for this are well rehearsed: the strong commitment to federalism evinced by many of the founders informed, and was influenced by, conflicts of interest arising from differing positions on the status of slaves and free black Americans. Internal migration therefore gave Americans as much cause for concern, and probably more, than the entry of hundreds of thousands of European nationals.

One could make the claim that a laissez-faire attitude toward immigration constitutes the American approach to border control. Leaving aside the question of whether an unarticulated laissez-faire policy can constitute a public philosophy, the fact remains that not all matters related to immigration can be resolved passively. In particular, refuge demands proactive policies and laws. The right of refuge requires that states formulate policies and programs in order to identify and protect eligible candidates for protection. There is much to suggest that refuge is an important element of American identity – from our founding as a refuge for religious minorities to the oft-referenced inscription on the Statue of Liberty. And yet institutional mechanisms that define and implement such protections have only come to exist in this country recently and in an entirely ad hoc fashion. In fact, until the cold war, the United States eschewed explicitly formulating a policy of refuge. While we encouraged the world to give us their tired, poor, huddled masses yearning to breathe free, we were not particularly interested in ferreting out anyone who might have been huddling voiceless in the dark recesses of poverty or political oppression. Only under the threat of appearing hypocritical, and with the incentive of weakening our cold war enemies, did the federal government institute a policy of refuge, and the terms of that policy limited the right to those fleeing communism.[10]

In addition to a relatively passive institutional approach to immigration, American politics has also rarely been shaped by conflict over immigration. While it is the case that the foreign-born have periodically been the subject of intense public scrutiny, this focus has rarely reached the levels experienced by many European countries. Furthermore, much of the conflict has centered on matters to do with alienage – the rights of the foreign-born who are already here and not the question of immigration and/or expatriation. Perhaps the closest we have come to party politics in which immigration played a dominant role was the brief period in the 1850s when the Know-Nothings held sway. However, the spell cast by their nativist rhetoric was broken by internal divisions over racial politics and, to date, while political parties have engaged immigrants as potential citizens and threats alike, none has predicated its existence on either defending or halting immigration.[11] This stands in sharp contrast to our European peer states that, upon discovering that they had become states of immigration in the post–World War II period, promptly generated political parties whose main reason for existence was connected to immigration. There is no American Kurt Waldheim, and there has never been an American Front National.[12]

Finally, as a matter of policy, it is simply the case that Americans did not seek to control or restrict access to their borders until relatively recently. Immigration was viewed as a necessity for much of American history – perhaps a necessary evil to some, but nonetheless inevitable. Restrictions for reasons of security, health, poverty, and criminality have existed, but the plain fact is that statistically these have prevented only an insignificant number of people from entering the country.[13] This pattern remained the case until the National Origins Quota Act was enforced in 1929, and following the 1965 Immigration and Nationality Act there has been a slow drift back toward increased immigration and lax border enforcement. "Illegal" immigration has tacitly been encouraged not simply through lax border enforcement but also by laws that facilitate the continued presence of undocumented individuals and their families. The paradigmatic example is the extension of *jus soli* to the children of the undocumented that accords citizenship to those born on U.S. soil regardless of the legal status of their parents. However, accommodations for the undocumented abound, ranging from the provision of education to their children to the licensing of undocumented drivers. Similar inconsistencies abound in the laws that govern the entry of legal immigrants. Family reunification and work changed places several times in the ranked list of immigration priorities institutionalized in 1965. If this indicates nothing else, it ought to make clear the fact that we do not know what we want our borders or the keepers of our gates to accomplish.

If it is an institutional, legal, and political fact that Americans lack a public philosophy of immigration, it remains to be explained why this is so. No doubt the reasons are manifold. Immigration is an issue that cuts across otherwise well-organized material and social interest groups.[14] Yet the moments at which immigration has been restricted and opened do not indicate that the material interests of any given class or set of classes are being systematically pursued via border control.[15] One might also suggest that the federal nature of the republic has prevented the development of a coherent philosophy of immigration. However, the demands of federalism alone cannot explain the failure of Americans to produce a public philosophy of immigration. The period following the nationalization of immigration has been the most schizophrenic to date. Furthermore, a country such as Germany has traditionally devolved many of the powers of immigration to the Länder and yet has maintained a consistent, if objectionable, philosophy of immigration in which the rights of refuge and return are honored, while traditional immigration is discouraged.

CITIZENSHIP VERSUS IMMIGRATION

Having established the counterintuitive fact of American inattention to immigration, I will draw upon the jurisprudential traditions that shaped American approaches to foreignness in order to offer an explanation of how a country so profoundly shaped by immigration has in turn considered immigration in such an unsystematic manner. But, before turning to the circumstances that led to the divergence of these two questions in the United States, a word about the general principles with which we can differentiate theories of citizenship from those of immigration is in order. Citizenship encompasses a broad and dense set of norms, policies, and laws that together govern what it means to be a member of a polity. This meaning includes rights, benefits, and expectations: the conditions of and for membership. Place of birth and/or nationality – the traits that distinguish immigrants from nonimmigrants – need not hold either a singular or a central place among these conditions. One tends to assume that because nation-states are in some senses reliant on sovereign borders for their existence, they must necessarily prioritize border-crossing issues in their definition of membership. Yet there is no reason that race or social class might not play a more central role in a philosophy of citizenship. That one is white or male or respectably employed in fact turns out to be crucial to many definitions of citizenship. One can be foreign without holding the passport of another nation and, at the same time, a nonnative Canadian may not be perceived as, be treated as, or even feel particularly foreign.

Americans have developed a philosophy of citizenship that, while keenly sensitive to notions of foreignness, does not fully resolve issues of immigration. We understand the degree to which the nation-state has the power to determine who enjoys the status of citizen, and we are extraordinarily self-conscious of the benefits conferred by our citizenship. But none of this dictates any particular response to entreaties from beyond our borders. One could examine this paradox through a number of lenses. Particularly illuminating is the distinction between immigration and alienage law discussed by Linda Bosniak in Chapter 6 of this volume. This distinction refers to the degree to which we have historically regulated the immigrants in our midst, as opposed to the act of immigration itself. While there was little in the way of a nationalized immigration policy, there have long been in place significant legal precedents that facilitated the control of aliens once admitted.[16] Alienage law, as opposed to immigration constraints, was very well developed early on in our history. From the founding onward, the rights of aliens were subjects of public debate.[17] While we did not seek to restrict immigration, as a nation we did recognize the need to control the foreigners in our midst. Alienage law, as opposed to immigration restriction, was prioritized both by the Framers, who sought to prevent those without citizenship from holding office, and by successive generations of American leaders. Even as we ignored our borders, we have always remained quite concerned with the foreigners among us.

The prioritization of debate regarding the rights of foreigners over discussion of immigration restrictions reinforces the idea that Americans have chosen to focus attention on citizenship rather than immigration. The primary concern of alienage law is the degree to which nonnationals may enjoy the rights of citizenship. To be sure, the threat of deportation looms large as an implication of alienage law; however, mass deportation has not played a particularly important role in the history of immigrants in the United States. More common has been a pattern of benign neglect of both legal and "illegal" immigration coupled with extensive use of alienage law as a tool to constrain the freedoms enjoyed by foreigners.

CALVIN'S CASE, THE ORIGINS OF THE AMERICAN CONCEPTION OF CITIZENSHIP, AND PREOCCUPATION WITH INTERNALLY GENERATED FOREIGNNESS

That foreignness can matter so much to Americans and yet not generate a better-articulated and more measured approach to border control would ostensibly seem to be unlikely, if not entirely irreconcilable. However, an examination of the origins of the American approach to citizenship yields a rationale for this very striking set of circumstances. American approaches to citizenship have long reflected a preoccupation with forms of discrimination that focus on race more than nationality. Perhaps the moment at which our skepticism about immigration was at its peak was the period surrounding the passage of the 1924 National Origins Quota Act, when we were concerned less with nationality and more with race. The bill itself was designed to encourage immigration from countries seen as racially and culturally in harmony with "Americanness" and simultaneously block further immigration of racially undesirable people. It was a law driven by sociobiology rather than sovereignty.

There are a number of routes to understanding why it is that race and other forms of internal differentiation have generated a philosophy of citizenship that lacks a focus on borders. I will now focus on the formative effects of the citizenship law bequeathed to the United States by the common-law tradition of Great Britain and in particular the influence of *Calvin's Case*. Nearly all scholarship on the origins of American citizenship acknowledges the singular importance of *Calvin's Case* in shaping the legal and philosophical principles upon which American citizenship was founded. *Calvin's Case* resolved the political status of people who had been born in Scotland after the ascent of a Scot, King James, to the British throne. The ruling accorded them subjecthood based on the principle of *jus soli* – their birth in territory considered to be a part of the British dominion. In so doing, it created two categories of people: *ante-nati* (persons born before the joining of the two kingdoms) and *postnati* (persons born afterward). The decision rendered the latter citizens and led to the development of naturalization rules and procedures for the former. Thus, common-law rules of citizenship were instantiated without any particular reference or relation to immigration across sovereign borders. In *Calvin's Case*, it was borders rather than people doing the migrating.

Insofar as it addressed the historically specific question of the citizenship of Scots who were newly incorporated into the political domain of England as a result of the ascent of King James to the throne, the case appears an odd one to have served such a significant role in shaping American jurisprudence. We were not a kingdom with an empire; we were a former colony that would continue to rely upon immigration to compose our population. *Calvin's Case*, with its emphasis on *jus soli*, could not help us with that. Given the lack of an American corollary to the status of the Scots in the British Empire, it is not entirely obvious why *Calvin's Case* became so important to American citizenship. Furthermore, the principle of *jus soli*, which *Calvin's Case* established, contradicts liberal consent, republican linkages of membership with civic virtue, or a contract-based notion of citizenship, which together embody the central philosophical influence on American citizenship doctrine.[18] Ascribing citizenship to persons based on *jus soli* (a rule based on place of birth) is almost entirely arbitrary. It deprives both the community and the individual of the opportunity to come to reasoned conclusions about membership.

It is tempting to leap to the conclusion that because the United States depended on mass immigration, *Calvin's Case* was crucial in establishing the means through which immigrants could become citizens because it gave the sovereign the right to naturalize noncitizens. Yet this reflects neither the spirit of *Calvin's Case* nor the use to which it was put for much of American history. Although *Calvin's Case* defended the king's right to naturalize subjects, it did not address itself directly to questions of immigration across sovereign national borders. Rather, it provided the means through which an expanding empire and its newly acquired members could understand their membership in relation to one another and to a shared sovereign. In the decision, Sir Edward Coke addresses himself to foreignness, citizenship, and problems of alienage. He does not take up the subject of transnational immigration. *Calvin's Case* not only established an ascriptive rule of *jus soli* but also generated a legal process of naturalization as a means through which citizenship could be granted to those not born with it. Scots born before the ascent of James had to be naturalized because the land upon which they were born had not been British territory at the time of their birth. Americans recognized that in order to remain sovereign they, too, would have to engage in ascription, if only because as a newly formed nation it was imperative that some justification exist for assigning citizenship to the people of the land, particularly loyalists to the British throne whose status might otherwise be indeterminate and threatening to the newborn union.[19]

Calvin's Case therefore trained an admittedly willing American eye to look inward in order to shape the borders of the nation. The decision applied the norms of an empire intent on colonizing territories and absorbing their populations into a single nation-state. It would therefore be an imperial understanding of citizenship, and not immigration, that would serve as the primary tool through which Americans would sculpt their populace. Thus, as the title of this chapter suggests, Americans have carved themselves from the inside out. This caused Europeans to remark, as Samuel Huntington notes, that we created a "consciousness among people" well before we ever formed what they would have legitimately called a state.[20]

The need to enfranchise the population following the establishment of the union was not the only distinctly American dilemma that *Calvin's Case* resolved. It also provided a means for addressing the presence of persons who may be desirable residents but not citizens. The ruling eschewed the ascription of citizenship to all Scotsmen. Rather, the ruling applied to two sets of persons: the *antenati* and the *postnati* – or those born before and after James's accession, respectively. The decision only granted automatic citizenship to those born after his accession. Most of the *antenati* were ultimately granted naturalization, but it was not ascribed to them. It is also the case that the persons to whom citizenship was ascribed by the new rule still had to be otherwise eligible for citizenship. *Calvin's Case* did not grant the Irish full subjecthood – they remained merely denizens. Thus, to call the precedent that *Calvin's Case* establishes an ascriptive form of pure *jus soli* is to mischaracterize it. In fact, it only selectively ascribed citizenship to segments of the population. The Irish in particular were left in the netherworld between full and noncitizenship.

There are therefore multiple legal statuses that denote "domestic foreignness" – birthright foreignness that is not produced by movement across sovereign national borders. This is supported by the conclusion affirmed in a subsequent case indicating that the rights of nonnative Scotsmen, who could be naturalized, were more extensive than those of nonnative Irishmen, whose status as a conquered people accorded them a weaker set of entitlements. Coke's reasoning in *Calvin's Case* allowed that "the conclusion that naturalization rested upon a legal fiction made it possible to distinguish among the various classes of subjects. Native Englishmen, *postnati* Scotsmen, and natural-born Irishmen were natural subjects."[21]

The analytical benefit of framing *Calvin's Case* thusly is that it reminds us that complicated questions of citizenship must be answered before a rule of *jus soli* can be invoked. In not automatically granting citizenship to *antenati*, *Calvin's Case* legitimized the existence of populations who would not hold citizenship despite their birth in a territory now subject to *jus soli*. It therefore raises the very likely possibility that *jus soli* leaves unanswered a range of ascriptive and substantive questions of citizenship. Understanding *Calvin's Case* thusly helps explain how Chief Justice Roger Brooke Taney, in writing the *Dred Scott* decision, was able to eschew the principle of *jus soli* that the case evinces. *Jus soli* would have accorded citizenship to free blacks. But the status of the Irish following *Calvin's Case* was similar to that of free blacks in the United States. Because no rule had changed, it was conceivable that the principle that excluded free blacks was still in effect in much the same way that some Irish continued to be excluded even after Coke's decision in *Calvin's Case* was issued. To bring us back to the initial premise of this chapter, *Calvin's Case* created an understanding of citizenship that accorded birthright citizenship based on *jus soli* to some, but not all, persons born in the territory.

Underlying the case is the presumption that rules affecting the contours of a citizenry can change and, when they do, complex negotiations will be necessary to determine to whom and how the rules ought to be applied. King James's ascent to the throne changed the rules under which subjecthood would be awarded. A rule had changed – in this case one involving borders, and one that affected a people's relationship to citizenship. This particular rule change affected this group in a way that made many of them eligible for citizenship. However, rule changes can take many forms, and one could easily imagine rule changes that would strip people of their right to citizenship. A border could contract rather than expand, ceding the citizenship of a set of people. Furthermore, rule changes that affect citizenship need not confine themselves to questions of sovereign borders. In the 20th century, rule changes granted citizenship to American women and (temporarily) deprived Japanese Americans of theirs. In this view, therefore, the rule of *jus soli* is secondary to the larger implication of *Calvin's Case*, namely that a range of circumstances can change and, in so doing, alter the contours of the population considered eligible for citizenship. Furthermore, when changes occur, the state will require and create procedures such as naturalization in order to regularize and govern the statuses they create.

The final outcome of *Calvin's Case* was the creation of procedures to transform people into citizens when rule changes entitle them to membership. *Antenati* had to be dealt with once the decision was rendered. The idea of naturalizing noncitizens predates *Calvin's Case* but had no legal precedent until Coke forced the issue by creating a large group of persons who needed to be naturalized. In adopting the entire jurisprudence that grew out of *Calvin's Case*, the United States therefore adopted not only *jus soli* but also a legitimation for multiple forms of citizenship and procedures for transforming noncitizens into citizens.

If we revisit the original question this chapter posed – why it is that we have such a well-articulated public understanding of citizenship that fails to answer basic questions about borders – we can now see that the jurisprudence out of which American citizenship was established was one that did not take up questions of immigration. *Calvin's Case* adopts ascriptive *jus soli* in a confined manner that does not apply universally. It actually legitimizes the simultaneous enfranchisement of immigrants and disenfranchisement of native and African Americans. Even as it dictated that a rule of *jus soli* be applied to *postnati* Scots, *Calvin's Case* simultaneously indicated that others be excluded.[22] It therefore framed questions of citizenship for the British and Americans who looked to it in ways that paid more attention to idiosyncratic and internally generated racial distinctions than to immigration. This functioned well within the unique context of the British Empire and fed into a long-standing American tradition of legalized racial citizenship hierarchies. But much as the British have had to execute a speedy gymnastic routine to address the influx of émigrés from former colonies following the dissolution of its empire, Americans, too, now find themselves forced to answer questions about immigration from within a tradition of citizenship that has more to say about how to distinguish between people of different races and nationalities than it does about the question of how to make immigration law.

CONCLUSION

For much of American history, our failure to develop a coherent philosophy of immigration was relatively unproblematic – in fact it may have served to allow vastly different visions of our nation to coexist. However, during the 20th century, this lacuna led to serious repercussions, leaving us now in the position of trying to forge a consensus on the basis of a set of apparently conflicting premises. Theorists of American political thought must reconcile the contradictions of massive, racially defined restrictions on immigration during the first half of the 20th century with equally extreme liberalizations during the second half. Do we wish to remain a nation that shapes itself from within, or are we in a moment of transition to a politics in which immigration controls will define the contours of future generations? Choosing the latter route will demand that the American people answer not Samuel Huntington's query of "Who Are We?" but the more difficult question, "Who do we want to be?" If the thesis of this chapter is correct, then we are in for more work than Huntington acknowledges, for the reply he offers us tells us who we have been. Who we ought to be and how we ought to achieve this remain as yet unanswered questions.

4

A Biblical Perspective on Immigration Policy

James R. Edwards, Jr.

It is not surprising that policymakers in the United States, the most religious nation in the Western world, often bring their faith to the table, as do faithful people in other cultures, and as many American statesmen have done since the nation's founding era. This chapter offers an approach to some of the most important immigration policy questions currently confronting the United States from the perspective of a biblically based Christian faith. As a Christian congressional staffer working for evangelical legislators, I have thought long and hard about many of these issues and have tried as conscientiously as I can to apply what I believe are the insights and commands of the Bible and the Judeo-Christian religious tradition to the many issues surrounding our current immigration problems.

I stress from the outset that deriving policy prescriptions from the Bible and other Christian sources is difficult business. Many complex issues are involved – theological, exegetical, and pragmatic. I do not claim that my own conclusions are infallible, and I realize that other believers may honestly and conscientiously reach conclusions different from my own. But I do believe that the *principles* that I outline here, as distinct from their specific application, are appropriate Christian biblical principles. And, as such, I believe they are the principles that should guide all Christians in making public policy judgments, even if we do not always agree as to their application in specific cases.

Before addressing the specific immigration controversy, the chapter considers three aspects of the Christian faith that provide background and context to the controversy itself: the biblical role of civil government; the distinction between ancient Israel and the United States;

and the role of Christianity and Reformation Protestantism in shaping America's political culture. After these issues have been addressed, the chapter looks at what the Bible specifically teaches about immigrants and immigration and concludes with an assessment of current immigration policy based on biblical principles.

WHAT IS GOD'S PURPOSE FOR CIVIL GOVERNMENT?

Christians hold the Bible, including both the Old and the New Testaments, as the source of moral authority. In terms of questions regarding government, the Bible presents many passages that indicate the purpose that God intends civil government to serve. A major theme in several of these passages is that civil government is divinely instituted for the protection of the innocent and the punishment of the guilty. Earthly authorities, the Bible says in Romans 13:4, act as God's sword bearer, as "an agent of wrath to bring punishment on the wrongdoer." Civil magistrates, in other words, are established to maintain law and order, and police forces and national armies exist to fulfill that purpose. According to the biblical view, civil magistrates hold responsibility under God for the protection of the people whom God has placed under their authority. Rulers owe a duty to God to faithfully carry out this trust. And the government's obligation is to protect all those under its care, both believer and unbeliever.

The government's power of the sword and its duty to punish evildoers have many implications. In addition to the duty to punish criminals, government has the duty to defend the nation against foreign invaders. There is also a duty to put down insurrection and to punish treason. All of these duties of government relate to preserving the rule of law, executing justice, protecting order, and defending the law-abiding. The government's obligation, moreover, is particularistic. It safeguards the public good for a particular group of people, in a particular geographic location, who belong to a particular body politic.

Throughout much of the history of Christianity, there have been pacifist sects that deny that government has any authority to use violence or coercive force to carry out its obligations. The pacifist Christians would deny government the power to use the sword to resist evil, claiming that Jesus's command to love our enemies precludes the use of government force. Such pacifism, however, is clearly inconsistent with the biblical teaching in either the Old or the New Testament. Throughout the Bible, government is seen as having a legitimate duty to use coercive force to protect the innocent from the results of human sinfulness. From a

biblical perspective, Adam and Eve's disobedience in the Garden of Eden
left human beings flawed in the depths of their nature. David writes in
Psalm 53:1, for instance, that "there is no one who does good." The consequences of this "sin nature" spill over beyond an individual's life; the
consequences affect the health and well-being of the entire social order.[1]
Therefore, it is necessary for a human society and its earthly rulers to adopt
laws for the public good, thereby checking human evil. For example, laws
protecting the infirm, putting violent criminals to death (or behind bars
for life), ensuring fairness in trade and commerce, and deporting criminal
aliens all seek to protect the innocent against wrongdoers and are appropriate activities of government – indeed, governments are *obligated* to do
these kinds of things.

For Christians, to try to deny to government the power of the sword –
the state's instrument for restraining evil – is to run against clear biblical
imperatives. As the Presbyterian scholar G. I. Williamson writes, commenting on St. Paul's teaching in Romans 13:1–5, "Those people who
advocate policies which virtually call upon our national government to
renounce the power of the sword, and to renounce all attempts to be a
terror to evil-doers, and to renounce the execution of revenge upon them,
advocate nothing less than the overthrow of the ordinance of God."[2]

Just as the government has an obligation to carry out the protective
purpose for which it exists, so, too, do those who are under the authority
of government to submit to the legitimate laws and commands promul-
gated by their government. "Submit yourselves for the Lord's sake to every
authority instituted among men," it says in 1 Peter 2:13–14 – "whether to
the king, as the supreme authority, or to governors, who are sent by him to
punish those who do wrong and to commend those who do right." Similarly, St. Paul in Titus 3:1 directs Christians "to be subject to rulers and
authorities." And in Romans 13:1, Paul says, "There is no [civil] authority except that which God has established. The authorities that exist have
been established by God."

The obligation of Christians to be subject to rulers and authorities is
well summed up in the Westminster Confession of Faith: "It is the duty of
people to pray for magistrates, to honor their persons, to pay them tribute
and other dues, to obey their lawful commands, and to be subject to their
authority for conscience's sake."[3] Christian duty does not give license to
disregard lawful statutes and may even require military service and other
forms of public service.

It is important to keep in mind that while the Bible commands us to
obey legitimately constituted authority, Scripture specifies no particular

form of government as being favored by God. Various forms of government have stood over different peoples and nations throughout history, and there is no claim in the Bible that one form – for instance, monarchy or democracy – is alone legitimate. The God of the Old and New Testaments has used everything from theocracy[4] in ancient Israel, to the later monarchy under the Israelite kings, to the Athenian republic, to the Roman Empire as the agency of his purpose. Christians, Israelites, and pagans alike have served as civil magistrates. Clearly, some rulers have fulfilled their responsibility better than others – consider the Old Testament accounts of those judges and kings who were faithful and those who were not. But the civic duty of citizens to obey civil authorities, except in certain restricted circumstances, remains constant.

ANCIENT ISRAEL AND THE MODERN UNITED STATES

The systems of government in Old Testament Israel and the United States differ substantially in form and operation. This, however, is not a problem for Christians, as we believe that God sanctions different forms of government for different people in different times and places. Many different forms of government can be agents of justice in their particular historical setting. Christians do believe that certain moral laws derived from the Bible, such as those embodied in the Ten Commandments, are universal in the sense of being binding on everyone, everywhere, and at all times. But this is not the case with the ceremonial and judicial laws in the Old Testament.

Christians generally believe that the ceremonial and judicial laws given to ancient Israel applied to that nation alone. Ephesians 2:15 says that Jesus Christ "[abolished] in his flesh the law with its commandments and regulations." The law that is meant here is clearly the ceremonial and judicial laws of ancient Israel, but not the universal moral commandments. G. I. Williamson points to Hebrews 7–10 as evidence of the ceremonial law's passing.[5] For example, Hebrews 9, he points out, speaks of the earthly priesthood and sacrificial system as a stopgap "until the time of the new order" (9:10), implying the Messiah's ultimate sacrifice. In other words, with the sacrifice, death, and resurrection of Jesus, the older Jewish sacerdotal system and its laws are superseded by a new dispensation under "the one Man, Jesus Christ," through whom "God's grace" did "overflow to the many" (Romans 5:15). Besides the ceremonial laws, the civil laws of Israel were also of a temporary character, as can be seen in the fact that many were clearly aimed at a particular local circumstance (e.g., Judges

18–19, where the Hebrew tribes are assigned to a particular region of Canaan).

While some Christian sects have seen the Old Testament form of government as a universal model for all Christian peoples to follow, this is clearly not the requirement of the Bible, which provides for greater flexibility and pragmatic wisdom in determining the best form of government in different historical circumstances. Our American form of government differs greatly from that of ancient Israel, but this does not mean that it is worse or that it has strayed from the biblical path. There is no single biblical path when it comes to the form of governance of different peoples, in different historical periods, under different political conditions. Even John Calvin, whose governance of the city of Geneva adopted many features of the Old Testament theological-political order, clearly believed that civil laws should be based on "the condition of the times, place, and nation."[6] Paul Marshall, author of one of the most illuminating books on Christianity and American politics, well sums up the situation for Christians when he says, "If we want to make a law, we need not only to know about laws in general, even divine laws, but we also need to know about these [particular] citizens, this [particular] legislature, this president, this constitution, these [specific] laws."[7] American government clearly allows for scriptural principles to inform its civil laws. This can occur because of the ingrained Christian aspects of U.S. history and culture, because of the influence of millions of Christian Americans doing their civic duty, and because of the public service of Christian officials. Yet we live in a democratic republic whose governing structure separates church and state and whose decision-making process is based on popular elections.[8] That is, though American civil laws should honor and reflect – even codify – God's moral laws, those civil laws are enacted through republican means that preserve the democratic process. Christians are obligated to honor that process and have a biblical obligation to obey the civil authorities under most circumstances, even if they are non-Christians. Non-Christian magistrates have every right to demand obedience by Christians to their lawfully enacted decrees.[9]

Here the United States differs not only from ancient Israel but from more contemporary regimes such as those that exist in Iran and certain other Muslim countries, where government is in the hands of ruling religious bodies. And it would be hard to argue that the United States is the worse for it. On the contrary, the consequences of not separating church and state in the modern world may be very harmful, as can be seen in the heavy-handed rule of the Taliban in Afghanistan, the excesses of the "morality police" in Iran, and the harmful influence of the Wahhabi sect in Saudi Arabia.

Besides biblical principles, the civil government of the United States also reflects features of English common law, Lockean liberalism, ancient Greco-Roman ideals, and the practical political compromises agreed to by the Founding Fathers who were charged with improving upon the Articles of Confederation.[10] America's Founders appreciated the need for keeping apart church governance and state rule. America's form of representative government allows for the exercise of prudential judgment by both Christian and non-Christian citizens and seeks to be fair to all. The American republic provides an orderly process for securing the "consent of the governed" on public questions, even though universal agreement on every law cannot be obtained. The system of checks and balances that we have – for example, the bicameral national legislature, the federal structure of the government, and the separation of powers at the national level into three co-equal branches – has been generally successful in "securing the blessings of liberty" for a huge population over a vast, continent-sized nation. We have moved far afield from the form of government of ancient Israel, but for a Christian, that is a prudential development, not a form of unfaithfulness to the Bible.

THE ROLE OF CHRISTIANITY IN AMERICAN POLITICAL CULTURE

One can understand much of American government and American political culture as a synthesis of two countervailing streams of thought, one deriving from the Enlightenment and the other from Christianity, particularly the Protestant Reformation.[11] The Enlightenment stressed individual rights and tended to downplay the need for social cohesiveness and common virtues. Taken to its extreme, the Enlightenment project could lead to the triumph of self-seeking individualism, the substitution of a deep religious faith by a false faith in progress, the general secularization of society, and the destruction of tradition and stability.[12] Much of the success of the American project can be attributed to the fact that these potentially destructive consequences of the Enlightenment were offset by the influence of both Christianity and the tradition of civic republicanism about which J. G. A. Pocock and many other scholars have written. As the Christian writer Os Guinness explains, "a combination of classical republicanism and Protestantism" constrained the Enlightenment's force of gravity. "Predominantly religious beliefs held in balance apparently irreconcilable opposites, such as self-reliance and community cooperation, daring enterprise and social stability."[13]

The Reformation, derived from Judeo-Christian principles, contributed a number of key ideals to American government. These included freedom of conscience, ordered liberty, the restraint of sinful passions, the rule of law, representative government from the bottom up rather than rule on the basis of a top-down hierarchy, and the need to restrain the governing elite no less than the governed. American civic ideals such as liberty, equality, individual responsibility, and justice under law derive from this heritage. These principles and ideals for government and society provided a means of achieving *unum* amid *pluribus* and prevented a free people from drifting away from their ethical moorings.

America's Founders sought to erect a limited civil government that would preserve liberty under law. But the only way limited government can work, they believed, is if the citizen body displayed a high level of self-government and self-restraint. Philosopher Francis Schaeffer has explained just how difficult it is for a government to achieve a healthy balance between order and liberty, or what he calls "form" and "freedom." We in the West, he says, "take our *form-freedom balance* in government for granted as though it were natural."[14] Historically speaking, however, it has been very unnatural, Schaeffer stresses, though the United States has been more successful than most other societies, he believes, in combining an emphasis on individual rights with an equally important emphasis on the fulfillment of social obligations. The success of the American experiment in ordered liberty, Schaeffer and others contend, can largely be attributed to the Judeo-Christian religious consensus that stresses the need for self-control and self-restraint and the need for God's guidance and God's grace in achieving these goals.[15] The Founders knew that only a people so restrained could ever remain politically free.

WHAT DOES THE BIBLE SAY ABOUT IMMIGRANTS AND IMMIGRATION?

With the foregoing knowledge in the background, we can now proceed to an understanding of what the Bible specifically has to say about immigrants and immigration. The first thing we notice when we consider the matter is that the Bible speaks much more about the treatment of immigrants – that is, the treatment of the stranger, the sojourner, or the foreign resident in our midst – than it does about immigration policy in the sense of the laws and customs that should regulate the influx of foreigners into a settled community. This distinction is important to keep in mind because many people erroneously confuse biblical teaching about the treatment of immigrants with the Bible's view of what is a moral and just immigration policy.

Certain Old Testament passages directly address the treatment of strangers and aliens. For instance, Leviticus 19:33–34a says, "When an alien lives with you in your land, do not mistreat him. The alien living with you must be treated as one of your native-born." A similar theme is raised in Exodus 22:21: "Do not mistreat an alien or oppress him, for you were aliens in Egypt." These verses have great significance for both Christians and Jews. This last verse has particular salience for Jews because the Jewish people were once enslaved and mistreated as aliens in Egypt during biblical times and have known similar hardship and mistreatment as foreigners during the many centuries of their existence in the Diaspora. Christians can also relate to such passages in a spiritual sense because the Bible declares us all "strangers and aliens" in this world (e.g., Ephesians 2:19; Philippians 3:20) – we are not fully at home, even in the land of our birth. The clear message of the Old Testament is that foreigners are not to be oppressed or mistreated and that God's moral law governs their treatment.

Foreign residents of ancient Israel were also seen as owing many of the same obligations to the community as the Jews. For instance, Deuteronomy 14:28–29 requires both Jews and Gentiles to share part of their agricultural produce every third year with a town's Levites, aliens, orphans, and widows, and Deuteronomy 16:9–15 stipulates a similar requirement for all residents, including non-Jews, to observe the Feast of Weeks and the Feast of Booths.

There are other scriptural passages, however, that place different obligations upon Jews and Gentiles. While "an alien living in any of your towns" may take for food an animal that has died (Deuteronomy 14:21), Hebrews could not eat it because they were "a people holy to the Lord your God." Similarly, while Hebrews were to relieve their fellow Israelites' debts every seven years, this commandment did not apply to transactions between Jews and Gentiles ("You may require payment from a foreigner [for credit loaned him]," it says in Deuteronomy 15:3). In these cases, God provided for distinguishing between citizens of Israel and noncitizens.

This distinction highlights what was said earlier about the difference between universal moral laws binding on all and the cultic, ceremonial, judicial, and other types of law that in the Old Testament apply only to

Israelites. Bible commentator Matthew Henry elaborates further on Jews' practice of giving or selling unclean food to foreigners: "It is plain in the law itself that [these precepts] belonged only to the Jews, and were not moral, nor of perpetual use, because not of universal obligation, for what they might not eat themselves, they might give to a stranger, a proselyte of the gate, that had renounced idolatry, and therefore was permitted to live among them."[16] In some circumstances it was thus appropriate to treat Jews and Gentiles differently – indeed, this was seen as God's command.

Of great relevance to the current immigration debate is the biblical view of the different nationalities of the earth and the places in which God has assigned them to reside. The division of the earth into specific geographic regions and the assignment of different peoples to these different geographic regions is first described in great detail in Genesis 10. It is alluded to later in Deuteronomy 32:8: "When the Most High gave the nations their inheritance, when he divided all mankind, he set up boundaries for the peoples according to the number of sons of Israel." Saint Paul takes up the same theme in Acts 17:26, when, in addressing the Athenians, he explains that "from one man [God] made every nation of men, that they should inhabit the whole earth; and he determined the times set for them and the exact places where they should live." It is clear from this that nation-state boundaries and the division of mankind into different peoples living in different geographic locations is something God ordained and part of a providential plan. It is not something sinful, immoral, or contrary to the divine intent.

WHAT IS A JUST, BIBLICAL IMMIGRATION POLICY?

If we move now from specific biblical passages to the current immigration controversy in the United States, we see Christians divided. In my positions as a congressional staffer, I often heard from lobbyists representing various religious groups who advocated what might be called the "brotherhood of mankind" position. It seemed to me, however, that in practice the policies these groups argued for were little different from the policies advocated by many liberal, secular political lobbies. Their policies were at odds with my own views and with the views of the evangelical legislators for whom I worked.

These liberal groups seemed to think it morally illegitimate for a nation's government to make distinctions in public policy on the basis of a person's citizenship, nationality, global residence, or place of birth. Some would base their claim on the spiritual universalism that is clearly present in the Bible, though they tend to ignore other biblical teachings that are not congenial to their claims. It is certainly true that the Bible proclaims a universal message of salvation that is available to all regardless of nationality, race, ethnicity, or any other human distinction. Scripture says that all human beings are created in God's image, and thus, despite their fallen or sinful nature, have inherent human value. And the New Testament announces in the most forceful manner that with Christians all human distinctions of race, ethnicity, socioeconomic class, and the like have little currency in the eyes of God. The New Testament proclaims a unity in Christ based on the belief that Jesus's sacrifice makes all those who call him their savior heirs of eternal salvation. To Christians, the differences that come into play on earth have little value in the Kingdom of God. As St. Paul says, all those who are made "sons of God through faith in Christ Jesus" are each "Abraham's seed, and heirs according to the promise" (Galatians 3:26, 29). Within the Christian community, he explains, "there is neither Jew nor Greek, slave nor free, male nor female," but all are "one in Christ Jesus" (Galatians 3:28).

The universalism inherent in the Christian Good News is easy to see. Individuals from all walks of life, from all over the globe, have become believers. They include prostitutes such as Rahab[17] (Hebrews 11:31), Roman centurions such as Cornelius (Acts 10), White House hatchet men such as Charles Colson, and, over the centuries, untold millions from every corner of the globe. But does this spiritual universalism translate into a biblical requirement for an open-borders policy of immigration as certain liberal Christians claim?

I do not believe that this is so, and I will try to explain why. The liberal Christians who advocate the open-borders policy on immigration make in my judgment three cardinal mistakes from a biblical point of view. They simultaneously (1) fail to acknowledge the special obligation we all have toward those closest to us and to the specific communities wherein we reside; (2) pay insufficient attention to the biblical obligation that civil authorities have to protect the people and the communities entrusted to their care; and (3) ignore the very real pragmatic harms that the policies they advocate would have on the health and well-being of American society.

SPECIAL OBLIGATIONS TO FAMILY, COMMUNITY, AND NATION

Recall what was said previously about the particularistic nature of nations and peoples and about the specific geographic locations wherein they reside. In Genesis 10, Deuteronomy 32:8, and Acts 17:26, it is explained how God determined the places on the earth where the different peoples that constitute humanity were to live. We are all seen as members of different tribes and nations living in different geographic locales, and our immediate obligations must clearly be to those concrete persons and groups nearest us rather than to tribes and persons living in different parts of the world. This is seen as part of the divine plan. Our first allegiance must be to specific human beings who are part of our own group, rather than to those who are members of other groups.

The situation with the family is one example. In 1 Timothy 5:8, Paul warns, "If anyone does not provide for his relatives, and especially for his own family, he has disowned the faith and is worse than an unbeliever." Here it is made plain that we each have a very special obligation to those who are closest to us by family and blood ties – that their needs and welfare must stand tops in our priorities. All of us who are members of families have obligations to the members of those families that are special and of a higher order than our obligations toward nonfamily members. However much we may love all human beings – and as Christians we are commanded to love all people – each of us nevertheless has a very special attachment to, and a very special moral obligation toward, the members of our own families and their well-being. A man who spent most of his time helping strangers but neglected the welfare of his own family would, in Paul's words, be disowning the faith. I have a more pressing obligation to provide for my family than I do for my neighbor's family, a more pressing obligation to help my relatives than to help strangers, and a more pressing obligation to be concerned with the well-being of the local civic community in which I reside than with the civic community in another part of my state.

And what is said here about the local civic community can also be said about the civic community on a larger scale. We as Americans have a greater and more immediate moral obligation to be concerned with the welfare and quality of life in the United States than in other countries, just as the residents of those other countries should be more concerned with what goes on there than in the United States. All peoples of the globe are part of various communities – nations, tribes, clans, families, local churches, and so on – and these communities have a certain corporate life, corporate independence, and corporate integrity that we honor and respect. Each of us has ties to very particularistic communities, and we must all acknowledge the legitimacy of those ties and the special obligation that we all have to direct our immediate attention to the welfare of those very special communities that each of us calls our own.

These facts are often ignored by defenders of open borders, who oppose all immigration restrictions and sometimes see nation-state boundaries as immoral. What they say is clearly out of tune with the biblical view that the division of the globe into territories inhabited by different nations and tribes is part of a God-ordained plan. Whatever God's ultimate plan for us may be in the triumph of his kingdom – where our glorified existence may be very different from our current one – in our present earthly situation, nations, families, tribes, and territorial states are a necessary component of orderly human existence and part of God's providential plan.

CIVIL AUTHORITIES' OBLIGATION TO PROTECT THE COMMUNITY

Just as we, as members of families, each have a special obligation to provide for our families' welfare, so statesmen and political leaders have a special obligation to look out for the well-being of the political communities that are entrusted to their care. The biblical basis for this view was pointed out previously. As stewards of the community welfare, political leaders have the obligation to protect the community from those who would do it harm and from those whose addition to the community for one reason or another would constitute an intolerable burden. Thus American Christians and their political leaders, from earliest colonial times, felt perfectly within their rights to exclude or deport public charges, prostitutes, disease carriers, anarchists, and the like.[18] When impoverished Chinese immigrants were flooding into the West Coast and undermining the wages of native workers in the latter part of the 19th century, Congress reacted with legislation that greatly restricted immigration from China. Similarly, in the early 1920s, after an enormous influx of immigrants from Eastern and Southern Europe, whose assimilation into mainstream America was a daunting challenge (especially because many were from rural peasant backgrounds and adhered to religions very different from the Protestant mainstream), Congress again passed severe immigration restrictions. These restrictions lasted until the 1960s, when our current immigration regime was put in place. These 1960s-era reforms arguably went too far and seemed to have been driven by people with a partisan political agenda.[19]

Magistrates and statesmen have an obligation to protect their own communities and if necessary to use the coercive power of the state to achieve this aim. This obligation includes the obligation to patrol national borders and to enforce immigration laws that are directed at the public good. Some liberal Christians believe that it is immoral for the Border

Patrol to stop illegal immigrants from flooding into the United States if all these immigrants seek is the opportunity to work and escape the impoverished conditions that exist in the lands from which they come. How can it be just or moral, they ask, to stop honest, hard-working people from coming to the United States when all they want is to improve their lot in life? What is wrong, they ask, with seeking a better life for oneself and one's family just as the ancestors of millions of Americans have done in the past? These are good questions – and there are good answers to them.

The problem with the huge influx of illegal immigrants into the United States today is that it has many harmful consequences for the quality of American public life. Some of these will be discussed shortly. Our political leaders have the obligation to enforce laws that are directed at the public good, and in regard to our immigration and naturalization laws, those who are not members of our political community have an obligation to respect those laws just as we have an obligation to respect the immigration and naturalization laws of other countries. While one can understand the desperation that motivates illegal immigrants, there are larger matters of the public good at stake here that make the actions of the illegal immigrants morally wrong. It is similarly morally wrong for a poor person to steal from a wealthier one – an action that we may well understand and even, in extreme circumstances, have sympathy with, but which, nevertheless, cannot be universally condoned. As Proverbs 6:30–31 says, "Men do not despise a thief if he steals to satisfy his hunger when he is starving. Yet if he is caught, he must pay sevenfold, though it costs him all the wealth of his house."

Paul Marshall sees the maintenance of borders as one of the obligations that governments have toward the well-being of those they govern. While he is sympathetic to the plight of poor immigrants, the welfare of the existing community, he believes, must be the first concern of government officials. Practical and prudential political judgments about the welfare of the community must be made through our democratic political process, Marshall believes, and once made, the rule of law requires that these judgments be enforced by appropriate officials. He writes on this:

While there are doubtless some thugs and thieves among them, as with all people, the majority of illegal immigrants entering the United States...simply desire a better life, and are willing to risk their lives in striving for it. If there were no border then who could object to what they do? It is the fact of a border, a political invention, that makes their action wrong.... Like all borders [America's borders] are a product of war, compromise, and accident. But if governments are to be able to govern, then there need to be some controls on who can enter a country through these borders. It is because of this necessary *political* restriction that an otherwise praiseworthy activity can become wrong.[20]

Thus the rightful power of the sword includes policing the nation's borders, as well as the arrest and deportation of immigrant lawbreakers, even when their only violation is of immigration status. The state is duty-bound to act in this manner because of the illegal alien's disregard for legitimately constituted authority and the adverse effect of his immigration upon the citizens whom the civil government is duty-bound to protect. We have here again a situation that comes under the Pauline injunction: "Everyone must submit himself to the governing authorities.... The authorities that exist have been established by God. Consequently, he who rebels against the authority is rebelling against what God has instituted" (Romans 13: 1–2).

This principle, it is true, can sometimes lead to tragic situations (tragic in the classical Greek sense, where following right principles leads to unavoidable suffering and even catastrophe). The Bible says that it is God who establishes governments and nations and societies. He places people within the care of temporal governments, imposing on them as individuals civic duties owed to that place where they hold earthly citizenship. They also are to love God and their neighbor. These dual obligations may pit believer against believer, each in service under God to his country, as in the touching story of a Belgian battlefield in World War I. On Christmas Eve 1914, English and German soldiers (with Christians on both sides) began a one-day cease-fire in a bloody battle with a million casualties. Impromptu, opposing soldiers sang the carol "Silent Night" together, but later resumed bitter combat.[21]

HARMS OF OPEN BORDERS AND THE NEED FOR MORE RESTRICTIVE IMMIGRATION

Immigration policy has an important effect in shaping the future of our nation. Currently, the United States admits a million legal immigrants each year, with illegal aliens adding another half million or more new residents annually.[22] These are historically high levels, even when compared with the Great Wave immigration that took place at the turn of the 20th century.[23] What has been the result of this massive influx? While there certainly have been net gains in some areas, particularly with the influx of highly educated and entrepreneurially talented foreigners, in many parts of the country the large-scale influx of often unskilled and uneducated immigrants who pay few taxes and draw heavily upon public services such as health and education has been a significant burden on the communities in which they have settled. They have imposed a fiscal burden on citizen taxpayers and in many areas have greatly increased urban congestion and crime. Even in purely economic terms, the net loss to our public treasuries from the mass immigration of unskilled immigrants is very large. Harvard economist George Borjas and several other scholars have documented this net economic cost well.[24]

In addition to the cost to the public treasury, the large-scale immigration of unskilled workers has put downward pressure on low-end wages. This may be a good thing for the middle-class person who hires an immigrant laborer to cut his lawn or care for his elderly parent, but it is not a good thing for America's own low-skilled workers. Uncontrolled immigration leaves low-skilled citizens vulnerable to such harms as direct job competition, wage depression, and flooded labor markets.[25] It aids foreigners at the expense of members of the polity and thus violates the principle of first looking out for the welfare of those closest to us. Those who have probably been most hurt by immigration have been America's poorest and most vulnerable, especially African Americans and our Hispanic citizen population.

But the greatest harm done by the kind of large-scale immigration that we have today in the United States may not be something that can be expressed in dollars and cents. The greatest harm posed by immigration on the enormous scale that we have today may be to our ability to preserve a sense of common culture and community in a rapidly changing world. While controlled immigration can benefit a nation, in extremis immigration can be destructive to the cohesiveness of a society and hamper the societal norms and mores that ensure its preservation.[26] This is particularly the case if immigrants are slow to assimilate or are averse to accepting the ways of the country to which they have moved. This latter development seems to be the case with at least some of the newer immigrants who have come to the United States in recent years. In ancient Israel, God required resident aliens to adopt the laws and customs of the natives, not the other way around (see Leviticus 18:26, 20:2, 24:22; Numbers 9:14, 15:14). The adverse consequence when this does not happen is seen in the curse described in Deuteronomy 28:43–44: "The alien who lives among you will rise above you higher and higher, but you will sink lower and lower. He will lend to you, but you will not lend to him. He will be the head, but you will be the tail."

Part of the cultural problem posed by current immigration comes from those hailing from countries with mores, customs, religions, and political systems different from our own. But the problem is exacerbated by the sheer size of the immigrant influx and its concentration in certain parts of the country. This effect of size makes assimilation much more difficult – it is much easier for a society to deal with a small number of people who need the support of social services and avenues to integrate into the wider society than it is to deal with a larger number. Immigration on the very large scale we have today endangers our ability to assimilate the newcomers into the mainstream of American life.

CONCLUSION

The current mass immigration of predominately unskilled people most directly harms our fellow Americans who lack skills and education.[27] A poor person from a third world country may become better off by immigrating, but he depresses the wages of the poorest Americans and competes directly for their jobs. The mass immigration of the unskilled can also be a drain on public services and a threat to the social and cultural stability of the United States. It is for these reasons that most Americans want to reduce to more manageable numbers the current large flow of immigrants.[28]

As a Christian, I believe that the governing authorities are established by God "as God's servant" to protect the population and provide for their welfare (Romans 13:1). A civil government should not cause the citizens under its protection to suffer economic, social, cultural, or financial upheaval through unchecked immigration. To the extent that our current immigration policies do these things, I think they are in need of great revision, as immigration critics such as George Borjas and Roy Beck have long argued. As U.S. citizens, we all have the obligation, regardless of our religious faith, to consider seriously the terms and conditions under which we allow aliens to enter, visit, and permanently reside in America, and attain citizenship. We need a great national conversation about our current immigration policies, and our conversation, if it is to lead to a wise course of action, must be guided by a high level of both prudence and sound judgment. Those of us who are Christians can bring to the table in this conversation our special grounding in the wisdom of biblical principles and the humility that comes from the recognition that we are all deeply flawed in our natures and are dependent upon God's grace to achieve whatever level of wisdom and insight we can attain. None of us should ever delude ourselves into believing that we are in possession of the whole truth on a prudential question such as that posed by our current immigration dilemma. In the spirit of Christian humility, we can move forward on this issue and make genuine progress.

5

The Moral Dilemma of U.S. Immigration Policy

Open Borders Versus Social Justice?

Stephen Macedo

IMMIGRATION POLICY AS A MORAL DILEMMA

How should we think about U.S. immigration policy from the stand-point of basic justice, especially distributive justice, which encompasses our obligations to the less well-off? Does a justifiable immigration policy take its bearings (in part) from the acknowledgment that we have special obligations to "our own" poor, our least well-off fellow citizens? Or, on the other hand, do our moral duties simply argue for attending to the interests of the least well-off persons in the world, giving no special weight to the interests of the least well-off Americans?

As is clear from other chapters in this volume, there are reasons to believe that recent American immigration policy has had a deleterious impact on the distribution of income among American citizens. According to influential arguments – associated with George Borjas and others – by admitting large numbers of relatively poorly educated and low-skilled workers, we have increased competition for low-skilled jobs, lowering the wages of the poor and increasing the gap between rich and poor

I am grateful for very helpful comments on versions of this chapter from Michael Blake, Rainer Forst, Matt Lister, Douglas Massey, Jamie Mayerfield, Philip Pettit, Walter Sinnott-Armstrong, and Leif Wenar. I also thank the participants in the Fellows seminar of the University Center for Human Values, Princeton University, in May 2005, especially Nir Eyal and Sanjay Reddy, for their extended comments. I am grateful to the discussants at workshops of the Program in Law and Public Affairs at Princeton and the Philosophy Department of the University of Utah in September 2005, and at the New York University Legal Theory Colloquium in December 2005, for which special thanks are given to Ronald Dworkin and Thomas Nagel, who raised a number of points that led to corrections and improvements to this chapter.

Americans. The high proportion of noncitizens among the poor may also lessen political support for social welfare policies.

How should we think about the apparent ethical conflict between, on the one hand, the cosmopolitan humanitarian impulse to admit less well-off persons from abroad who wish to immigrate to the United States and, on the other hand, the special obligations we have to less well-off Americans, including or especially African Americans? Those with liberal sensibilities need to consider whether all the things that they might favor – humanitarian concern for the world's poor, an openness to an ever-widening social diversity, and concern for distributive justice within our political community – necessarily go together.

These are vexing questions not only in politics but in contemporary political theory and moral philosophy, and what I say will be controversial, though the perspective I defend is shared by some others. I argue that if high levels of immigration have a detrimental impact on our least well-off fellow citizens, that is a reason to limit immigration, even if those who seek admission seem to be poorer than our own poor whose condition is worsened by their entry. Citizens have special obligations to one another: we have special reasons to be concerned with the distribution of wealth and opportunities among citizens. The comparative standing of citizens matters in some ways that the comparative standing of citizens and noncitizens does not. Of course, distributive justice is only one consideration bearing on immigration policy, though a weighty one.

I argue against what is sometimes characterized as a "cosmopolitan" position with respect to distributive justice and defend the idea that distributive justice is an obligation that holds among citizens, a position that has also been defended by Michael Walzer, John Rawls, and David Miller, among others.[1] What is the basis of these special obligations among citizens? I argue that it is as members or co-participants in self-governing political communities that we have special obligations to our fellow members.

Do we conclude, therefore, that the borders should be closed and immigration by the poor restricted? That conclusion would be far too hasty. For one thing, we do have significant moral obligations to poor people abroad, although these are different from what we owe to fellow citizens. In addition, measures designed to "tighten up" the borders may do more harm than good. On balance, we should perhaps accept ongoing high levels of movement back and forth across the U.S.-Mexico border, as Douglas Massey recommends. But we also need to consider whether high levels of immigration by low-skilled workers make it less likely that we will fulfill our moral obligations to the poorest Americans. The distributive impact of immigration policy is important.

This chapter proceeds as follows. The first part describes why it is reasonable to think that we face a dilemma in shaping U.S. immigration policy. I feature the sorts of claims advanced by George Borjas not because I am sure he is right but because he raises important moral questions. In the next section, I consider the debate between "cosmopolitans" – who argue against the moral significance of shared citizenship and in favor of universal obligations of distributive justice – and those who argue for the existence of special obligations of justice among citizens. I seek to clarify the moral grounds for regarding shared membership in a political community as morally significant but also emphasize that we do have significant cosmopolitan duties. In the final section, I return to the moral dilemma of U.S. immigration policy and offer some reflections on policy choices.

One point is worth making before moving on. The perspective adopted and defended here is politically liberal. John Rawls and Michael Walzer (whose ideas I treat in some detail) are philosophers of the Left in American politics. It might be thought that this limits the relevance of my argument, but this may not be so. For one thing, the vast majority of Americans profess a belief in some liberal principles, such as equality of opportunity. While Americans are less supportive than Europeans of measures designed directly to reduce income disparities between the wealthy and the poor, they overwhelmingly affirm that institutions such as public education should ensure that every child has a good start in life, irrespective of accidents of birth.[2] The question of whether we have special obligations to our fellow citizens is important independently of the details of one's convictions about what justice requires among citizens. Even those who believe that "equality of opportunity" mandates only a modest level of educational and other social services may still think that the mandate holds among fellow citizens and not all of humanity. The general thrust of my argument should therefore be of relevance to those who do not accept the specific prescriptions of Rawls and Walzer.

THE CONTOURS OF THE IMMIGRATION DILEMMA

Over the last 40 years, American immigration policies and practices have become, in some respects, more accommodating to the less well-off abroad. Some argue that this "generosity" has exacted a significant cost in terms of social justice at home.

The basic facts are striking. Whereas in 1970, 5 percent of the general population was composed of immigrants, that figure is now 12 percent, the highest in nearly 80 years. By 2002, there were 56 million immigrants and first-generation Americans (children of immigrants), comprising 20 percent of the U.S. population in 2000, the highest overall number in U.S. history according to the Census Bureau, though not the highest percentage.[3]

The composition of the growing immigrant pool has changed markedly in recent decades, with the skill level and earnings of immigrants declining relative to that of the native U.S. population. Whereas in 1960 the average immigrant man living in the United States earned 4 percent more than the average native-born American, by 1998 the average immigrant earned 23 percent less. Most of the growth in immigration since 1960 has been among people entering at the bottom 20 percent of the income scale. This is partly because, as George Borjas observes, "[s]ince the immigration reforms of 1965, U.S. immigration law has encouraged family reunification and discouraged the arrival of skilled immigrants."[4] At the same time, the ethnic makeup of immigration has also changed, with the percentage arriving from Europe and Canada falling sharply and the percentage from Latin America and Asia rising.[5]

In Borjas's influential if controversial analysis, recent decades of immigration have worsened income disparities in the United States. Immigration from 1980 to 1995 increased the pool of high school dropouts in the United States by 21 percent while increasing the pool of college graduates by only 4 percent, and this, argues Borjas, has contributed to a substantial decline in the wages of high school dropouts. He argues that immigration between 1980 and 2000 had the effect of lowering wages overall by about 4 percent while lowering wages among those without a high school diploma (roughly the bottom 10 percent of wage earners) by 7.4 percent. To put it another way, it is widely agreed that in the United States in the 1980s and early 1990s there was a substantial widening of the wage gap between more and less well-educated workers. Borjas argues that nearly half of this widening wage gap between high school dropouts and others may be due to the increase in the low-skilled labor pool caused by immigration.

Steven A. Camarota, in Chapter 10 of this volume, associates recent immigration with employment losses among Americans: from 2000 to 2004, unemployment among native-born Americans increased by more than two million, while more than two million immigrants entered the labor force (half of them illegally).[6] A study funded by the Congressional

Black Caucus Foundation argues that labor force participation among African American males with low levels of education has fallen especially steeply, with immigration being one possible contributing factor.[7]

Of course, all Americans have benefited from cheaper fruits and vegetables and other products that immigrants (including undocumented workers) help produce.[8] But wealthier Americans have also benefited from increased access to cheap menial labor – such as service work performed by nannies, gardeners, and others. Firms have also benefited from cheap labor. However, Borjas argues that native-born African American and Hispanic workers have suffered disproportionately because they have disproportionately lower skills and education, own few firms, and often compete directly with low-skilled immigrants for jobs.[9]

Let me add one other element to this admittedly controversial account before moving on. Nations with notably more progressive domestic policies often have immigration laws that are quite different from those of the United States. American immigration policy emphasizes family reunification (including children, spouses, parents, and adult siblings), with a very small percentage of immigrants – around 5 percent in recent decades – receiving visas based on the possession of desirable skills. Canada, by contrast, has a quota system that gives greater weight to educational background, occupation, and English-language proficiency of applicants for admission. Canada's policy favors better-educated and higher-skilled workers, and this seems likely to have distributive effects that are the opposite of U.S. policy. By increasing the pool of skilled workers relative to the unskilled, Canadian policy tends to lower the wages of the better-off and to raise the relative wage levels of the worse-off.[10]

Finally, recent patterns of immigration to the United States may also tend to lower public support for social welfare and redistributive programs. Economic inequality in the United States has increased sharply since 1970, but this has not led to increased pressure for redistribution. If anything, the reverse would seem to be the case: the real value of the minimum wage has fallen, and taxes paid by the better-off have been cut, including top marginal tax rates and the estate and capital gains taxes. Congress restricted alien access to many federally funded welfare benefits in 1996;[11] nevertheless, immigrants to the United States receive various forms of public assistance at a higher rate than native-born Americans. Nolan McCarty, Keith T. Poole, and Howard Rosenthal argue that recent patterns of immigration help explain why increasing inequality has come about without an increase in political pressure toward redistribution. Since 1972, the percentage of noncitizens has risen and their incomes relative to those of other Americans have fallen.] According to McCarty, et al., "From 1972 to 2000, the median family income of non-citizens fell from 82% of the median income of voters to 65% while the fraction of the population that is non-citizen rose from 2.6% to 7.7%."[12] Over this time, the incomes of the median voters – the voters likely to be the "swing voters" who decide close elections – have not fallen. Increasing economic inequality has left these median voters no worse off in terms of relative income. Meanwhile, the income of the median family living in the United States (including voters and nonvoters) has fallen on account of the sharp decline in the incomes of noncitizens. According to this analysis, immigration to the United States has made the median voter better off relative to the population as a whole (including voters and nonvoters), decreasing the median voter's likelihood of supporting redistribution.

There are yet other ways in which immigration might have an impact on distributive justice. I have not considered the argument that welfare states benefit from the presence of a shared culture, a position ably defended by David Miller.[13] There is evidence suggesting that cultural diversity leads to lower trust among groups and declining support for the provision of public goods.[14] We have enough on the table to raise some relevant ethical questions, though I should also emphasize that all of these empirical questions cry out for additional investigation.

The questions before us include the following: if U.S. immigration policies appear to be liberal and generous to the less well-off abroad (or at least some of them), does this generosity involve injustice toward poorer native-born Americans, including – or perhaps especially – African Americans? If we have special obligations to our poorer fellow citizens – obligations that are sufficiently urgent and weighty – then U.S. immigration policy may be hard or impossible to defend from the standpoint of justice.

Of course, the question of how we should respond to this – if it is true – is not straightforward. It does not follow that greater justice argues for more restrictive immigration policies. It may be that justice requires us to change the laws and policies that allow the immigration of low-skilled workers and thus generate adverse effects on the native-born poor. The inegalitarian distributive effects of immigration could be offset via a higher minimum wage or improved education and training for the unemployed along with other social benefits for all of the less well-off. And yet we have seen that high levels of low-skilled immigration may also lower public support for social welfare. This sharpens the dilemma.

COSMOPOLITAN VERSUS CIVIC OBLIGATIONS?

[If the better-off have moral obligations to help the least well-off, why shouldn't those obligations focus on the least well-off of the world? Can we justify special obligations to our own poor, even if they are less poor than many others in the world?]

Consider two ways in which we might care about the condition of the poor and seek to do something about it. We might care only about their absolute level of poverty or deprivation, or we might care about relative deprivation: the gap between the lives of the poorest and those of the richest. In response to the first concern, we would engage in *humanitarian assistance* and seek to establish a floor of material well-being: a standard of decency below which no one should fall. In response to the latter concern, we would articulate and enforce principles of social or *distributive justice*: standards to regulate the major institutions of taxation, inheritance, social provision, wage policies, education, and so forth that help determine over time the relative levels of income, wealth, and opportunity available to different groups.

Most people seem to accept that wealthy societies owe the first sort of concern to human beings generally. Via humanitarian assistance, wealthier societies should pool their efforts and seek to lift poorer countries at least up to a level of basic decency; exactly what level is adequate or morally required is an important question. This sort of cosmopolitan moral concern has been likened to the duty we all have to be "Good Samaritans."[15]

The latter species of concern – social or distributive justice – requires the establishment of institutions to regulate market inequalities: systems of progressive taxation, inheritance taxes, and the provision of social services. As noted, most Americans profess a belief that every child born in the United States should have a fair chance to attain a good job – to compete based on his or her talents and effort – and this requires that governments raise taxes in order to provide good schools for all.] Virtually everyone accepts some degree of progressiveness in the tax structure, so efforts to promote fair equality of opportunity are typically redistributive and constitute part of a system of distributive justice. Opportunity is one of the things we "redistribute" by building public institutions – including tax-supported schools – alongside market institutions. As we have seen, immigration policies may also have an impact on the distribution of opportunities and rewards in society.

Do we have special moral obligations to our fellow citizens, especially obligations falling under the rubric of distributive justice? The question is whether, and if so, how, national borders matter with respect to our fundamental moral obligations to one another.

There are, roughly speaking, two opposing lines of thought. One emphasizes the moral arbitrariness of borders and the universality of our obligations to the less well-off. The other argues that borders are morally significant, that we have special obligations to poorer fellow citizens, and that obligations of distributive justice in particular apply only among citizens. The first position is often referred to as a form of moral "cosmopolitanism;" the latter position – for which I argue – goes under various names, and I will refer to it as the "civic view."

I want to join those who argue that we have special obligations of mutual justification to our fellow citizens and that distributive justice often has special force among fellow citizens. With respect to people in the rest of the world, our duties are different, though still quite important: fair dealing – including curbs on the exploitative potential of our corporations and doing our fair share to address common problems (e.g., environmental dangers such as global warming); more specific projects of historical rectification and redress in response to particular past acts of injustice; and humanitarian assistance to help lift other societies (insofar as we can) out of poverty.

Michael Walzer strikingly asserts that, "Distributive justice begins with membership; it must vindicate at one and the same time the limited right of closure, without which there could be no communities at all, and the political inclusiveness of existing communities."[16] It seems to me that Walzer is on the right track here, though he is not very clear about the moral grounds for his claims. He has a distinctive approach to the practice of justifying moral claims in politics to one another, and this helps explain why he argues that obligations of distributive justice apply within political communities only. Walzer famously argues that moral arguments in politics should avoid philosophical system building and abstraction; arguments of political morality should take the form of interpreting "shared social meanings." We should, he says, think about principles of justice in light of "the particularism of history, culture, and membership." Social goods should be distributed according to criteria internal to their social meanings, and these shared social meanings are located within particular political communities.[17]

Given this account of the nature of moral argument and distributive justice, it is not surprising that Walzer should argue that distributive justice applies within ongoing political communities that are the natural homes of shared meanings. For Walzer, the rejection of cosmopolitan obligations of distributive justice goes hand in hand with the claim that common understandings of values are shared within particular political communities but not across them.

Walzer's argument may contain part of the truth, but it is also puzzling. Achieving shared meanings with respect to justice is a worthy aspiration. But while shared meanings are an important goal of public argument, an achievement to be worked toward, the extent of shared meanings is not the proper ground for circumscribing claims of social justice. Publicly justified "common meanings" seem more like a goal of public argument and deliberation rather than the basis (or the presupposition) of political obligations.

Shared social meanings – common understandings, shared assumptions of various sorts – are important for sustaining a political system based on discussion and mutual justification, but they would seem not to be the central criterion for demarcating the range of those to whom we owe justice. The range of those with whom we should seek to establish common and publicly justified principles of justice consists of those with whom we share a system of binding laws.

Walzer sometimes lays too much emphasis on consensus and shared meanings in another way as well: what we should want is a justified consensus that is the result of criticism and testing. Critical argumentation (which I would characterize as philosophical) is essential to this project of public justification because what we should work toward are common understandings that are sound, and their soundness is essential to their authoritativeness. The mere fact of agreement, the mere existence of conventions, is not enough.

David Miller has argued eloquently for the advantages to political communities of a shared national culture and a common language because these can help support a collective identity and bonds of mutual sympathy and understanding: "Social justice will always be easier to achieve in states with strong national identities and without internal communal divisions."[18] Social scientists are only beginning to explore systematically the relationship between heterogeneity, social capital, and social justice.[19]

Particular political societies – at least when they are well ordered rather than tyrannical, oppressive, or desperately poor – will tend to generate common understandings among members, including standards for how disputes and disagreements should be resolved.[20] They may generate a plethora of disagreements and conflicts, but these will be manageable if the society has set standards and practices for how disagreements should be dealt with and a reserve of rough agreement on other matters sufficient to sustain a common willingness to continue to share a political order.

In his *The Law of Peoples*, Rawls cites and endorses Walzer's discussion of the moral significance of membership and borders. He argues that the political community – or "people" – is the appropriate site of distributive justice: there are no obligations of distributive justice simply among human beings. We have humanitarian duties to relieve those in distress – as mentioned earlier – but both Walzer and Rawls agree that we have no obligations across borders to regulate the relative well-being of better- and worse-off people (or to create institutions capable of doing so).

Why does Rawls embrace Walzer's view of the limited scope of distributive justice? Rawls does not as a general matter share Walzer's emphasis on the authority of shared social meanings. Moreover, Rawls's general method seems designed to encourage us to transcend the limited perspective of morally arbitrary accidents of birth, so there is a puzzle here.

When Rawls argues about domestic justice, the guiding thought is that when we consider principles of justice to regulate the "basic structure" of a polity, we should regard each other as free and equal persons and put aside moral claims based on morally arbitrary differences and accidents of fate. We put aside claims to unequal rewards based on advantages flowing from accidents of birth, including the good fortune of being born into a well-off family or with a superior genetic endowment. We do this by imagining ourselves in an "original position" behind a "veil of ignorance": we ask which principles of social justice we would choose if we did not know the social position we would occupy.[21] This helps us consider which principles of justice for regulating the design of the basic structure are fair to all and so capable of being freely accepted by reasonable people regardless of the position they occupy in society. To affirm mutually justified principles to regulate basic social institutions is to affirm that we regard one another as moral equals.

The upshot of Rawls's thought experiment is his argument that two basic principles of justice would be chosen by citizens of modern pluralistic democracies:

1. Each person has an equal claim to a fully adequate scheme of equal basic rights and liberties, which scheme is compatible with the same scheme for all; and in this scheme the equal political liberties, and only those liberties, are to be guaranteed their fair value.

2. Social and economic inequalities are to satisfy two conditions: (a) They are to be attached to positions and offices open to all under conditions of fair equality of opportunity; and, (b) they are to be to the greatest benefit of the least advantaged members of society.[22]

Principle 2 (b) is also known as the "difference principle."]

What is the relevance of all this to obligations across borders? If being born into a well-off family or with especially advantageous genes is to be regarded as morally arbitrary when thinking about justice, surely it seems equally arbitrary whether one is born in New Mexico or Mexico. One's place of birth with respect to nationality or political community seems quintessentially arbitrary. And yet Rawls follows Walzer in arguing that obligations of distributive justice (such as the difference principle and the principle of fair equality of opportunity) apply only within the borders of a political community and only among co-participants in a shared political order. What can justify this?

[Like Walzer, Rawls mentions the fact of greater diversity on the international scale, the fact that reasonable pluralism "is more evident within a society of well-ordered peoples than it is within one society alone."[23] Some have supposed that this invocation of diversity signals a retreat in Rawls's later writings with respect to his ambitions regarding justice. Suffice it for these purposes to say that I think this interpretation is wrong, and in any event we should seek a better one if we can find it.[24]]

[The diversity-based argument for limiting obligations of distributive justice to particular political communities would appear to be a nonmoral account of why justice's sails need trimming, a matter of bowing before unfortunate necessities, a pragmatic or prudential concession rather than a full moral justification. I believe there is a moral justification for confining obligations of distributive justice to co-participants in particular political communities. But what might it be?]

THE MORAL SIGNIFICANCE OF COLLECTIVE SELF-GOVERNANCE

Borders are morally significant because they bound systems of collective self-governance.[25] As Michael I. Blake has emphasized, the arbitrariness of the location of borders does not stop them from being of great moral significance.[26] Co-participation in governance is an important moral relation. As members of a political community, we are joined in a collective enterprise across generations through which we construct and sustain a comprehensive system of laws and institutions that regulate and shape all other associations, including religious communities and families. We are born into political communities and are formed by them. From cradle to grave (and beyond), our interests, identities, relationships, and opportunities are pervasively shaped by the political system and the laws that we collectively create, coercively impose, and live within. The basic values of our political order pervasively shape the lives of those who reside within it.

The governments of self-governing political communities – at least so long as they are legitimate – are recognized by members to be capable of authoritatively resolving conflicts and of making decisions that bind us as members of the political community: our government as our agent enters into treaties, makes alliances, declares war, and conducts various undertakings in our name. As Henry Richardson has emphasized, legitimate governments are capable of putting citizens under new duties, and this is an awesome moral power.[27] We can be held collectively liable as citizens for the actions of our government, recognized by us and others to be our collective agent.[28]

Citizens have powerful obligations of mutual concern and respect, and mutual justification, to one another because they are joined together – as constituent members of a sovereign people – in creating binding political institutions that determine patterns of opportunities and rewards for all.[29] A self-governing political society is a hugely significant joint venture, and we understand it as such. We have strong common obligations as fellow citizens because we collectively govern one another: we collectively make hugely consequential decisions. This could not simultaneously be true of the international society, and it is not. Membership in international bodies does not have the same significance because that membership is mediated by membership in primary political units, namely the "Member States" of the United Nations or its peoples: individuals are not governed directly by multilateral institutions.[30] International institutions deal with a limited range of subjects.

Cosmopolitan distributive justice (as opposed to a duty to assist other peoples to become self-governing) makes no sense absent a cosmopolitan state and a cosmopolitan political community, for which hardly anyone seriously argues and we are not obliged to bring into being, though there are good reasons for strengthening international institutions. It is, moreover, hard to understand the reasonableness of making people responsible for the welfare of others without also making them responsible for their governance. It would be strange and unreasonable to sever ongoing responsibilities for the provision of health, welfare, and education from responsibilities for governance with respect to these matters. ⌐

To argue that membership in a political collectivity is morally significant in the ways I have begun to describe raises further questions. Which political collectivities qualify? Does every political community have equal moral standing, and if not, which ones do? The traditional answer is to say that all sovereign and independent regimes have full moral status in international law. Rawls, in *The Law of Peoples*, in effect offers an account of full legitimacy that seems to me to be on the right track. Respect for basic human rights is one crucial threshold condition of legitimacy. Liberal democracies qualify for full respect, but so do certain not fully liberal and democratic regimes, which Rawls calls "decent" peoples. We need not go into the details here, but suffice it to say that the theory of legitimacy at work here is the following: *we ought to fully respect states that effectively protect citizens and provide working legal arrangements and within which (a) basic human rights are respected and (b) there are effective processes for giving everyone a say, for ensuring that all groups within society are listened to, responded to, and effectively included in collective self-rule.*[31] To respect such political societies is to respect distinctive forms of collective self-rule, forms of collective self-rule that may deviate from some of the features that we understand to be aspects of liberal democracy but nevertheless observe basic rights and take all members' interests seriously into account. If such communities go wrong in some of the respects identified here, we can nevertheless say that the mistake is theirs to make. Such political communities can be regarded as the fit custodians of the interests of their own citizens.

WHAT DO WE OWE TO NONMEMBERS?

Space does not permit an extensive discussion of what the civic view might say about obligations to nonmembers, but it may be helpful to round out the account before returning to the problem of immigration.

First, societies have general duties of *fair dealing* with one another, and this would include nonexploitation, the avoidance of force and fraud, and the duty to curb the capacity of one's citizens or corporations to harm or exploit others. This general duty of fair dealing would seem to include doing our fair share to address common problems (avoidance of free-riding), including environmental problems such as global warming, disaster relief, and humanitarian assistance.

Second, societies have specific obligations to other countries or groups growing out of particular relations of exploitation, oppression, or domination, which give rise to specific obligations of *rectification and redress*; that is, if we have exploited or oppressed poorer and weaker societies, or if we have allowed our corporations to do so, then we have debts to these other societies that require some sort of recompense.

I should emphasize that these first two categories almost certainly generate strong demands for serious reform of the ways in which countries such as the United States conduct themselves in international affairs.[32]

Finally, it seems right to say that well-off societies have general *humanitarian duties* to relieve those in destitution or distress and to respond to gross and systematic violations of human rights. Our duty is to do what we can to relieve distress, to end suffering, to stop gross violations of human rights, and to get a society on its feet so that it can look after its own affairs. These duties may involve substantial resource commitments, and they certainly require rich countries such as the United States to spend more than they currently do on assistance. It is crucial to specify the target: the proper target of aid could be such that all members of a given society are capable of leading good lives; while Americans and other consumerists might disagree, Aristotle was right to note long ago that the good life does not require vast amounts of wealth.

Crucially, members of wealthier societies do not owe to all the people of the world precisely the same consideration that they owe to fellow citizens. The reason is that fellow citizens stand in a special moral relation with one another: they share extensive institutional relations of shared governance.

U.S. IMMIGRATION POLICY AND DISTRIBUTIVE JUSTICE

[As we have seen, it is not implausible to think that U.S. immigration policy of the last 40 years has been bad for distributive justice within the United States. It may have worsened income inequalities by admitting large numbers of poor people. Those poor immigrants are better off for having been allowed to immigrate, but the burdens of funding some social welfare programs are increased, and those programs may be less politically popular as a consequence.]What, from an egalitarian perspective at least, could possibly be wrong in making the United States more like Canada by reducing overall levels of immigration and giving greater priority to immigration by the better-educated and higher-skilled?

Howard Chang rightly observes that the civic, or "liberal nationalist," policy on immigration seems anomalous:

If the welfare of all incumbent residents determines admissions policies, however, and we anticipate the fiscal burden that the immigration of the poor would impose, then our welfare criterion would preclude the admission of unskilled workers in the first place. Thus, our commitment to treat these workers as equals once admitted would cut against their admission and make them worse off than they would be if we agreed never to treat them as equals. A liberal can avoid this anomaly by adopting a cosmopolitan perspective that extends equal concern to all individuals, including aliens, which suggests liberal immigration policies for unskilled workers.[33]

Chang admits, of course, that the morally justified cosmopolitan immigration policy may be politically infeasible because Americans seem unwilling to embrace the right sort of cosmopolitan moral attitude.

I have argued, however, that there are good reasons for believing that we have special obligations for our fellow citizens, obligations arising from membership in a self-governing community. In shaping immigration policies, concerns about distributive justice are relevant and urgent, and these concerns are inward-looking rather than cosmopolitan, emphasizing the special obligations we have toward our poorer fellow citizens. If the United States were to move toward a more Canadian-style immigration policy, this could improve the lot of less-well-off American workers. Considerations of distributive justice – taken in the abstract – argue for the superiority of the Canadian system: this would mean limiting immigration based on family reunification (perhaps limiting that preference to spouses and minor children), placing greater weight on priorities for education and other skills, and curbing undocumented or illegal immigration.

However, sound policy recommendations in this vexing area of policy need to take into account a great deal more of the relevant context, including geography and the heavy residue of historical patterns and practice. The United States is not Canada, and the costs of pursuing a Canadian-style immigration policy in the United States could be prohibitive. Empirical description, and careful analysis and prediction, must be combined with moral judgment. I can only sketch a few of the relevant considerations here.

The United States shares a 2,500-mile border with Mexico, and that border represents vast differences in development, income, and wealth. For more than 60 years, there have been high levels of migration from Mexico to the United States, and the United States has periodically welcomed massive influxes of migrant workers. In the period 1965–1986,

1.3 million Mexicans entered the United States legally along with 46,000 contract workers, but 28 million entered as undocumented migrants. The vast majority subsequently returned to Mexico, yielding a net migration to the United States of around five million during this time.[34] These patterns of immigration and return are self-reinforcing: migration prepares the way for more migration as language and labor market skills are acquired, along with personal contacts, including Mexicans who remain in the United States.[35] In 2000, there were eight million American citizens who were born in Mexico. Estimates of the number of undocumented persons working in the United States illegally vary widely. Stephen Camarota puts the total number of illegals at 9.1 million as of March 2004, with about 5.5 million illegal workers. In addition, 3.4 million Mexicans enter the United States yearly on nonimmigrant visas, and there are 213 million short-term border crossings. The United States and Mexico (along with other Western Hemisphere nations) are committed to policies of open markets and free trade.[36] The costs of trying to close the border would be quite high.

What is the most ethically defensible way of responding to concerns about immigration, including concerns stemming from social justice within the United States? The answer is far from simple. We must, however, consider the humanitarian costs of attempts to massively alter long-standing patterns of movement across a long and long-porous border.

One approach is to try to limit legal migration and stop illegal immigration by more vigorously controlling the southern border, by constructing a security fence, and by other means.[37] Would this be effective? It could just lead to a surge in illegal migration by tunnel, sea, and air. It is far from obvious that a fence by itself would accomplish anything useful.

A more feasible way of curtailing illegal migration by poor workers would focus on stemming the demand for migrant workers in the United States. We might institute a national identification card, increase penalties for forging identification papers, and vigorously punish employers who hire undocumented people. None of these proposals are new, and some have been tried before.[38] Obviously, if such policies were implemented effectively, the cost of low-skilled labor would increase considerably in many areas, especially in agriculture, but that would appear to be good insofar as wages rise at the bottom of the income scale. It is often said that illegal migrants do work that Americans are unwilling to do, but of course the reality is Americans are unwilling to do the same work at the prevailing low wage, and that is just the problem from the standpoint of distributive justice.[39]

An alternative approach would be to accept and regularize the flow of migrant labor, as Douglas Massey, Jorge Durand, and Nolan J. Malone recommend. Their proposals include increasing the annual quota of legal entry visas from Mexico from 20,000 (the same as for the Dominican Republic) to 60,000 and instituting a temporary two-year work visa, which would be renewable once for each Mexican worker. They propose making available 300,000 such visas per year. This would regularize the flow of migrant workers and rechannel the flow of illegal migrants into a legal flow. The work visas would be awarded to workers, not employers, so that workers are free to quit. Fees for these visas plus savings in the Immigration and Naturalization Service budget could generate hundreds of millions of dollars a year that could be passed along to states and localities with high concentrations of migrants to offset the costs of some local services. Finally, Massey and his colleagues would curtail the priorities that are now provided to family members of those who become naturalized Americans: they would eliminate the priority given to adult siblings of naturalized citizens, and they recommend making it easier for Mexican relatives of U.S. citizens to get tourist visas so they can visit and return home more easily.[40]

One advantage of this approach is that it seems to deal directly with the underlying force generating migration to the United States from Mexico: poverty in Mexico. Massey and his colleagues emphasize that immigration is part of the development process and is temporary. The poorest nations do not send out migrants – witness sub-Saharan Africa. Developing countries typically send out immigrants for eight or nine decades until growth at home relieves the pressures to leave. Facilitating short-term migration and return would help promote growth in Mexico, and it is consistent with the general emphasis of the North American Free Trade Agreement on the integration of North American markets.

One moral problem with this approach is that it regularizes a system that would seem to impose downward pressure on low-wage jobs in the United States. It takes seriously the interests of poor people in a neighboring country – with whom we have long-standing ties and very likely unpaid historical debts – and it benefits American employers, American consumers, and better-off Americans, but it does not address the special obligations we have to our poorest fellow citizens. The distributive justice problem could be dealt with by explicitly coupling these reforms with measures designed to improve the condition of poor Americans; that would be appropriate and overdue in any case.[41] But as we have seen, high levels of immigration by low-income people may make transfer payments less politically popular and, if so, that is a liability of the proposal, perhaps one that can be partially addressed by excluding guestworkers from many public benefits.

Another possible problem with this policy is the intrinsic status of guestworkers. Adequate protections must be built into any guestworker program so that workers are not exploited and oppressed. The fact is that wages and work conditions among agricultural workers in the United States are currently awful, and a regulated guestworker program ought to be coupled with measures to require decent wages and work conditions, basic health care, protection from poisoning by pesticides, and so on.[42] However, if a guestworker in the United States becomes seriously ill, the program might be designed so that he or she is entitled to a trip to the emergency room and then a one-way ticket home. Such provisions seem likely to be part of the price of getting Americans to accept a guestworker program, and they seem legitimate so long as work conditions, wages, and protections are such that we can regard the conditions of work as humane and reasonable. (If such provisions led workers to conceal and postpone treatment of serious illnesses, then we would need to rethink the acceptability of the provision.)[43]

CONCLUSION

There is reason to believe that current patterns of immigration do raise serious issues from the standpoint of social justice: high levels of immigration by poor and low-skilled workers from Mexico and elsewhere in Central America and the Caribbean may worsen the standing of poorer American citizens. Furthermore, such immigration may lessen political support for redistributive programs. Nevertheless, as we have also seen, the costs of "tightening up" the border could be extremely high: border security efforts have imposed great hardships and expense on migrant workers without stemming the tide of immigration. Employer sanctions could be a more humane enforcement mechanism, though it remains to be seen whether Americans have the political will to impose such measures. In addition, it is not clear how many poor Americans would be interested in doing the agricultural work done by many migrants, though independent of all other considerations, work conditions and wages for migrant agricultural work should be improved.

[I have argued that U.S. immigration policy presents us with the necessity of grappling with the tension between two important moral demands: justice to our fellow citizens and humanitarian concern with the plight of poor persons abroad.]I have argued that we do indeed have urgent reasons to shape major public policies and institutions with an eye toward the distributive impact. Justice demands that we craft policies that are justifiable not simply from the standpoint of aggregate welfare – or the greatest good of the greatest number. We must consider the justifiability of policies from the standpoint of the least well-off among our fellow citizens. John Rawls's theory of justice stands for the proposition that the political equality of citizens requires this sort of "distributive" justification among citizens: it is not reasonable to expect our less-well-off fellow citizens to accede to a policy on the grounds that it makes those with the luck of superior endowment by nature and birth even better off. Immigration policy – as part of the basic structure of social institutions – ought to be answerable to the interests of the poorest Americans. An immigration policy cannot be considered morally acceptable in justice unless its distributive impact is defensible from the standpoint of disadvantaged Americans.

And yet, we must also consider the collateral costs of border security measures given the long border and long-standing patterns of migration from Mexico. It is possible that the best combination of policies would be something like the Massey proposals involving guestworkers, coupled with more generous aid to poorer Americans. But we also need to consider whether immigration policies themselves significantly affect the political saleability of aid to the poor; they may well do so. Of course, it is possible that under current conditions the prospects of doing anything serious for poorer Americans are dim, and given that, we should simply do good where we can and for whom we can. The proposals by Massey and his colleagues hold out the prospect of doing some real good for hundreds of thousands of migrant workers and for Mexicans and Americans as a whole.

PART II

LAW AND POLICY

6

The Undocumented Immigrant

Contending Policy Approaches

Linda Bosniak

Although parties to the immigration debate are bitterly divided over policy, virtually everyone agrees that the presence of a large class of unauthorized immigrants in the United States is undesirable. However, enactment of the kind of policies that would be required to fully eliminate the class of undocumented immigrants – whether through exclusion or through legalization – is politically unlikely and probably unachievable in the near term. The current population of undocumented immigrants in the United States is estimated to stand at 10–12 million, an all-time high. Even if Congress manages to pass a guestworker program in the coming period, the population of undocumented immigrants will likely continue to renew itself by way of both unauthorized entry and visa violations.

This being the case, Americans find themselves facing a set of policy questions that go beyond border policy proper. These questions have to do with the proper treatment and status of undocumented individuals once, and while, they are here. In fact, a great deal of the debate over unauthorized immigration in this country is tied up with issues of status and treatment.

Technically speaking, there are two distinct *kinds* of questions that arise concerning the status and treatment of undocumented immigrants. There are, first of all, questions pertaining to the treatment of these immigrants within the immigration regulatory system itself. At issue are federal policies concerning admission and exclusion of foreigners to and from territory and membership. Here, the focus includes matters such as the grounds for deportability, eligibility for asylum, the conduct of removal proceedings, immigration detention practices, and enforcement practices at the territorial border. A second set of questions has to do with the status and treatment of the undocumented beyond the domain of immigration law proper. At issue here is the access of resident noncitizen immigrants, or "aliens," in legal terminology, to legal rights and protections and to social benefits in a wide range of social relations, including criminal process, politics, the workplace, education, and welfare.

It is important to keep the distinction between "immigration questions" and "alienage questions" in mind when we debate policy concerning undocumented immigration. For one thing, each of these contexts has its own set of relevant government policymakers and administrators. Immigration policy is federal policy, usually administered by officials of the agency dedicated specifically to border regulation and immigration control. (This was formerly the Immigration and Naturalization Service [INS] but is now various branches of the Department of Homeland Security [DHS].) Alienage policy, in contrast, is a composite of rules and standards set by both state and federal law across a wide variety of regulatory domains; and here, aliens are only one of many groups subject to regulation.

Furthermore, and more significantly, the legal norms relevant in each area are substantially different. In the immigration enforcement context, the federal government enjoys extraordinarily broad powers. Although unauthorized immigrants enjoy certain procedural protections in the immigration process on constitutional grounds,[1] the government's exclusionary power in the sphere of immigration regulation is exceptionally unconstrained. This is especially true in relation to the government's substantive rules about who may stay and who must go, which have been held by the courts to be essentially nonreviewable.

Within the domain of alienage law and policy, by contrast, the balance of power between government and immigrant is more complex. The country's constitutional commitment to *personhood* as the fundamental basis of rights has produced certain zones of protected status for the undocumented, notwithstanding their irregular status under the immigration laws. Additionally, undocumented immigrants have been extended certain rights and protections for instrumental reasons, borne of a desire to avoid some of the social pathologies associated with the existence of an entrenched marginalized class. That is not to say that the unauthorized immigration status of these individuals is regarded as *irrelevant*; in fact, this status has been treated as a legitimate basis for justifying discriminatory or exclusionary treatment against the undocumented in a host of areas. Still, undocumented immigrants are formally afforded a host of important rights in both the federal and state contexts, including the

rights to contract, to own property, and to sue. They are also formally entitled to claim a range of statutory and common-law protections extended
generally to residents, consumers, and employees.

Current policy debates in the United States about the status and treatment of undocumented immigrants concern issues that fall on both sides
of the immigration/alienage line. We are preoccupied, on the one hand,
with issues such as border deaths of undocumented immigrants, human
trafficking, immigration detention policies, and the criminal grounds for
deportation – all traditional immigration issues. Also on the agenda are
debates over questions such as whether undocumented immigrants should
be able to access in-state tuition at state universities, back pay remedies for
labor law violations and workers' compensation insurance, and driver's
licenses – all traditionally alienage issues.

But there is another kind of question that is central to the current policy agenda – and is the focus of the present chapter. This question is not
debated outright but rather is implicit in and serves to structure all of the
other debates on undocumented immigrants' status and treatment. This
question has to do with how the regulatory domains of immigration and
alienage stand in relation to one another. What is the nature of the relationship *between* the regulatory regimes associated with immigration and
alienage, and what should it be? This question arises because, as a practical matter, the legal norms associated with each regime are often simultaneously applicable and relevant in a given context. The lives of undocumented immigrants are governed at times by liberal individual rights
norms, at times by exclusionary border norms, and very often by both at
once. The jurisdiction of these regimes, in other words, is overlapping.

The *fact* of this overlapping jurisdiction, notably, has had significant
consequences for the functioning of each regime individually. On the one
hand, the border control authority of the state has in some respects been
constrained by the rights that the undocumented enjoy as persons and residents in the United States. Despite the extensive immigration enforcement
authority enjoyed by the state, border enforcement practices have been
subject to certain formal limits. And because these immigrants are able
to lead lives that are, in many respects, indistinguishable from those of
other members of the national society, it is often difficult for immigration
authorities to identify them for border enforcement purposes.

On the other hand, the rights undocumented immigrants formally
enjoy as persons and as residents are always held in the long shadow
of the government's immigration enforcement power. An undocumented
immigrant worker can formally claim a right to receive the minimum

wage, for example, but her willingness to press for the fulfillment of that
right (assuming she is aware of it at all) is commonly undermined by her
fear of coming to the attention of the immigration authorities and being
subjected to deportation. And, like all aliens, the undocumented may be
deported for otherwise constitutionally protected conduct (e.g., certain
forms of speech and association).

I have argued elsewhere that making sense of the law concerning the
status and treatment of undocumented immigrants in the United States
requires an understanding of the complex interplay between the immigration and alienage regimes to which they are subject.[2] But making sense
of the various policy debates about unauthorized immigration likewise
requires attention to this interplay. Indeed, many of the recent policy disputes can best be understood as disputes *about* the relationship between
immigration regulation and alienage regulation. Most often, the question
presents itself as a question about the proper regulatory and normative
jurisdictions of "the border." How far does the political community's
domain of border control legitimately extend? We know that border control is not confined to the actual territorial threshold; it extends as well
into the nation's interior. But in precisely what respects and into precisely
what domains? Is an undocumented immigrant, by virtue of *being* undocumented, legitimately subject to the exclusionary border-enforcement
regime at every moment and in every respect? Where within the national
society does border regulation properly begin and end?

At the risk of oversimplifying, I want to propose that the parties to
this debate tend to cluster around two opposing positions in response to
this question. One side seeks to confine, or circumscribe, the jurisdiction
of the border. For both pragmatic and justice-oriented reasons, their view
is that undocumented immigrants must be guaranteed a degree of insulation from the reach of the nation's border-regulatory laws. The second
side aspires to an expansion of the border's jurisdiction. To ensure both
national self-protection and a coherent administrative policy, they hold
that the federal government needs to be far less obstructed than it is in
the exercise of its border control functions.

The difference between these two perspectives might be described in
this way: advocates of border confinement seek to erect or reinforce fire-
walls between the immigration and alienage domains, whereas advocates
of border expansion seek to tear those walls down wherever possible.

The question of the border's scope – where the border legitimately
begins and ends – is today being debated in relation to two broad and
contrasting kinds of policy initiatives. The first set of initiatives are those

that seek to insulate the immigrant from the imperatives of the border in certain circumstances. Many of these take the form of what we might call confidentiality policies. Under a confidentiality policy, an agency or institution of government makes a determination that it will not inform the federal immigration authorities of any contact its representatives may have with individuals whose status is unauthorized under immigration laws. Confidentiality policies themselves can take various forms. The government entity may determine that it will not inquire into a client's immigration status – a kind of "don't ask, don't tell" approach. Alternatively, the government entity may decide to maintain as confidential any information that it may have acquired, by whatever means, about an individual's (regular or irregular) immigration status. A confidentiality policy, furthermore, may be a matter of informal practice, or it may be formally announced and publicly defended.

The best-known examples of government confidentiality policies are cases of cities and counties declaring their intention to maintain as confidential any information they acquire about their residents' unauthorized immigration status when they are seeking medical treatment, public benefits, police assistance, or other city services (except in cases of criminal law enforcement).[3] But there are other such policies. Many police departments around the country have independently determined that they will not inquire about the immigration status of crime victims and crime witnesses. The Labor Department, in enforcing the wage and hour laws on behalf of undocumented immigrants, maintains a policy of nonreporting to immigration authorities.[4]

The rationales articulated by defenders of confidentiality policies are usually instrumental and practical in nature. The argument is that undocumented immigrants who fear possible exposure to the immigration authorities will fail to make use of the protections or services the nonreporting entity provides and that this, in turn, will undermine the vital interests of the community as a whole. To the extent that community residents are afraid to contact the police in response to crime, public safety will suffer; to the extent that workers are unwilling to press for enforcement of the wage and hour laws, the working conditions of all employees are undermined; and so on. These instrumental arguments are sometimes accompanied by arguments about the demands of liberal democracy: it is unjust to subject persons who contribute to this society to "the ever-present threat of deportation."[5] Ensuring these immigrants some insulation from this threat is necessary as a matter of fairness and essential in order to fulfill our society's own anti-caste commitments.

Opponents, on the other hand, find confidentiality policies incomprehensible. The nonreporting entities are seen as working to affirmatively impair the authority and effectiveness of the nation's immigration enforcement branches. Critics commonly characterize these policies as "sanctuary" policies, pursuant to which some government entities are protecting undeserving lawbreakers from the legitimate force of the federal immigration laws. These policies of protection, as they see it, represent an absurd form of national self-handicapping in relation to border enforcement; it is government undoing with one hand what it is attempting to do with the other. All of this bodes badly for the country's security, which depends on unimpaired coordination of law enforcement functions.

Another recent initiative protecting undocumented immigrants from the imperatives of the border was the guarantee issued by the September 11th Victim Compensation Fund that undocumented immigrants could seek benefits under it without fear of immigration reprisals. Here, the Fund elicited an agreement by the INS itself that it would refrain from enforcing the immigration laws against undocumented claimants for survivors' benefits based on information acquired by the Fund.[6] Some commentators saw this announced guarantee as an absurd form of amnesty;[7] others who had pressed for the policy regarded it as both morally and practically essential. Given the relatively small number of individuals involved, the significance of this decision may seem limited. But it represents a striking example of border confinement; this is policy that expressly served to insulate the undocumented from the reach of the immigration laws – with the country's border enforcement authorities in this case agreeing to constrain their own jurisdiction in order to protect the immigrants' rights.

If one set of recent policy initiatives has been directed at confining the scope of the government's immigration authority, a second, contrasting set of policy efforts has sought to expand it. Measures seeking to extend the border's jurisdiction into formerly insulated domains of alienage regulation have become increasingly common. These initiatives most often take the form of verification and reporting requirements.

Verification requirements are mandates imposed by either the federal or local government requiring that government service providers – or, in some cases, nongovernmental entities – demand proof of lawful immigration status as a condition of providing services or entering into a contract. Reporting requirements further require service providers to convey to the immigration authorities whatever information they acquire about an individual's/client's unauthorized immigration status.

Sometimes the verification requirements are imposed alone. For in stance, the federal authorities sanction provisions requiring that employers formally inquire about prospective employees' immigration status (in this case, authorization to work) before hiring, but they do not require the employer to report apparently negative results to the immigration authorities.[8] Likewise, federal authorities are now required to verify the immigration status of applicants for certain federal benefits such as (nonemergency) Medicare and Food Stamps before issuing benefits but are not required to report those who are found unqualified. Some states have similarly required the state Department of Motor Vehicles to verify the authorized immigration status of applicants for driver's licenses before issuing the license, though they have not required officials to contact INS/DHS in case such verification yields negative results.

Sometimes, however, the law requires both verification and reporting. The best-known version of such a dual requirement was California's Proposition 187, a 1994 state initiative that would have required schools, hospitals, and other state agencies to verify the immigration status of all individuals seeking services *and* to report irregular results to the INS. Proposition 187 was struck down by the courts in 1997 on grounds that it constituted a "scheme of immigration regulation" and thereby invaded an exclusively federal domain. However, many of its key provisions, including its reporting and verification provisions, are reprised in Arizona's Proposition 200, which was passed by a majority of state voters in November 2005. Proposition 200 requires that individuals prove legal status in order to obtain public benefits[9] and imposes criminal penalties on state and local officials who fail to alert federal immigration officials, in writing, of suspected illegal immigrants who seek those benefits. The proposition's supporters hope it will fare better in the courts, though as a purely legal matter, it is not clear why it should.[10]

But fights over reporting and verification requirements are not always fights over national versus state power. Reporting and verification requirements are becoming increasingly common among agencies *within* the federal government as well. Recent statutory and regulatory provisions require the Social Security Administration, Department of Health and Human Services, and Department of Housing and Urban Development to report to the DHS the identity of an immigrant whom they "know" is not in the United States legally.[11] Also notable is the congressional effort (so far unsuccessful) to require that hospitals report to the immigration authorities undocumented immigrants for whom they provide emergency care as a condition for obtaining federal reimbursement.[12]

Supporters of verification and reporting requirements advance several rationales for these policies. First, they claim that, however firmly the country purports to stand against unauthorized immigration, such immigration is encouraged when undocumented immigrants are entitled to benefits without fear of immigration reprisals. Reporting and verification requirements therefore rationalize immigration policy overall by eliminating the benefits incentive. In effect, they ensure that the nation's left brain and right brain (as supporters conceive them) are working together rather than at cross-purposes. Second, and relatedly, supporters maintain that government border-enforcement efforts have been inadequate and that verification and reporting requirements serve as an indispensable enforcement supplement. In the case of state-imposed reporting requirements, supporters point out that the federal government's failure to adequately enforce the immigration laws means that states are unfairly left with the social and financial burdens to which they must be empowered to respond. Finally, many supporters maintain that these measures properly deter a class of lawbreakers from accessing benefits to which they are not morally entitled in any event.

Opponents of these requirements, on the other hand, press several criticisms. First, they point out that such policies do not deter the entry and residence of undocumented immigrants, but they do engender widespread fear and mistrust of official authority in immigrant communities. Such mistrust, in turn, only functions to undermine rather than reinforce national security and public health and safety – and most likely increases immigrants' desirability among predatory employers as well. Critics further maintain that it is unfair to deprive "hard-working, contributing members of our community ... from receiving basic services"[13] and that it is inappropriate to force social service providers "to become de facto federal immigration officers"[14] – something they are entirely unequipped to do in any event.

Beyond verification and reporting requirements, there is another recent and highly controversial policy initiative that presses for the expansion of the border's jurisdiction into formerly insulated domains of alienage regulation. These are the efforts by the federal government to enlist state and local law-enforcement agencies to engage in the direct enforcement of immigration laws. Soon after the terrorist attacks of September 11, the Bush administration's Department of Justice concluded that, contrary to long-held understandings, state officials possess "inherent authority" to enforce federal immigration laws.[15] Officials of the DOJ have urged local police departments to exercise that authority in the case of civil and criminal immigration law violations, including violations pertaining to unauthorized presence. Legislation is also pending in Congress that would mandate state and local police enforcement of immigration laws as a condition for receipt of certain federal funds (the proposed Clear Law Enforcement for Criminal Alien Removal [CLEAR] Act).[16]

Supporters of state involvement in immigration enforcement defend these policies as an essential means of ensuring coordinated policy responses among law enforcement branches across the country to fight terrorism nationally. Opponents, meanwhile, find themselves invoking the (often otherwise reviled) federalism jurisprudence of the Rehnquist Court to insist that "[t]he constitution requires a distinction between what is truly national and what is truly local."[17]

While this debate is most certainly a debate about the legitimate scope of federal and state power, its significance extends beyond federalism questions. Arguments over immigration and federalism have often served as stand-ins for arguments about the status of noncitizen immigrants in our society. On the theory that national immigration power may be plenary but only within its sphere, federalism doctrine has long served as a kind of insulating wall against the enforcement of border control in the nation's interior and thereby protects not just state power but immigrants' rights. Current efforts to dismantle this wall (from both the state and national sides) reflect a desire to radically recast the status of aliens – especially the undocumented – in the United States. As state and local officials become more involved in aspects of border enforcement, the zones of protection that the undocumented have enjoyed by virtue of their personhood and residence will become increasingly curtailed. This is precisely the intention of dismantlement's supporters.

While policy arguments over confidentiality policies, reporting requirements, and enforcement mandates implicate a variety of political considerations and institutional actors, they are organized around the same structural questions: What is the proper scope of the country's immigration-enforcing authority? Is the undocumented immigrant always fair game for such enforcement? Does the border, in effect, follow the undocumented immigrant wherever she goes, or are there limits on the border's legitimate domain of action? Should we reinforce walls between the spheres of immigration and alienage regulation, or should we be tearing them down?

As we have seen, the debate on this question is characterized by dramatically contrasting views. Despite the differences between them, however, there is one respect in which these views are not in disagreement at all.

This is not a debate between immigration restrictionists and open-borders advocates; both sides assume the legitimacy of the border in the first instance. Instead, this is a debate between two sets of advocates who at least accede to the norm of border closure but who disagree on the particular wheres and whens of the border's enforcement.

There is, of course, a great deal to be said about the normative legitimacy of the commitment to national borders in the first instance. But as a practical matter, these national borders – whether confined to the territorial threshold or permitted to pervade all social relations – are not going to prevent large numbers of people from coming to this country and residing and working as undocumented immigrants. The idea that enforcement of borders themselves can make the class of undocumented immigrants disappear is a vain hope. As many analysts have made clear, global and domestic conditions are such that immigrants are going to continue to arrive. And it is *because* they will continue to arrive that the debate between advocates of border confinement and border expansion is significant – for both immigrants and the rest of us.

7

Good Neighbors and Good Citizens

Beyond the Legal–Illegal Immigration Debate

Noah Pickus and Peter Skerry

The year 2006 will go down in history as the year when immigration moved definitively to the center stage of American national politics. For more than 20 years, political elites have been able to contain and marginalize this intractable and emotional issue, dealing with it discreetly and episodically. But over time, the number of newcomers – both legal and illegal – has continued to grow and is now reaching historic proportions. Meanwhile, the dispersion throughout the United States of immigrants formerly concentrated in a few gateway states has contributed to the nationalization of this issue.

The politics of immigration changed fundamentally in 2001, when the George W. Bush administration seized on the issue in order to build support among Hispanics and to open a dialogue with Mexico's president, Vicente Fox, one of the few heads of state eager to do business with the new president. This was the rare occasion when a major national political figure did not merely react to events or seek the protective cover of a study commission but grabbed immigration with both hands to further his own objectives. Sidelined by the terrorist attacks of September 11, 2001, Bush's immigration initiative reemerged in January 2004 with his proposed guestworker program. That proposal jump-started a debate over illegal immigration that was then fueled by tough enforcement legislation passed by the House of Representatives in December 2005. That bill provoked unprecedented demonstrations by illegal immigrants and their supporters in cities across the nation, resulting in a flurry of counter-activity on conservative talk radio. The debate rages on even as we write during the summer of 2006.

At the center of this controversy are the approximately 12 million illegal immigrants now living in the United States. This number is unprecedented, as is the group's homogeneity: almost 80 percent of illegals are Latinos.[1] Furthermore, there is a broad gap in attitudes toward illegal immigration between the vast majority of ordinary Americans and our social, economic, and political elites.[2] Indeed, we believe that part of what is fueling the current reaction is anger among many Americans that their concerns and complaints about illegal immigrants have for too long been ignored by elites.

We are also critical of our academic colleagues for being insufficiently attentive to the building public outrage over what increasingly looks to be the largest influx of immigrants in our nation's history. More to the point, the American public's anxieties about immigration are not fairly or prudently reduced to racism or nativism. We take our cue here from the late John Higham, the dean of immigration historians and author of the standard work on nativism, *Strangers in the Land: Patterns of American Nativism 1860–1925*.[3] Although his book continues to be widely and approvingly cited by those concerned with underscoring the history of prejudice and intolerance toward newcomers to the United States, Higham himself repeatedly and eloquently distanced himself from such use of his work. In fact, two years after *Strangers in the Land* first appeared in 1955, Higham declared, "I propose that research on the conflicts associated with foreign elements in American society should take a new line. The nativist theme, as defined and developed to date, is imaginatively exhausted."[4] More than 40 years later, Higham was still making this same point.[5]

Following Higham, we believe that a fuller understanding of immigration politics requires moving beyond long-dominant academic preoccupations with irrational prejudices and distorting ideologies as the presumed mainsprings of negative reactions to immigrants. Instead, we advocate focusing on the concrete processes and structures of daily life. As Higham acknowledged, this approach entails paying less attention to dramatic and passionate outbursts and more to the mundane contexts of neighborhoods and cities. This is where a myriad of quite rational conflicts of status and interest play out between immigrants and nonimmigrants, as well as among various immigrant groups themselves.[6]

Yet this is not to say that the views of Americans – or of the politicians representing them – about immigration should be taken at face value. Even opinions with rational origins can be distorted by perverse political dynamics. Contemporary policy debates often get stuck in frames that politicians and advocates find comfortable but that do not lead to discussion of meaningful policy options. Immigration is an issue area that seems particularly prone to such distortions.

A case in point is the American public's current preoccupation with illegal immigration. All parties to the current debate share the same unexamined assumption: that legal immigration is benign or even beneficial, while illegal immigration is problematic.[7] Here, we will argue to the contrary that the real challenges do not stem exclusively or even primarily from illegal immigration but from mass migration itself. Specifically, those challenges involve the social strains and disorder that inevitably accompany any movement of large numbers of unskilled migrants into advanced democratic societies. Were it possible to stop illegal immigration tomorrow, most of the concerns expressed by so many Americans would remain unaddressed.[8]

The high-decibel popular debate over illegal immigration has proceeded simultaneously with a more muted elite discussion over the meaning of citizenship in contemporary America. Some have expressed concern that immigrants are not naturalizing as quickly or as eagerly as they might. Others are suspicious of the motives of those becoming citizens, in part because of the increased visibility of dual citizenship. Overall, many Americans are convinced that immigrants are "gaming the system" and naturalizing not out of commitment to our values and ideals but for crass, instrumental reasons.

These are different issues, but each reflects widespread anxiety that immigrants are taking advantage of the system, that things are out of control, and that American national identity is being challenged. The parallel debates over illegal immigration and citizenship also both hinge on similar formalistic dichotomies – legal immigrants versus illegal immigrants, citizens versus noncitizens. These categories are hardly incorrect. Indeed, they have intuitive appeal and legal grounding that policymakers ignore at their peril. However, in the contemporary context, they get used as legalistic shorthand that obscures the true dilemmas facing us. In our view, rigid adherence to these simple dichotomies has gotten in the way of creative policy responses to the complexities of today's immigration predicament.

In this chapter, we will elaborate on the limitations of the legal–illegal and citizen–noncitizen dichotomies; examine why these have nevertheless become so entrenched in the current debate; and offer an alternative way of thinking about these issues that supplements the prevailing preoccupation with the formal, vertical ties between individuals and state institutions with a focus on informal, horizontal relationships. While the current debate asks whether immigrants can be good citizens, we argue that to many Americans the more immediately pressing question is whether immigrants can be good neighbors. To be sure, many communitarians do emphasize this horizontal dimension of civic membership, but they typically neglect the vertical dimension. We argue that both dimensions are critical and that only by paying attention to both can policymakers hope to make rational and fair public policy in this extremely contentious area.

ILLEGAL IMMIGRATION: NUMBERS AND CATEGORIES

The public's anxiety over illegal immigration is hardly unfounded. The Pew Hispanic Center reports that of the 12 million "unauthorized migrants" estimated to be in the United States today, 40 percent have arrived since 2000. During the first half of the 1990s, about 450,000 illegals arrived here every year. Since 2000, that annual figure has jumped to 850,000.[9]

Over the same period, illegal immigrants have dispersed across the land. In 1990, California had the largest share of the nation's illegals: 45 percent. By 2004, the Golden State still led the nation, but its share had dropped to 24 percent. Meanwhile, the proportion of illegal immigrants ending up in states such as North Carolina, Georgia, Tennessee, and other nontraditional destinations more than tripled. As a result, a regional concern has become a national one.[10]

Long before the current furor, it was evident to those who would look that Americans were particularly vexed by illegal immigration. In the early 1990s, a *New York Times* poll found that Americans greatly exaggerated the proportion of all immigrants who were in fact illegal.[11] In 1994, California's Proposition 187, which would have banned most public services to illegal immigrants, was passed with support from almost three-fifths of the state's voters, including about one-fifth of Hispanic voters and an even greater proportion of Asians.[12]

In 1998, Alan Wolfe reported in *One Nation, After All* that ordinary Americans otherwise uncomfortable with strong moral judgments were not at all reluctant to express moral outrage toward illegal immigrants. Indeed, based on his in-depth interviews across the United States, Wolfe concluded that the divide between legal and illegal immigrants "is one of the most tenaciously held distinctions in middle-class America; the people with whom we spoke overwhelmingly support legal immigration and express disgust with the illegal variety."[13]

But the watershed event here was Proposition 187. The federal courts eventually gutted this draconian measure. Nevertheless, this was a political earthquake that continues to define the terrain – such that legal immigration is generally regarded as benign, while illegal immigration is seen as the source of most problems.

Before Proposition 187, most politicians – indeed, most officials – studiously avoided the issue of immigration, period. It took a politician as shrewd, tough, and desperate as California Governor Pete Wilson to seize on it. Indeed, Wilson salvaged his doomed reelection bid by acknowledging what a majority of Californians felt – that illegal immigration was a critical problem that had to be addressed.

Of course, the price Republicans paid for Wilson's boldness is now political legend. Universally overlooked, however, is that Proposition 187 also chastened immigrant advocates. Before its resounding passage, they vigorously resisted the drawing of any bright lines between legal and illegal immigrants and rejected labels such as "illegal immigrant" and "illegal alien" in favor of more neutral or positive terms such as "undocumented immigrant" and "undocumented worker." But with their backs to the wall after Proposition 187's victory, immigrant advocates retreated to the legal–illegal dichotomy and accepted the fall-back position that attributed negative outcomes associated with immigration to illegals and positive outcomes to legal immigrants. Hence, the still dominant paradigm "illegal immigrants, bad; legal immigrants, good."

Immigrant advocates are hardly the only ones to have this mind-set. They are joined by skittish politicians and political elites of varied persuasions who have found this to be a relatively safe way to address a technically complex, emotionally charged issue that they would prefer to avoid completely. For their part, immigration restrictionists went through the obverse process and learned to narrow an array of objections about immigration generally to the problem of illegal immigration specifically. Thus, at some point restrictionists figured out that it was more costly politically to inveigh against Hispanic immigrants than against illegals.

If one must address "immigration," then illegal immigrants – relatively small in number and definitely not well organized or vigorously defended – represent the path of least resistance. To be sure, Proposition 187 taught Republicans that even the illegal immigration card can be overplayed. Nevertheless, illegal immigration – particularly when not explicitly linked to a specific ethnic group – remains the safest way for policymakers and politicians to address this intractable issue.

Now, in recent months immigrant advocates have been arguing for amnesty for millions of illegal immigrants. Does this mean that the line between legal and illegal immigration is becoming less bright? Not really. In fact, the opposite is more nearly true. After all, the case for amnesty has been made on the grounds that illegal immigrants live a separate, second-class existence in a netherworld.

Consider the rhetoric across the political spectrum. A liberal columnist depicts illegals as "living in the shadows."[14] A conservative commentator refers to them as a "huge, subterranean population" that exists in fear of one day being "whisked away by government agents."[15] A Los Angeles religious leader bemoans their exploitation at the hands of "unscrupulous employers" who know they "are reluctant to seek legal recourse."[16] Finally, President Bush has characterized undocumented workers as dwelling "in the shadows of American life – fearful, often abused and exploited."[17]

In a moment, we will argue that such characterizations are misleading – that in fact illegal immigrants are much more integrated into American life than is typically understood. But right now, our point is that those arguing for amnesty – to relieve the undeniable burdens on illegal immigrants – actually end up reinforcing that bright line between legals and illegals. And this is just one of many ways that this line gets relied on by political elites.

In fact, the legal–illegal dichotomy makes much more political sense than policy sense. To be sure, illegal immigrants working in remote citrus groves in south Florida[18] or in chicken-processing plants in rural Arkansas fit the stereotype. Yet such workers routinely gravitate to urban areas – which is why their employers routinely push for fresh infusions of foreign labor. Once in the cities, illegal immigrants join other immigrants, documented and undocumented alike, in low-paying and arduous service or manufacturing jobs.

One undeniable outcome of this phenomenon is that 59 percent of adult illegals lack health insurance, compared with 25 percent of adult legal immigrants and 14 percent of natives.[19] Similarly worrisome is the infrequently noted fact (about which immigrant advocates are understandably discreet) that 78 percent of illegals are from Latin America, 56 percent from Mexico alone.[20] While approximately four-fifths of Latinos are *legal* residents or citizens, the danger nevertheless looms that the public will equate being Latino with being illegal.[21]

Despite such troubling indicators, the dominant image of illegal immigrants as a distinctive and isolated group "living in the shadows" is overdrawn. After all, hundreds of thousands have – at least until recent restrictive legislation – applied for and obtained driver's licenses. And how vulnerable could illegal workers be if, as is the case, they have been joining unions in significant numbers? As UCLA sociologist Ruth Milkman observes, undocumented Latinos "have been at the core of the L.A. labor movement's revival."[22]

Similarly suggestive is the number of illegal immigrants who are homeowners. In a study for the American Immigration Law Foundation, Rob Paral presents what he considers a generous estimate of 429,000 undocumented Latino homeowners.[23] A survey of undocumented Mexicans by the Pew Hispanic Center found that at least 10 percent are homeowners.[24] These are necessarily guesstimates. But one way or another, undocumented homeowners number in the hundreds of thousands.

This figure is all the more striking because mortgages held by illegal immigrants are not, as a matter of policy, purchased on the secondary market by Fannie Mae or Freddie Mac. Pressure from the housing industry to tap into this growing market may change this. But in the meantime, individual taxpayer identification numbers are being issued to millions of illegal immigrants by the Internal Revenue Service and functioning as an alternative to the social security number necessary to open a bank account and establish a credit rating.[25]

In those homes owned by illegals live many legal immigrants and even citizens. Of the approximately 15 million individuals who live in households where the head or spouse is illegal, about one-fourth are legal. Most of these are children who are U.S. citizens.[26] Looking beyond such households to their relatives and friends, one finds more legal immigrants and citizens, whose presence and support encourage illegals to come here in the first place. In this same vein, the pervasive media image of people sneaking across the Mexican border hardly applies to all 12 million illegals. In fact, as many as 45 percent entered *legally* through a port of entry – as shoppers, workers, or tourists – and then overstayed their visas.[27]

On the other side of the ledger, over the decades there have been several amnesties. The last one, in 1986, legalized some 3 million aliens.[28] Up until a few years ago, illegal immigrants with children born here (who are therefore citizens) were routinely awarded green cards. Nowadays, every year 50,000 lucky individuals – many of whom are already residing here illegally – win a green card in Homeland Security's Diversity Lottery.[29] Indeed, according to the New Immigrant Survey at Princeton, in a typical year (1996) about one-third of all adult legal immigrants in the United

States had prior experience here as undocumented immigrants; two-thirds of adult legal Mexican immigrants did.[30]

Then there are the 1 million–1.5 million among those 12 million illegals who University of Virginia law professor David Martin estimates to be in "twilight status." Of these, more than 300,000 have Temporary Protected Status (TPS), a category Congress devised in 1990 as a way to avoid either repatriating or granting refugee status to individuals from countries (such as El Salvador or Nicaragua) beset by civil war and other unsafe conditions. Some Liberians have been here "temporarily" for 14 years. In any event, those afforded TPS are usually counted among the undocumented.[31]

Martin also points out that as of May 2003, another 617,000 persons were caught up in processing delays waiting to be granted adjustment to "lawful permanent resident" status. All but a small fraction of such persons typically get approved, but they are nevertheless included among the illegals and are technically deportable.[32]

Martin's analysis hardly accounts for all 12 million illegal immigrants in the United States today, but it does underscore the fact that a nontrivial number of them are illegal for reasons not entirely of their own making. Indeed, errors and delays by immigration bureaucrats are notorious and arguably contribute to undermining the rule of law as much as the presence of millions of illegals. In fairness to those bureaucrats, immigration law is a complicated maze of exceptions and deadlines carved out by Congress to accommodate diverse constituencies. These are not only difficult to administer; they are hard to comply with and easy to run afoul of.

Therefore, the conventional understanding of illegal immigrants as conscious lawbreakers hardly accounts for all the facts on the ground. While many, indeed most, illegals actively committed a crime – or, to be sure, a misdemeanor – by entering or remaining in the United States without authorization, many others have become entangled in a complicated system of rules and regulations that confuses everyone.

BORDER PATROL EMPATHY

There is another, more fundamental source of ambiguity about the line between legal and illegal immigrants. It has surfaced readily and repeatedly in conversations and interviews that one of us has had with scores of Border Patrol (now Customs and Border Protection) agents. Given the opportunity to express their views about the individuals they are charged with apprehending, these federal law enforcement officers routinely volunteer, almost without exception and nearly verbatim: "If I were in their shoes, I would be doing the same thing, coming across that border and trying to better things for me and my family." Ironically, this observation comes from men and women who also readily express frustration about their low status in the federal law enforcement hierarchy and are therefore generally eager to enhance their standing relative to other agencies. Yet just imagine your neighborhood cop similarly empathizing with drug dealers or even petty thieves and opining that, "If I was in that guy's situation, I'd be pushing cocaine, too!"

This ambiguity lies at the heart of our immigration policy dilemmas. For example, how can one ask Border Patrol agents to risk their lives apprehending illegal immigrants if in an elemental, gut-level sense they and their superiors do not consider the violation in question to be a crime? The answer of course is that one cannot – which is why the Border Patrol long ago abandoned its policy of engaging immigrant smugglers in high-speed pursuits on U.S. highways. Too many serious accidents and fatalities clarified the calculus that the costs far outweighed the perceived benefits from successful pursuits and apprehensions. As a Border Patrol supervisor at a highway checkpoint north of San Diego explained, "The life of one of my agents or of one American citizen is not worth the apprehension of a whole truckload of illegals or of their smuggler."[33]

Border Patrol agents do not need the Catholic bishops or the *New York Times* to tell them that illegal immigrants are not typically criminals.[34] Still, they do their job and detain illegals when they find them.[35] Nevertheless, the trade-offs and moral ambiguities of immigration control pervade all that the Border Patrol does. They clearly contribute to high turnover and low morale at the agency.[36] They also help explain why, for example, agents in the field are so readily drawn into pursuing drug smugglers who operate along our borders – about whose status as "*really bad guys*" there is little or no ambiguity.[37]

If the line between legal and illegal immigration is much fuzzier than it appears, what is bothering Americans? Is it possible that their concerns are both broader and deeper than anyone has bothered to notice? In this connection, it is certainly noteworthy that in one breath Americans denounce illegal immigrants, while in the next they complain about job competition, overcrowded schools, chaotic hospital emergency rooms, and noisy neighborhoods where nobody speaks English – all problems that have more to do with mass migration per se than with its strictly legal component.

Take, for example, the views of independent congressional candidate Jim Gilchrist. Running in a special run-off election in Orange County, California, in December 2005, Gilchrist won 25 percent of the votes in a protest campaign focused exclusively against illegal immigration. But when asked by the *Wall Street Journal* to elaborate, Gilchrist immediately cited concerns about Spanish-speaking newcomers not assimilating, multiculturalism, and overpopulation.[38] Pollsters report similar complaints. Two-thirds of respondents in an April 2005 *Fox News* poll agreed that illegal immigrants "take jobs away from U.S. citizens," while 87 percent claimed that illegals "overburden government programs and services."[39] In a January 2006 *Time* magazine survey, 63 percent expressed concern that illegals "take jobs away from Americans," and 60 percent agreed that "there are already too many people in the United States."[40]

Whatever their specific merits, none of these or similar problems are unique to illegal immigrants. Indeed, these concerns are explained by readily identifiable factors common to both legal and illegal immigrants: low levels of education and skills, low average age, the strains from the transience of migration, and that historically a high concentration speak only Spanish. To be sure, some of these may beset illegal more than legal immigrants. But there is simply no reason to believe that legal and illegal immigrants are starkly different with regard to such salient characteristics. In fact, because there are more legal immigrants than illegal immigrants, the former arguably contribute more to such problems than the latter.

Some of these complaints are wide of the mark in other respects. For example, while immigrants themselves may not be learning as much English as Americans would like, the evidence is that their children and grandchildren certainly are.[41] Neither is there much reason to believe that immigrants are competing directly in the labor market with large numbers of American workers. (The obvious exceptions are low-skilled individuals, including more settled immigrants, especially Latinos, and many African Americans.)[42]

It would be easy therefore to dismiss many such complaints as misguided and ill-informed, even as nativist and racist. Our own reading of the evidence certainly leads us to the conclusion that the United States is *not* as threatened by the current influx of immigrants as many clearly believe. We do not believe that our society is unraveling.[43]

Yet to cling to expert opinion here is to miss a larger, more important political reality. Both legal and illegal immigrants have become the human face of two sweeping forces: the fraying of local community ties and the decline of national sovereignty. The title of Robert Putnam's controversial book *Bowling Alone*[44] has become a national metaphor for the perceived decay of social bonds and traditional institutions that have helped to make a diverse democracy function. At the same time, transformations in communication and transportation have resulted in an increasingly interconnected globe that leaves us unsure about who is part of "our community," as more people live both here and there. However ineptly or even at times harshly they express themselves, large numbers of Americans *do* feel that "things are out of control" and that immigrants are straining the social fabric. Such concerns are not completely unfounded.

Consider day-labor hiring sites, one of the most contentious immigration issues in communities across the nation. For many Americans today, the image of immigrants that most readily comes to mind (aside from shadowy figures running across the border) is of male laborers hanging out near a Home Depot, waiting to be hired by contractors or homeowners. To some, such scenes are evidence of ambition and hard work. But to many others, they represent the annoying, even threatening behavior of unkempt men leering at passing women, darting out into traffic to negotiate with potential employers, drinking and urinating in public, perhaps dealing drugs, and sometimes worse.[45]

Here again, not all such complaints should be taken at face value. Nor should we overlook that day laborers are often mistreated by employers, which is confirmed by findings from the National Day Labor Study at UCLA.[46] That research also indicates that while most day laborers are illegals, one-fourth are legal immigrants.[47]

Yet the UCLA study also confirms that virtually all day laborers are males, more than three-fifths of whom are single or unattached. So, it is not without reason that for many Americans, day laborers have come to personify the transience and social disorder associated with mass migration. At times, such individuals have even been the fodder for civil disturbances that have broken out among immigrants in cities such as Miami; Washington, D.C.; New York; and of course Los Angeles.[48] Noting that 51 percent of those arrested during the 1992 L.A. riots were Hispanics, RAND demographers Peter Morrison and Ira Lowry point to "the availability of a large pool of idle young men who had little stake in civil order" as one reason why in multiethnic states such as California "we ought to expect more riots."[49]

CITIZENSHIP: THE VERTICAL AND THE HORIZONTAL

Similar, though hardly identical, issues arise over the naturalization of today's immigrants. On the one hand, these reflect concerns that the United States has reduced citizenship to a thin, one-dimensional relationship, shorn of emotional commitment and focused more on the rights of individuals than on their obligations to the political community. But there is also the perception that immigrants themselves have come to view citizenship in cramped, instrumental terms.

Political scientist Stanley Renshon has written persuasively that in the contemporary world, the real possibility of multiple national memberships renders frequently cited indicators of immigrant economic success insufficient evidence of meaningful attachment to the United States.[50] The analyst who has raised such questions to the highest visibility is, of course, Samuel Huntington. In his controversial volume *Who Are We? The Challenges to America's National Identity*, Huntington focuses much of his critical energy on denationalized American elites, who in his view have fostered the weak national commitments that immigrants are now taking advantage of. Notably, Huntington argues that "naturalization is the single most important political dimension of assimilation."[51]

Concerns with the quality of contemporary citizenship are found more among elites than among the population at large. They have typically led to calls for more meaningful naturalization ceremonies and more rigorous citizenship exams.[52] Yet the more salient point is that, like popular worries about illegal immigration, elite concerns about citizenship reflect a preoccupation with formal legal categories. Such categories are of fundamental importance, needless to say. But as John Higham reminds us, America's pluralist values call for a "lack of precision in social categories, and a general acceptance of complexity and ambiguity."[53]

Both concerns also reflect the top-down administrative rationality that the contemporary bureaucratic state inevitably imposes on dense, informal social relations.[54] Thus, when finally compelled to address the issue of immigration, political actors enmeshed in the logic of the administrative state offer responses and "solutions" appropriate for and suited to the tools at their disposal. In the current context, they have focused on refining categories and then policing the new boundaries – whether between legal and illegal immigrants or between citizens and noncitizens.

Such tendencies have been reinforced in recent years by the dramatically increased attention and resources expended on immigration enforcement. Immigration bureaucrats have had to account for themselves. But what if the problems at hand transcend the categories that bureaucrats and politicians have seized upon, or if those problems are not addressed simply by revised citizenship exams and ceremonies? What if they also depend on the horizontal ties between individuals or between individuals and local private or public institutions? Unlike the vertical ties between individuals and the state, which are formal and tend to be episodic, these horizontal relationships are informal, day-to-day, and ongoing.[55]

In our view, the prevailing emphasis on vertical ties overlooks what is at least equally salient to the public about immigrants – regardless of how this public actually articulates its concerns. Most Americans are less worried about immigrants having proper documents or being able to answer questions about American history and politics than their behaving like responsible members of the community. Are immigrants making too much noise? Are they attempting to communicate in English? Are they parking their cars where there is supposed to be grass? Are they crowding too many people into their living quarters? Are they cluttering the neighborhood with abandoned shopping carts or cars? In sum, we believe that when Americans complain about immigrants, their concern is less about immigrants failing to be good *citizens* than about their failing to be good *neighbors*.

Of course, such informal horizontal relations are open to highly subjective, even arbitrary, judgments. They can become the basis for harassment and exclusion of minorities. This is why we are not suggesting that horizontal ties should be looked at exclusively. Indeed, we maintain that citizenship should be defined along *both* the vertical and horizontal axes.

Yet this insight is overlooked by all sides in the current debate. Occasionally, advocates stress immigrants' vertical ties, particularly that they pay taxes. More typically, advocates highlight the horizontal ties that immigrants establish, especially good relations with their employers or their children's teachers.[56] But, by themselves, these are insufficient, for the matter at hand concerns membership in a political community that can never be reduced simply to social relations.

For their part, immigration critics are preoccupied with the vertical dimension – illegals' lack of formal status. But, as we have seen, they are also upset with immigrants' poor horizontal relations. The basic shortcoming of the critics – and of the debate whose terms they have established – is that they ignore the vital distinction between the two dimensions of citizenship and implicitly collapse all their concerns onto the vertical axis.

SOCIAL ORDER IN A POLITICAL COMMUNITY

How do we address these constraints? How do we move beyond the unhelpful and misleading formalism and legalism of the current immigration debate toward a meaningful revaluation of citizenship?

A starting point would be to recognize that this is hardly a new problem. Social theorist Philip Selznick reminds us that the liberal theorists who provide the conceptual foundations of our society are heavily reliant on abstractions, including the state of nature, natural rights, and atomized individuals detached from society, culture, and history. In this same vein, Selznick emphasizes that we are prone to think in terms of walls of separation – between individual and society, law and morality, private and public, church and state.[57]

More to the point, Selznick argues for an alternative way of thinking about contemporary society. Reminiscent of Higham, he points out that pluralism necessarily implies a certain messiness: "All societies are composed of different, often contending groups based on kinship, age, occupation, and inequalities of property and power. Pluralism finds in this natural diversity a benign disorder, a vital source of energy and safety."[58] Selznick consequently points to the advantages of boundaries that are *not* bright and rigid: "A common life is furthered when boundaries are blurred – for example, between parenting and teaching, work and recreation, religion and social work."[59] Overarching such specific points is Selznick's broader argument against abstraction in favor of, as he puts it, "the primacy of the particular."[60] He calls for an alternative "conception of individuals as socially embedded persons, products of history and culture, neither idealized nor abstract."[61]

The relative importance of informal horizontal relations over formal vertical ties emerges in varied contexts. The military is a case in point, as underscored by the research of sociologists Edward Shils and Morris Janowitz. In their classic essay "Cohesion and Disintegration in the Wehrmacht in World War II," Shils and Janowitz found that the effectiveness and cohesion of the German army was traceable not to ideological zeal or indoctrination from above but to the strong and satisfying primary group relations, especially among infantry and junior officers, fostered by the social dynamics of the German army. As in most settings, the appropriate conclusion is not that formal, vertical relations do not matter. On the contrary, those relations have a lot to do with how well horizontal relationships function. But the broader point is, as Shils and Janowitz noted, that "most men are members of the larger society by virtue of identifications which are mediated through the human beings with whom they are in personal relationships. Many are bound into the larger society only by primary group identifications."[62]

Immigration is the *locus classicus* of these enduring issues. The formalism and legalism of today's complaints about illegal immigrants and citizenship certainly echo those articulated by Progressives in the period leading up to World War I, when the number of immigrants (as a percentage of the population) reached its highest point in our history. Then, as now, Americans were alarmed that newcomers were too preoccupied with their own private concerns and were insufficiently attentive to broader community and national goals. Barriers to naturalization were even lower than those today, and the process was prone to abuse and corruption. Not unlike today, there were anxieties that citizenship was being devalued and that immigrants were becoming Americans out of the crassest motives. Looming over all such concerns for most Americans was the specter of powerful urban political machines that drew immigrants into the voting booth by catering to their private needs.

Progressive outrage at such abuses led to reforms inspired by a high-minded, dualistic notion of the private and the public. From this perspective, the goal was to reinforce the boundary between the two realms. Requirements for citizenship were raised, as were barriers to electoral politics. Voter registration was instituted as a disincentive to immigrant voting, which remained depressed for a generation until the New Deal. Patronage hiring was curtailed by civil service reforms that reflected the Progressive view that the influence of disinterested scientific experts housed in legal-rational bureaucracies needed to be enhanced. Not all of these reforms were equally effective, but the intellectual ethos that informed them was clear: to cleanse the public domain of petty private interests. The overall objective of such reforms – sometimes intended, sometimes not – was to exclude immigrants and their families from the civic realm on the grounds that they were inadequately prepared for it.[63] Ultimately, this perspective led many Progressives to advocate immigration restriction.[64]

By contrast, Jane Addams represented a different current of Progressivism. As Jean Bethke Elshtain explains in her biography of the founder of Hull House, Addams was as troubled about the integration of immigrants into American civic life as her fellow Progressives. But unlike many of them, Addams saw the domestic arena as a springboard into wider civic life rather than an inhibition to matters civic.[65] Unlike the principled reformers and dogmatic socialists who either denigrated or just ignored the narrow, even petty, concerns of uneducated immigrants, Addams used those private preoccupations to draw them into the civic arena. Among the immigrant wives and mothers with whom Addams often worked, those preoccupations were strictly domestic and rigidly defined. Nevertheless, Addams taught such women how their families' health and well-being – for example, with regard to garbage collection – depended on much more than keeping their own homes clean.

Accordingly, Addams got embroiled in "the garbage wars" in Chicago's 19th Ward, to the point of being appointed garbage inspector. No mere bureaucratic sinecure, this meant getting up at six in the morning to make sure that the garbage collectors were doing their job. Addams did this by enlisting the help of the immigrant women who were her neighbors at Hull House. Over time, the results were impressive. Eventually, the death rate in the ward was reduced.[66]

Yet those efforts definitely clashed with how immigrant women defined their duties and responsibilities. As Addams explained in *Twenty Years at Hull House*:

Many of the foreign-born women of the ward were much shocked by this abrupt departure into the ways of men, and it took a great deal of explanation to convey the idea even remotely that if it were a womanly task to go about in tenement houses in order to nurse the sick, it might be quite as womanly to go through the same district in order to prevent the breeding of so-called 'filth diseases.'[67]

Such attempts to build bridges between the private concerns of immigrant women and the broader public realm led Addams to her notion of "municipal housekeeping." As Elshtain explains, this did not imply that politics could be replaced by housekeeping on a grand scale. Rather, Addams's point was to socialize politics by bringing some of the concerns and virtues of the private realm, especially as experienced by wives and mothers, into the public arena.[68]

In a similar way, Addams resisted the heavy-handed efforts of the Americanization movement, which sought to integrate immigrants and their children by encouraging them to make a sharp break with the history and culture of their country of origin.[69] On the contrary, Addams encouraged immigrants to respect and build on their past while pursuing integration into the American culture.[70] As Addams wrote, "We were often distressed by the children of immigrant parents who were ashamed of the pit whence they were digged, who repudiated the language and customs of their elders, and counted themselves successful as they were able to ignore the past."[71]

To such immigrants, Addams and her Hull House colleagues held up the example of an American such as Abraham Lincoln as someone who relied on his appreciation of the past to guide his current and future actions.[72]

Perhaps the most apt support for the point we are making about the importance of informal horizontal ties comes from social scientists who have in recent decades developed an alternative understanding of crime and ways to address it. James Q. Wilson began his 1968 study *Varieties of Police Behavior* by observing that "the patrolman's role is defined more by his responsibility for *maintaining order* than by his responsibility for enforcing the law."[73] Written by a conservative in the midst of a nationwide crime wave that was leading to widespread demands for "law and order," this is a striking observation. It suggests that in the midst of today's demands to get tough on illegal immigration, it would be similarly helpful to move beyond the legalistic terms of the current debate. And it once again suggests that the public's anxieties ought not to be dismissed as racist, but neither should they be taken at face value. What lurks just beneath the surface of Americans' inarticulate, and sometimes harsh, rhetoric are not-unreasonable concerns that record numbers of immigrants are threatening the maintenance of social order.

Twenty years after his initial insight, Wilson and a colleague, George Kelling, published the widely cited article "Broken Windows."[74] In the subsequent book by that title, Kelling and Catherine M. Coles called for nothing less than the reconceptualization of crime, away from formal status criteria and toward behavioral criteria. They argued that law enforcement should be less concerned with *loiterers* and more focused on *behaviors* that are associated with loitering but are nevertheless specific offenses – such as petty vandalism, public urination, or drunken and disorderly behavior.[75]

These insights about order maintenance and crime suggest to us that we should be less concerned with whether immigrants are here legally or why they are naturalizing. Instead, we should focus more on whether they are *behaving* like responsible, law-abiding members of the political community. For example, are they steadily employed? Are they making sure their children attend school regularly? Are they seriously attempting to learn English? Are they learning about American culture, history, and politics so that they might become knowledgeable, active citizens? Are they involved in local community life? Are they avoiding difficulties with the law? In other words, are immigrants demonstrating through their actions that they intend to become part of the social and political fabric of America, or are they behaving as if they are here provisionally with some other end in view?[76]

Fragments of the perspective being outlined here can be identified in a few programs and proposals. In Chicago, for example, a consortium of predominantly Mexican-immigrant Catholic churches called The Resurrection Project provides housing opportunities – both rental and owner-occupied units – to parishioners. Eager to avoid becoming a mere service provider, the Project requires beneficiaries of its housing programs to meet specific behavioral conditions. In the case of rental housing, these conditions include the protection of the property and attempts to prolong its life. The Project is concerned with developing a stronger sense of commitment, particularly among immigrants who do not always exhibit those traits either because they are too busy struggling to make ends meet or because they may be planning to return home to Mexico.[77] As the chief executive officer of the organization put it, "When our residents buy one of our houses, they are buying part of our community."[78]

The state of California's Little Hoover Commission has proposed what would be another example. In a report entitled *We the People: Helping Newcomers Become Californians*, the Commission called for the establishment of "The Golden State Residency Program," in which all immigrants – regardless of their formal legal status – could participate. The guiding principle here would be to commit governmental resources to immigrants who demonstrate through their behavior that they intend to become responsible members of the community. The report mentions several criteria by which to judge immigrant behavior:

> Responsibility to the local community, as indicated by a history of paying taxes, remaining in good standing with law enforcement agencies, and where appropriate, being employed or engaged in workforce development and training
>
> Proficiency in English, as demonstrated by actual skills or enrollment in appropriate programs
>
> Participation in civic affairs, for example in public, volunteer and community-based programs
>
> Responsibility for children and other family members, as demonstrated by care for dependent family members and enrollment of children in school and health plans

In return for satisfying such criteria, immigrant enrollees would become eligible for benefits that might include a driver's license, in-state tuition at public colleges and universities, eligibility for public health insurance, and even welfare support.[79]

The Commission even suggests that participants in the Golden State Residency Program be put on track for citizenship – even those who are here illegally.[80] This would clearly be controversial, and perhaps ill-advised. But any such program component could be optional, with specific details tailored to the preferences and values of individual states.

Programs providing benefits to illegal immigrants could even coexist with rigorous enforcement of our immigration laws, especially by federal authorities along the borders and ports of entry as well as at workplaces.

We have no illusions that this would be easy. Tensions and inconsistencies would arise. But if efforts like the Golden State Residency Program were allowed to address gnawing but unacknowledged problems, then that would be better than the status quo, which is also rife with inconsistencies.

A further advantage of programs such as those the Little Hoover Commission has proposed is that they would make more explicit the terms of the bargain struck between immigrants and American society. This would be helpful to everyone – immigrants and nonimmigrants alike. Immigrants would benefit because such programs would make clear to them what Americans expect of them. Indeed, nonimmigrants tend to overlook the confusing signals this diverse society sends out to newcomers. Certainly, in recent decades we have taken a decidedly laissez-faire approach to the integration of immigrants.[81] As one astute immigrant organizer in Chicago put it, "I wish to hell someone would make it clear how we're supposed to act here!"[82]

But endeavors like the Golden State Residency Program would be even more helpful to nonimmigrants. If Americans want immigrants to join our political community, then we need to show them how to do that. Yet this is precisely the area where we have the most cause for self-reproach. Contrary to the usual complaints, Americans are not particularly guilty of racial or ethnic prejudice toward immigrants. But we *are* guilty of a certain smug complacency. All too often, we unthinkingly assume that because immigrants have gained an opportunity for which there is clearly an oversupply of takers, they should be content just to be here, and that we have fulfilled our end of the bargain. Initiatives like the Golden State Residency Program require us to turn vague assumptions into conscious choices and to negotiate an explicit, realistic bargain that asks something of both sides.

In this chapter, we have been concerned with highlighting the importance of informal, horizontal relations in the current debate over illegal immigration. Ultimately, though, the bargain described here speaks to the *political* community, whose formal, vertical ties of membership benefit from explicit articulation and choice. It would behoove America's newcomers to express clearly both their desire to become members of the American political community *and* their commitment to its terms. But that cannot happen unless those who already belong to that community do a better job of defining just what those terms are.

8

Alien Rights, Citizen Rights, and the Politics of Restriction

Rogers M. Smith

THE HARSH VIEW OF AMERICAN IMMIGRATION POLITICS

Scholars of American immigration policies have long understood that they characteristically emerge from a "strange bedfellow" politics comprising opposing political coalitions that, in Daniel Tichenor's words, "cut across familiar partisan and ideological lines."[1] Many employers and free market economic conservatives support expansive opportunities for immigration, often in alliance with pro-immigrant cosmopolitan liberals and ethnic American advocacy groups. Cultural conservatives generally favor restrictive immigration policies, and historically they have often been joined by many unions and others on the Left who have wished to protect American workers from competition with cheap immigrant labor. The latter groups – cultural conservatives, American workers, and those who identify with them – have usually greatly outnumbered the former groups among the general public, so opinion polls traditionally show majority support for more restrictive immigration policies.[2]

But the United States has often had relatively generous immigration policies nonetheless, accompanied by large numbers of undocumented aliens. I am among the somewhat cynical who have explained this apparent anomaly by arguing that the proponents of more open immigration, especially employers but also in the last quarter-century ethnic advocacy groups, have generally been more intensely active on the issue and more politically powerful than their opponents. Thus they have been able to get their way in substance. The fact that American majorities have favored restrictive immigration, though more diffusely and less intensely, has meant only that policymakers in the United States have set some partly symbolic limits on immigration that could gratify cultural conservatives without much helping American workers. In fact, those generally symbolic limits have often served employer interests instead. Although they did not prevent immigrants from coming to this country, they often did restrict the rights of aliens once here. As a result, in those times when either labor surpluses or the political radicalism of immigrant workers curbed employer desires for their presence, officially restrictive policies often assisted in deporting the nation's troublesome excess immigrant population.

Thus, when the intercontinental railroads had been completed and anti-Chinese racism mounted in the late 19th century, the United States excluded first Chinese laborers and then virtually all Asians. Later, in the 1920s, the race-based national origins quota system also kept many Southern and Eastern Europeans out, including often politically radical Jews. But employers easily replaced their inexpensive labor with Mexican workers, against whom no restrictions applied except the general ban on immigrants who might be vagrants and public charges – so that when Mexican workers were not needed, they could be deported.[3] Certainly, from the standpoint of would-be Chinese immigrants and, later, other potential Asian immigrants, these restrictions mattered greatly. It is also likely that the history of the United States, China, and perhaps many other places would have been significantly different if these restrictions had not occurred. But from the standpoint of overall immigration levels and, most pertinently, from the standpoint of employer interests, the bans first on Chinese and then on virtually all Asians, along with other exclusions in the national origins quota system, all represented immigration limits that were more symbolic than real.

The pattern of "symbolic restrictions on entry, real restrictions on rights, extensive practical openness for cheap labor" has historically also been visible in the fact that, in relation to its border patrol responsibilities, the old Immigration and Naturalization Service (INS) was probably the most underfunded, understaffed, demoralized, inefficient, and sometimes corrupt agency in the whole federal bureaucracy.[4] In a kind of perverse functionality, these characteristics meant that those who sought to immigrate legally but who lacked political connections often faced frustrations and delays so great that they sometimes gave up, thereby constraining the total number of immigrants. But immigrants who simply sought to slip across the border had little to worry about in the way of either border or in-country enforcement of the immigration laws, so employers still got their workers. And those workers' undocumented status, their lack of any legal right to be in the United States, made them even more conveniently deportable if they ever sought to be anything more than cheap labor.

This harsh view of American immigration policies and politics may well be unduly negative and overdrawn. I do not wish to deny that the United States has accepted and assisted millions of immigrants in its history, providing many with an asylum from oppression and many more with economic opportunities far beyond any they could dream of having in their home countries. But I lay out the less-flattering account at the start in order to be able to ask: Is something like this pattern of immigration politics visible in the last decade or so of American politics, a period that saw major immigration laws in 1996 and major new executive actions and judicial decisions affecting immigrants after the 9/11 attacks? Is this pattern likely to characterize American policies and legal doctrines affecting immigrants in the foreseeable future?

My answer is that many recent developments do fit this pattern, and the post–9/11 "war on terrorism" has resulted in renewed legitimacy for discriminatory policies toward immigrants and reductions in their legal rights. Those reductions have been so great that they in fact also endanger the rights of American citizens. The division of the old INS into separate services within the new Department of Homeland Security (DHS), moreover, so far seems little more than a change on paper. The heightening of security concerns has far outrun the growth in resources devoted to immigration control, so in terms of state capacity, the United States still does not have the means to patrol its borders effectively or process applications efficiently. It has really added only greater legal and administrative powers to detain and deport the immigrants, legal and undocumented, that the United States decides it does not want. As of this writing, House Republicans are again clamoring for more restrictive measures, and the Bush administration is promising to implement them – so long as it also gets a guestworker program that can satisfy employer demands.[5] Those positions promise to replay the past.

But as Tichenor and others have shown, immigration politics is complex, and today there are important factors that countervail these tendencies. Bush administration officials see a real opportunity to continue to increase the Republican share of the Hispanic vote if the GOP is not perceived as too anti-immigrant – although this goal does not greatly constrain policies aimed at Islamic and Arab immigrants, nor is it likely to produce policies threatening employer interests. That is a major reason why President George W. Bush has sought "comprehensive" immigration reforms that would include some kind of "road to citizenship" for undocumented aliens who are long-term residents, a position Republican conservatives have virulently opposed. Moving beyond the GOP, many of those seeking to revive the contemporary labor movement are striving to make it more transnational, and they are increasingly trying to make common cause with immigrant workers rather than opposing them. Although many workers and some unions are still restrictionists, many more union leaders are now championing immigrant rights and sometimes even higher levels of immigration. And the Supreme Court has also made clear that it will not agree to give up its basic institutional powers and prerogatives in deference to executive security concerns about immigrants, though whether the Court's rulings will provide much substantive protection for immigrant rights, as opposed to precedents upholding the Court's jurisdiction, very much remains to be seen.

THE 1996 LAWS: AEDPA, PRWORA, AND IIRIRA

The early 1990s saw mounting anti-immigrant sentiments in the United States. Polls appeared to show some rise in the degree and salience of the long-standing public opposition to the prevailing level of admissions. Governor Pete Wilson of California, who had supported guestworker programs in the 1980s, championed Proposition 187, a referendum proposal that sought to deny public benefits, including education, to undocumented aliens.[6] Probably the most widely read writer on immigration in those years was Peter Brimelow, who published various essays and then a book, *Alien Nation*, devoted to concerns about the "ethnic and racial transformation" that public policies were "inflicting" on the country. He insisted that "race is destiny" in American politics and life.[7] But though Brimelow sold books and Proposition 187 won at the polls, a federal court declared it unconstitutional, and the United States did not lower immigration levels. Thus many observers concluded that the nation had experienced one of its periodic spasms of anti-immigrant anxieties but that its basically receptive policies and practices remained unaltered.

Congress did, however, pass three laws in 1996 that arguably represented significant victories over these receptive policies and practices and put "the government seal of approval" on the "wave of widespread anti-immigrant feeling," even though the laws also served employer interests.[8] In June 1996, Congress passed the Antiterrorism and Effective Death Penalty Act (AEDPA) of 1996. This act greatly restricted federal habeas corpus review of state and federal prisoners and created a one-year statute of limitations for raising such claims. It also expedited the exclusion and arrest, punishment, and removal of those suspected of being alien terrorists or criminals by authorizing a special removal court, limiting judicial review of deportations, speeding up the timetable for deportation processes, limiting the discretion of the attorney general to admit or grant asylum to suspect aliens, and making many immigration law offenses subject to the expansive punitive measures authorized by the Racketeer Influenced and Corrupt Organizations Act (RICO).[9]

In August, President Bill Clinton signed the Personal Responsibility and Work Opportunity Reconciliation Act (PRWORA). This historic measure ended the Aid to Families with Dependent Children program established in the original New Deal Social Security Act, replacing it with Temporary Assistance to Needy Families (TANF) block grants to the states. It thereby reduced the federal social assistance rights of all citizens. But it also made immigrants arriving after its enactment ineligible for all federally funded means-tested benefit programs such as TANF and Medicaid for five years, with a state option to restore them thereafter; it further denied them Supplemental Security Income and food stamps altogether. Immigrants could regain eligibility by naturalizing.[10]

In September 1996, the Illegal Immigration Reform and Immigrant Responsibility Act (IIRIRA) increased resources for immigration law enforcement, including detentions, further streamlined procedures to expedite exclusions and deportations, further limited the attorney general's discretionary authority to grant entry to the needy via "parole," banned Social Security benefits for undocumented aliens, authorized states to limit public assistance to aliens, mandated new data collection on aliens, including requirements that educational institutions report on their foreign students, and authorized heightened worksite investigations, among other measures.[11]

Collectively, these laws meant that even though the United States did not restrict legal admissions during a decade when immigration was rising rapidly, it cut back sharply on the public benefits that immigrants could receive, even as it reduced the social rights of its citizens somewhat less severely. These policies made it more likely that aliens would take any sort of employment on any terms offered; and if they failed to find employment, the laws also made it easier to deport them. Scholars agree that the laws succeeded in sharply reducing the number of immigrants who received various forms of public assistance, and many argue that problems of ill health, inadequate nutrition, and poverty are on the rise in many immigrant populations as a result.[12] These laws also prompted the states to undertake additional financial burdens of immigrant support that many have found difficult to sustain.[13] Even so, the laws seem to have partly satisfied many critics of high immigration levels without jeopardizing the availability of cheap immigrant labor.

THE POST–9/11 INNOVATIONS

Then came September 11, 2001. It showed that, despite the 1996 law and other measures, the United States had failed horrendously to prevent the entry and operations of foreign terrorists. Almost overnight, a wave of new measures affecting immigrants began that have continued to proliferate up to the present. Most importantly, administration officials quickly compiled many existing proposals to strengthen the nation's antiterrorist capabilities into the USA Patriot Act, which Congress passed even more rapidly, so that President Bush signed it into law on October 26, 2001.[14] Section 411 of the Act permitted denials of entry to aliens perceived as having "endorsed" terrorism, and Section 412 authorized the detention of aliens on a renewable basis if the attorney general had "reasonable grounds to believe" that an alien was engaged in terrorist activities. Then, on November 13, President Bush issued an executive order authorizing trials of noncitizens suspected of terrorism in new military tribunals, without most of the procedural protections constitutionally guaranteed in ordinary criminal trials.[15] On January 11, 2002, the administration opened its detention camp for unlawful enemy combatants at the U.S. naval base in Guantanamo, Cuba, where it claimed the right to hold suspected combatants in indefinite detention without individualized determinations of their status required by the Third Geneva Convention of 1949.[16] We also now know that, sometime in 2002, President Bush secretly authorized the National Security Agency (NSA) to monitor without warrants the international phone calls and e-mails of those suspected of links to Al Qaeda, aliens and citizens alike; and the NSA also reportedly secretly obtained millions of phone call records from several major telephone companies, analyzing calling patterns to identify suspected terrorists.[17]

Then, on the symbolic date of September 11, 2002, the INS began a "Special Registration Initiative" targeted at noncitizens from Arab and Islamic nations, beginning with those from Iraq, Iran, Syria, Libya, and Sudan. The Initiative led to the questioning of roughly 130,000 male immigrants and alien visitors, the deportation of some 9,000 undocumented aliens, the arrest of more than 800 criminal suspects, and the detention of 11 suspected terrorists, without any convictions, before it was officially ended on April 30, 2003 (though many of the new practices in fact

continued).[18] On November 25, 2002, Congress authorized the creation
of the new DHS, meant to absorb, reorganize, and coordinate some 22
federal agencies, including the INS. It officially opened in January 2003,
though most agencies under the DHS have continued to operate in their
preexisting locations.

In June 2003, an internal report led the Department of Justice's inspector general to testify to Congress that some immigrant detainees had been
treated abusively in ways that amounted to serious civil rights violations.[19]
Many private groups and journalists also reported a wide range of discriminatory actions against aliens. In this context, not only civil rights groups
but labor unions began to step up campaigns to protect the rights of immigrants. The AFL-CIO, which had begun to emphasize organizing immigrant workers in the mid-1990s, led a coalition in the summer of 2003
that sponsored the Immigrant Workers Freedom Ride, a bus caravan that
traveled across the country to Washington to call for legalization of undocumented farmworkers and greater civil rights for noncitizens generally.[20]
Perhaps partly in response, on January 7, 2004, President Bush proposed his new temporary workers program as a means of reducing the
immigration backlog that hampered security checks, and he indicated
that undocumented aliens in the United States with good work histories
could be eligible for this program. Conservative critics have claimed that
this would mean de facto amnesty and perhaps access to naturalization,
though the administration disagrees. The plan won the approval of the
Mexican government and remained part of Bush's reelection platform,
but Congress did not act, and Bush set it aside until he felt compelled in
2006 to respond to heightening calls from his own party for tighter border
security and deportation of immigrants.[21] Many still contended that his
"comprehensive" approach would not work to deter illegal immigrants
and would only continue to serve employer interests.

One development did at least appear to modify historic patterns. In
June 2004, the Supreme Court decided three cases that rejected some of
the administration's claims for inherent executive authority to detain suspected terrorists, both citizens and aliens, without procedural protections
or judicial review. Those rulings merit closer attention.

THE SUPREME COURT DECISIONS

The Bush administration's initial measures aimed at immigrants suspected
of terrorism, embodied in the USA Patriot Act, the executive order for
military tribunals, and the Special Registration Initiative, all relied on

doctrines going back to the *Chinese Exclusion Case* and the *Insular Cases*, denying that aliens were entitled to anything more than the most minimal forms of due process rights. But indefinite detentions on the basis of reasonable suspicion alone, without specific charges or evidence and without the detainee having access to an attorney, seemed to many to violate even that undemanding standard, and the administration also soon sought to hold citizens suspected of being involved with terrorism indefinitely in the same fashion. Consequently, executive branch officials came to rely heavily on the heretofore obscure precedent of *Ex parte Quirin*, 317 U.S. 1 (1942), to justify their measures.

In *Quirin*, the Supreme Court had upheld secret military trials for all persons, whether citizens or noncitizens, who fell in the previously undefined category of "unlawful enemy combatants," persons engaged in forms of belligerency that violated the laws of war. The unlawful enemy combatants in question were Nazi saboteurs who had landed covertly on Long Island and in Florida with the intent of blowing up American weapon-production facilities. The Court said that they had no claim to ordinary Fifth and Sixth Amendment procedural guarantees. The decision that came before the Geneva Conventions elaborated the rights of lawful combatants in international wars, but it clearly indicated that whatever rights might come to be established for legitimate soldiers, they did not apply to unlawful enemy combatants. The Bush administration claimed plausibly enough that all terrorists should be seen as unlawful enemy combatants, so that the Guantanamo detainees, and even U.S. citizens suspected of terrorism, could all be treated like the Nazi saboteurs in *Quirin*. Indeed, in the eyes of the executive branch, the president's national security powers and that precedent virtually precluded any judicial review of the detentions of persons so designated.

But in *Rasul v. Bush*, 542 U.S. 466 (2004), Justice John Paul Stevens ruled for a six-justice majority that the Guantanamo detainees had a statutory right to present habeas corpus petitions to U.S. courts whether or not they were U.S. citizens. (Sharif Rasul was a British citizen who had actually been released by the time the case reached the Supreme Court. The remaining petitioners were Australian and Kuwaiti citizens.) In the Court's view, all the detainees were persons who were not nationals of countries at war with the United States and who were being detained indefinitely in a location that, the Court ruled, was under U.S. jurisdiction. None had received any formal process to determine if they were indeed unlawful enemy combatants. Because the Constitution and federal statutes promised due process rights and habeas corpus review for all persons detained by the United States within its jurisdiction, or at least all those who are not technically enemy aliens, the propriety of those detentions had to be reviewable by federal courts.

Justice Antonin Scalia's dissent argued that Stevens had failed to distinguish *Johnson v. Eisentrager*, 339 U.S. 763 (1950), where the Court had denied that civilian courts had any right to review cases of enemy alien combatants in a declared war who had been captured and tried by military forces outside of U.S. jurisdiction. Scalia thought ruling otherwise extended "the habeas statute to the four corners of the earth," and he insisted there was a sharp line between citizen and alien rights. Only U.S. citizens were entitled to habeas corpus review if detained by U.S. agents outside the United States. The majority, however, refused to find such a chasm between citizen and alien rights, and in this case the Court insisted that aliens also receive the larger share of rights Scalia would have confined to citizens.

In response, military officials established review boards, currently termed Combatant Status Review Tribunals, to provide individual determinations of whether each detainee was indeed an unlawful enemy combatant. After releasing some detainees, they then proceeded with military trials for others. Lower courts ruled in conflicting ways on the propriety of these procedures and over the question of whether the right to petition for habeas corpus review upheld in *Rasul v. Bush* carries with it a right to have habeas review actually granted and a civilian trial held.[22] As of this writing, the Supreme Court is completing review of the case of *Hamdan v. Rumsfeld* (No. 05–184, 2005), brought by lawyers for a Yemeni, Salim Ahmed Hamdan, who is still being detained in Guantanamo. His attorneys contend that he is covered by the Third Geneva Convention and the U.S. Constitution as construed in *Rasul v. Bush*, so he is entitled to habeas corpus relief and cannot be subjected to trial by a military commission.[23]

In taking the case, the Court appeared to stand by its 2004 rulings and to reject continuing administration contentions that such military detentions and trials are simply unreviewable. But Congress has since passed the Detainee Treatment Act of 2005, which denied the federal courts all habeas corpus review of the detention of aliens at Guantanamo.[24] It did permit the decisions of Combatant Status Review Tribunals to be appealed to the U.S. Court of Appeals for the District of Columbia, which was authorized to consider the compliance of those tribunals with the standards and procedures established for them by the secretary of defense. The legislation was in part an effort to override *Rasul v. Bush* and render *Hamdan v. Rumsfeld* moot, and in principle it reduces the habeas rights of both aliens and citizens should they be detained as "unlawful enemy combatants." As of this writing, the Act has not come before the Supreme Court.

If and when it does, the decision may have implications for an equally important companion case to *Rasul v. Bush* that involved the rights of citizen, not alien, detainees: *Hamdi v. Rumsfeld*, 542 U.S. 507 (2004). There the Court held that Yaser Hamdi, an American citizen born in Louisiana but raised largely in Saudi Arabia, where he also held citizenship, had access to habeas corpus relief until and unless Congress suspended the writ. He was also entitled to "receive notice of the factual basis for his classification" as an enemy combatant and "a fair opportunity to rebut the Government's factual assertions before a neutral decisionmaker," though that hearing did not have to be accompanied by all the procedural protections required in criminal trials. In the wake of this ruling, officials decided that there was no longer a need to detain Hamdi. He was sent to Saudi Arabia after agreeing to relinquish his U.S. citizenship.[25]

Similarly, for well over a year, the courts refused to offer any but the most limited judicial review of the conditions of confinement imposed on José Padilla, also known as Abdullah al Muhajir, an American citizen and long-term resident arrested at O'Hare airport. He was detained incommunicado for some months as a "material witness" to terrorist activities, and though officials then accused Padilla of having been sufficiently involved in a "dirty bomb" plot to qualify as an unlawful enemy combatant, he continued to be incarcerated in a military facility in South Carolina without formal charges. Two judges of the Second Circuit Court of Appeals held in 2003 that the *Quirin* decision did not authorize the U.S. government to detain a U.S. citizen in this matter (*Padilla v. Rumsfeld*, U.S.C.C.A., 2d Cir. 02–7338, December 18, 2003). On appeal, after deciding *Rasul* and *Hamdi*, the Supreme Court ruled 5–4 that Padilla's petition had been filed in the wrong federal court (*Rumsfeld v. Padilla*, 543 U.S. 426 [2004]).

A three-judge panel of the U.S. Fourth Circuit Court of Appeals then ruled that Padilla's continuing detention without charges was perfectly constitutional (*Padilla v. C. T. Hanft*, U.S.C.C.A., 4th Cir. 05–6396, September 9, 2005). But when Padilla's lawyers sought to appeal to the U.S. Supreme Court, the president ordered that he be released from military custody and transferred to the control of the attorney general, to be tried in a Florida federal district court on lesser criminal charges of associating with terrorists, without any mention of his alleged involvement in a "dirty bomb" plot. Outraged, Judge Luttig of the Fourth Circuit Court sought to prevent the transfer as an apparent effort to evade Supreme

Court review of his court's pro-executive ruling (*Padilla v. C. T. Hanft*, U.S.C.C.A. 4th Cir. 05–6396, filed December 21, 2005). But the Supreme Court declared the case moot, at least until such time as Padilla again faced the threat of a military trial (*Padilla v. C. T. Hanft*, 126 S. Ct. 1649 [2006]). As a result, it seems certain that the Supreme Court will not readily concede that it is without power to consider whether detainees are receiving a minimally adequate hearing to determine if there is an appropriate basis for their detention. But whether detainees, citizen or noncitizen, will really benefit from having their cases reviewed, or whether the courts will in the end show great deference to executive judgments of national security needs, remains unclear.

That uncertainty arises in part from the fact that in the 2004 election President Bush won a narrow but decisive victory, in part by promising to continue to take aggressive actions against terrorism and in part by increasing his share of the Hispanic vote from 35 percent in 2000 to 41 percent, according to the National Annenberg Election Survey.[26] As I have noted, he has continued to champion his guestworker program and to resist deportation schemes, satisfying both employers and his Hispanic constituents, even as he has also promised heightened border controls. At the same time, his administration has also contested adverse judicial rulings asserting the rights of immigrant detainees and has sought to enhance further its powers to track, detain, and deport noncitizens in a great variety of ways, including renewal of the USA Patriot Act.

What do all these somewhat conflicting developments suggest concerning the prospects for alien rights in the years ahead? I believe they provide some confirmation of the bleak depiction of American immigration policies I sketched at the outset. The 1996 laws took away many rights of immigrants to public benefits, and a whole range of post–9/11 actions made immigrants even more vulnerable to detention and deportation, with few procedural protections. Yet despite some increases in human and material resources for border patrols, the United States is still countenancing the arrival of millions of undocumented alien workers each year. And though the administration is facing rising political pressures as a result, it still appears most concerned with maintaining access to immigrant labor, even as it trumpets a few new efforts to prevent aliens from coming into the country for illicit reasons. On balance, the nation has taken and is taking many actions that may reassure those who fear immigrants for cultural or national security reasons, but not many that are likely to reduce immigration significantly or to enhance national security against immigrant terrorists substantially. In the process, however, the executive branch has adopted positions that make even citizens vulnerable to indefinite detentions without access to an attorney on the basis of "reasonable grounds" to suspect that a person is engaged in terrorism or even simply a material witness to terrorist activities.

Clearly, this is not a bright picture from an immigrant rights standpoint, a citizens' rights standpoint, or indeed a national security standpoint. Yet as I noted at the outset, there are countervailing features present. As governor of Texas and as president, Bush has undeniably resisted the most strident anti-immigrant voices in his party in ways that have certainly responded to his many supporters among employers of foreign workers but also in ways that he has presented as embodying his "compassionate conservatism." His success in winning a larger share of the Hispanic vote in 2004, in a country where Hispanics are the fastest-growing minority, undoubtedly strengthened his resolve to resist harsh anti-immigrant policies at all times except when he fears he is in danger of losing his conservative base. He has all the more incentive to resist his more extreme constituents because more compassionate policies also may make Hispanic workers less susceptible to the intensified recruitment efforts of the AFL-CIO and many other unions today. They would do so, however, only if those policies included genuine acceptance of at least some of the demands for restored immigrant rights that the unions are advancing.

At the same time, Islamic and Arab immigrants are not a fast-growing voting base or a promising community for union recruitment. They are, in post–9/11 America, deeply suspect in the eyes of many. Despite the efforts of civil liberties and ethnic advocacy groups, there has been no general outrage at the abusive practices and denials of due process rights that have now been elaborately detailed not only at Abu Ghraib but at Guantanamo and in detention facilities in the United States and abroad – with the details provided not only by the administration's international and domestic critics but by internal reports within the executive branch itself. This absence of mass protests is not surprising. The United States did fail to prevent foreign terrorists from committing the 9/11 attacks, and it does need to do better in the future. For many Americans, that inescapable reality makes even extensive infringements of immigrant rights reasonable. But, by the same token, the current political environment gives us little basis to expect that these immigrants, in particular, will have their civil liberties securely protected in the future.

What about the current legal environment? The Supreme Court decisions in June 2004 came as a surprise to many in the administration, and their reach is still being contested. The modern Supreme Court has shown in other regards that it does not like to have its authority challenged, as when, for example, a former chief justice criticized legislation reducing judicial discretion over sentencing.[27] That is why I think it is likely that the Supreme Court will continue to reject claims that executive branch actions in the war on terrorism are entirely exempt from judicial review. And as the release of Hamdi and many of the Guantanamo detainees shows, that rejection by itself can sometimes be sufficient to free many who are being held on dubious grounds.

But in the history of the United States, the courts have rarely gone far in challenging executive actions justified in the name of national security, as not only *Ex parte Quirin* but also *Korematsu v. United States* and the Supreme Court's unwillingness to review the constitutionality of the undeclared Vietnam War all show. It is hard to believe that a Supreme Court predominantly appointed by conservative Republican presidents is going to do much to restrain the substantive security measures of kindred administrations as long as the "war on terror" continues, at least not after the justices have acted to protect their own institutional authority.

Consequently, it seems likely that the United States will remain a country open to those from impoverished nations who seek significantly improved, though often still relatively meager, economic opportunities. It may well come to be increasingly shaped by a politics that promotes access to full citizenship, and thus public benefits, for those who prove over time to be productive and law-abiding. Many of these immigrants may also benefit from the advocacy of labor unions as well as civil liberties groups and ethnic associations concerned with their rights. But we are likely to face ongoing difficulties with abuse of Islamic and Arab immigrants in particular at the hands of American law enforcement and military forces, and the ways they are denied procedural protections may continue to rebound to erode the rights of American citizens generally. The harsh picture is therefore not the whole story. But it is enough of the story to ensure that eternal vigilance remains the price of civil liberties for citizens and noncitizens alike.

PART III

ECONOMICS AND DEMOGRAPHICS

9

Borderline Madness

America's Counterproductive Immigration Policy

Douglas S. Massey

S. 1/3

The year 1986 was pivotal for the political economy of North America. In that year, two events signaled the end of one era and the beginning of another. In Mexico, a new political elite succeeded in overcoming historical opposition within the ruling party and orchestrated the country's entry into the General Agreement on Tariffs and Trade. Then the Mexican president approached the United States to forge a new alliance that would create a free trade zone stretching from Central America to the North Pole. As U.S. officials worked jointly with Mexican authorities to integrate North America economically, however, they simultaneously and unilaterally acted to prevent the integration of its labor markets. Rather than incorporating the movement of workers into the new trade agreement, the United States insisted there would be no migration in North America, and to underscore its resolve Congress in 1986 passed the Immigration Reform and Control Act (IRCA).

Since then, the United States has pursued an escalating politics of contradiction, simultaneously moving toward integration while insisting on separation. Even as it moved headlong toward a consolidation of markets for capital, goods, commodities, services, and information, it somehow sought to keep labor markets separate. In the ensuing years, the U.S. government would spend increasing financial and human resources to demonstrate to the American public that the border was *not* porous with respect to migrants, even as it was becoming more permeable with respect to an increasing variety of flows.

MOVING TOWARD INTEGRATION

The economic regime imposed on Mexico by its ruling party naturally met with great favor in Washington – indeed, U.S. officials had long pushed for it. Still, there was the troubling problem of institutionalizing the reforms and making them permanent. To solve this problem, President Carlos Salinas de Gortari turned toward the United States, proposing to join the free trade agreement that had recently been negotiated between Canada and the United States. This move would tie his neoliberal reforms to a treaty with Mexico's powerful northern neighbor. It would be extremely difficult, if not impossible, for a future Mexican president to abrogate a treaty with the United States.

The administration of George H. W. Bush warmly embraced Salinas's overture and began talks to expand the North American Free Trade Agreement (NAFTA). The treaty was successfully negotiated and ratified by the U.S. Senate in 1993, with strong support from Bush's successor, Bill Clinton. NAFTA took effect on January 1, 1994, and from that date forward, the United States has been officially committed to a policy of economic integration between itself and its neighbors to the north and south.

The imposition of neoliberal reforms in Mexico after 1986 accelerated cross-border flows of all sorts, and they increased even more dramatically after NAFTA was enacted in 1994. Total trade between Mexico and the United States increased by a factor of eight between 1986 and 2002. According to data published by the U.S. Office of Immigration Statistics, over the same period, the number of Mexicans entering the United States on business visas increased almost fourfold and the annual number of intracompany transferees grew more than five times. Meanwhile, the number of Mexicans admitted as investors increased more than 50 times, going from just 73 in 1986 to 3,983 in 2002.

The growth of trade promoted other cross-border movements as well. In 1986, the annual number of legal border crossings (short-term crossings for business, pleasure, or recreation) stood at roughly 114 million per year. Thereafter, the volume of border traffic increased sharply, peaking at 290 million in the year 2000. The number of official exchange visitors likewise increased dramatically, going from 3,000 in 1986 to nearly 6,700 in 2002, while over the same period the number of Mexicans admitted as temporary legal workers (America's little-known guestworker program) surged by a factor of nearly ten, reaching 119,000 persons in 1998.

INSISTING ON SEPARATION

As envisioned under NAFTA, therefore, North American integration has proceeded rapidly and cross-border traffic has multiplied accordingly. Although the United States has committed itself to integrating most markets in North America, it has paradoxically sought to prevent the integration of one particular market: labor. Indeed, since 1986 the United States has embarked on a determined effort to restrict Mexican immigration and tighten border enforcement, an effort that intensified around 1994, just as NAFTA took effect, and has become even more intense since 9/11.

Beginning in the 1980s, border control was framed by U.S. politicians as an issue of "national security," and illegal migration was portrayed as an "alien invasion." As a result, between 1986 and 1996, the Congress and the president(s) undertook a remarkable series of actions to reassure citizens that they were working hard to "regain control" of the Mexico-U.S. border.[1] The new era was heralded by the passage of IRCA in October 1986, which sought to combat undocumented migration by expanding the Border Patrol, imposing sanctions on employers who knowingly hired undocumented workers, and giving the president authority to declare an "immigration emergency" if large numbers of undocumented migrants had embarked or were expected to embark for the United States.

Despite expectations that IRCA would somehow slow unsanctioned Mexican immigration, by 1990 it was clear that the legislation was not working. With both legal and illegal migration from Mexico still on the rise, Congress returned to the drawing board and in 1990 passed another major revision of U.S. immigration law. The 1990 Immigration Act again focused strongly on border control, authorizing funds to hire more Border Patrol agents, tightening employer sanctions, streamlining deportation procedures, and increasing penalties for numerous immigration violations.

Early in the Clinton administration (1993–1994), the Immigration and Naturalization Service (INS) developed a new border strategy known as "prevention through deterrence." The basic idea was to prevent Mexicans from crossing the border illegally in order to avoid having to arrest them later.[2] The strategy had its origins in September 1993, when the Border Patrol chief in El Paso, Texas, launched Operation Blockade in an all-out effort to prevent illegal border crossing within El Paso. Within a few months, immigrants had been induced to go around the imposing wall of enforcement, and traffic through El Paso itself was dramatically reduced.

Officials in Washington, D.C., took note of the favorable outcome and incorporated the operation into the Border Patrol's national strategic plan for 1994. In October of that year, the INS launched a second border operation, this time along the busiest stretch of the Mexico-U.S. border, in San Diego.

Operation Gatekeeper installed high-intensity floodlights to illuminate the border day and night, as well as an eight-foot steel fence along 14 miles of border from the Pacific Ocean to the foothills of the Coastal Range.[3] Border Patrol officers were stationed every few hundred yards behind this formidable wall (which came to be known as the "tortilla curtain"), and a new array of sophisticated hardware was deployed in the no-man's-land it fronted.[4] As in El Paso, the operation was a success. Formerly the busiest point on the entire border, San Diego became relatively tranquil, as migratory traffic slowed dramatically.[5]

The buildup of enforcement resources on the border was further accelerated by Congress in the Illegal Immigration Reform and Immigrant Responsibility Act (IIRIRA) of 1996. Once again, the legislation focused heavily on enforcement, authorizing funds for the construction of two additional layers of fencing in San Diego and enacting tougher penalties for smugglers, undocumented migrants, and visa overstayers. It also included funding for the purchase of new military technology and provided funds for hiring 1,000 Border Patrol agents a year through 2001, to bring the total strength of the Border Patrol up to 10,000 officers.[6]

The succession of restrictive policies enacted between 1986 and 1996 proved to be bureaucratically beneficial to the INS, particularly to its enforcement branches. In the space of a few years, the Border Patrol went from a backwater agency with a budget smaller than that of many municipal police departments to a large and powerful organization with more officers licensed to carry weapons than any other branch of the federal government except the military.[7] By 2002, the total INS budget was *thirteen times* its 1986 level, and the Border Patrol budget was *ten times* its former level, with three times as many officers.

The additional resources and personnel allocated to the INS after 1986 had a pronounced effect on the agency's enforcement efforts. Linewatch hours – the number of person-hours spent patrolling the Mexico-U.S. border – began to grow, and after 1992 this growth accelerated dramatically. By 2002, the Border Patrol was devoting *eight times* as many hours to patrolling the border as in 1986. As a result of an aggressive new judicial approach to smuggling and repeated illegal entries, formal deportations of Mexicans also exploded after 1986, increasing nearly tenfold by 2002.

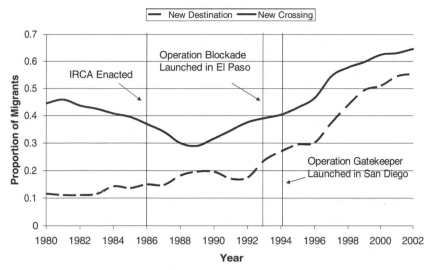

FIGURE 9.1. Proportion going to new crossing points and destinations.

THE COSTS OF CONTRADICTION

Before the buildup at the border, most undocumented Mexican migrants entered the United States through two narrow corridors – San Diego and El Paso – which together comprised only a tiny fraction of the 2,000-mile border. In response to the geographic concentration of undocumented migration, the Border Patrol's enforcement resources were likewise concentrated. Agency operations focused overwhelmingly on these two sectors, and when the massive militarization of the border began in 1993, these two districts naturally led the way. As a new "tortilla curtain" went up in these areas, migrants naturally began to go around the reinforced portions of the border, prompting U.S. authorities to extend their lines of enforcement outward.

This pattern of deployment, response, and counterdeployment influenced the geography of migration in two ways. First, Operation Gatekeeper, by far the largest deployment of enforcement resources, deflected migrants away from California toward new crossing points in Arizona, New Mexico, and more dangerous sections of the Río Grande. Second, within heavily traversed corridors, such as San Diego/Tijuana, the new militarization channeled migrants away from built-up, settled areas and redirected them to a more remote and desolate country.

Figure 9.1 illustrates the changing geography of Mexican immigration using data from the Mexican Migration Project (MMP).[8] The solid line at the top shows the proportion of Mexican migrants entering the United States through a nontraditional crossing point (i.e., not Tijuana/San Diego or Juarez/El Paso). Clearly, from 1980 through 1989, undocumented migration was channeled increasingly through these two traditional gateways. The proportion of undocumented migrants in places other than El Paso or San Diego fell steadily from around 45 percent in 1980 to about 30 percent in 1989.

As the Border Patrol began to expand in the wake of IRCA, the share of border crossings at nontraditional points edged upward, going from 30 percent to 40 percent between 1989 and 1993. With the launch of operations Blockade and Gatekeeper, however, the shift to new crossing points accelerated markedly, and by 2002 nearly two-thirds of all migrants were avoiding San Diego and El Paso entirely. It was precisely at this time that the Border Patrol began to report a sudden increase in traffic through Arizona.

[Not only were undocumented migrants deflected away from traditional crossings, but once in the United States they kept on going. Historically, the vast majority of Mexican migrants went to just three states: Texas, Illinois, and especially California.]The dashed line at the bottom of Figure 9.1 shows the proportion of migrants traveling to states other than these three. Until 1993, no more than 20 percent of migrants ended up at a nontraditional destination. But with the launch of the border blockades in 1993–1994, the share suddenly shot upward until, by 2002, around 55 percent of migrants settled outside of the big three states.

Relative tranquility in the San Diego sector did not mean that the Border Patrol's strategy of "prevention through deterrence" was really working. On the contrary, by pushing migration away from urbanized areas toward sparsely populated sectors, the Border Patrol effectively channeled migrants toward portions of the border where they were *less likely* to be caught, for in addition to being less inhabited, the new crossing points were also *less patrolled*. Figure 9.2 plots annual probabilities of apprehension.[9] Historically, studies have shown the odds of apprehension for undocumented migrants to be about one in three,[10] and these were indeed the relative odds that prevailed during the pre-IRCA period. As shown in Figure 9.2, the probability of apprehension was fairly steady at .30–.35 through the early 1980s. After 1986, however, the probability *fell steadily* to reach record lows of .20–.25 in the period 1990–1994. Although the launch of Operation Gatekeeper in San Diego in 1994 produced a short-term upsurge, after 1996 the probability of apprehension fell once again and by the end of the 1990s was moving rapidly

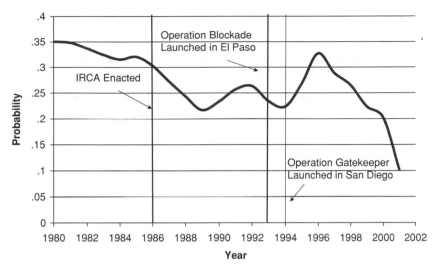

FIGURE 9.2. Probability of apprehension.

downward. There is little evidence, therefore, that the Border Patrol's string of post-1993 enforcement operations were successful in raising the probability of apprehension.

Under these circumstances, one would not expect much of a deterrent effect stemming from Operation Gatekeeper and its extensions. This expectation is indeed borne out by Figure 9.3. The dotted line shows the annual probability that a Mexican male left for the United States in undocumented status between 1980 and 2001. As can be seen, the probability of undocumented migration is small and the trend is relatively flat, fluctuating around .02 per year. At no point in the past 20 years has there been a rising tide of undocumented migration from Mexico. Indeed, the rate of undocumented entry has not changed in several decades. The only thing that changed is U.S. border policy, which, as we have seen, acted to shift migrants to new crossing points and new destinations.

Not only were undocumented migrants dispersing more widely in the wake of the new enforcement regime, they were also staying longer in the United States. A perverse consequence of border enforcement is that for two reasons, it does not deter would-be migrants from leaving so much as it discourages those who are already in the country from returning home. First, even though the costs of border crossing are not increased to the point where migration becomes uneconomical, they *are* nonetheless increased. According to data from the MMP (not shown here), the cost of

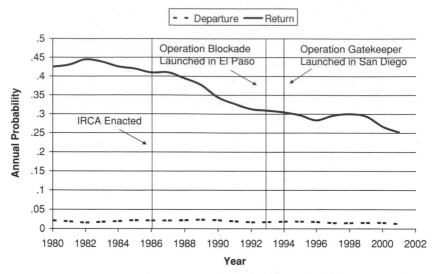

FIGURE 9.3. Probability of undocumented departure and return.

hiring a border smuggler, or coyote, increased from around $300 before 1993 to around $1,200 at present. Raising the out-of-pocket costs of undocumented migration increases trip lengths because migrants have to work longer before the trip becomes profitable. Second, by pushing migrants away from urban areas and into more remote sectors of the border, operations Blockade and Gatekeeper increased the physical risks of border crossing. According to Massey, Durand, and Malone,[11] the rate of death during undocumented border crossing tripled after 1993, and in 2005 the Border Patrol reported a record 415 migrant deaths. It is hardly surprising that migrants, having run the gauntlet of border enforcement and made it into the United States, are loath to repeat the experience.

The end result of the border buildup has thus been to lower the probability of return migration and push migrants toward permanent settlement. The net effect of rising costs and risks of border crossing is evident in the solid line plotted in Figure 9.3, which shows the probability of returning to Mexico within 12 months of an undocumented entry. Historically, the probability of return was about .40–.45, but since the militarization of the border began with IRCA, the odds of returning home within a year have steadily dropped, reaching a historic low of .25 by 2001.

Obviously, if the rate of migration out falls while the rate of migration in remains constant, as demonstrated in Figure 9.3, only one outcome is

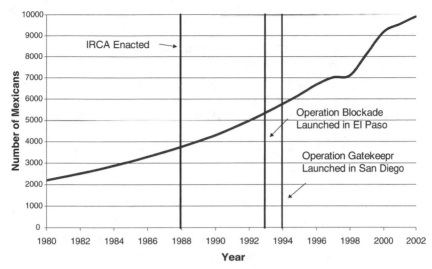

FIGURE 9.4. Number of Mexicans in the United States, 1980–2002.

possible, more rapid growth of the U.S. undocumented population, and this is precisely what has happened. Figure 9.4 draws upon U.S. census data to show the inevitable result of declining rates of return in the face of constant rates of entry: a sharp acceleration in the rate of Mexican population growth after the mid-1990s. From 1980 through the mid-1990s, the Mexican population of the United States grew at a steady if rapid rate, roughly tripling in the 15 years between 1980 and 1995. After 1990, however, there is a sharp discontinuity in the curve and the rate of Mexican population growth shifts sharply upward, with the population growing from 7 million in 1997 to around 10 million in 2002, an increase of 43 percent in just five years. After results from the 2000 U.S. census were published, it was evident that Hispanics had overtaken blacks to become the nation's largest minority far earlier than most demographers had predicted.

THE WORST OF ALL POSSIBLE WORLDS

If the United States had set out to design a dysfunctional immigration policy, it could hardly have done a better job than what it has accomplished over the past two decades. U.S. immigration and border policies have had no detectable effect in deterring undocumented migrants from seeking to come to the United States or in preventing their entry. They have been effective, however, in causing hundreds of needless deaths each year and transforming what had been a seasonal movement of workers focused on three states into a settled population of families dispersed throughout the country. In the end, we have the worst of all possible worlds: continued Mexican migration under conditions that are detrimental to the United States, its citizens, and the migrants themselves.

These negative consequences fundamentally stem from the unwillingness of Americans to accept the reality of North American economic integration. In NAFTA, the United States committed itself to a joint framework for the continent-wide integration of markets for goods, capital, information, commodities, and services, but since then it has refused to recognize the inevitable fact that labor markets will also merge in an integrated economy. In practical, if not logical, terms, it is impossible to create a single North American market characterized by the free movement of all factors of production except one.

Rather than bringing labor migration into the open and managing it in ways that might maximize the benefits and minimize the costs, the United States has employed increasingly repressive means and growing amounts of money to drive the migration flows underground to maintain the illusion of a "controlled" border – one that is miraculously porous with respect to all movements except those involving labor. As we have seen, however, maintaining this pretense is very costly. The time is thus ripe for the United States to abandon its illusions and to accept the reality, indeed the necessity, of North American integration.

10

Immigrant Employment Gains and Native Losses, 2000–2004

Steven A. Camarota

Concern that immigration harms the job prospects or wages of native-born Americans has existed throughout the nation's history whenever immigration levels have been high. With more than 34 million immigrants (legal and illegal), the United States is in the midst of a great surge of immigration. Prior to the economic slowdown that began in 2000, most research that found a negative impact on natives has also found it on earnings.[1] While the debate over earnings continues, since the economic slowdown that began in 2000, a growing body of research has raised the possibility that immigrants may also be displacing natives in the job market.[2] This chapter will explore the relationship between immigrant and native employment between 2000 and 2004 using data collected by the United States Census Bureau over this period. Overall, there is evidence that immigration is adversely impacting the employment of native-born workers.

DATA SOURCE AND METHODS

The information for this chapter comes from the March *Current Population Surveys* (*CPS*) collected by the Census Bureau.[3] The foreign-born or immigrant population in the *CPS* is estimated to include 90 percent of the illegal aliens in the country, who comprise slightly more than one-fourth of the total immigrant population. For the purposes of this chapter, foreign-born and immigrant are used synonymously. This chapter examines employment patterns among adult workers (18 years of age and older). Although persons of age 15 through 17 often do work, it is adults who comprise the vast majority of full-time workers and almost always are the primary income source for a household. Thus the labor market situation of adult workers is central both to the economy and to American families. At various times in the study, I examine labor force participation among workers in the 18–64-year age category. When considering labor force participation, it is standard practice to confine the analysis to those under the age of 64 because the overwhelming majority of Americans retire by the time they are 65. Persons in the labor force are both those who are working and those who are unemployed but looking for work. All other individuals are considered to be outside the labor force.

OVERALL EMPLOYMENT, 2000–2004

Declining Native Employment

Table 10.1 examines the labor force status of adult natives and immigrant workers in the United States. The top of the table shows that the number of employed natives was about 500,000 fewer in March 2004 than in March 2000. In contrast, there was a net increase of 2.3 million in the number of foreign-born workers holding jobs over this same time period. Put another way, there was a net increase of 1.7 million in the total number of adults working in the United States, but all of that increase went to foreign-born workers. The middle section of Table 10.1 reports the number of unemployed natives and immigrants. It shows that there were almost 2.3 million more natives unemployed in 2004 than there were in 2000. While it would be a mistake to assume that there is a one-to-one relationship between immigrant employment gains and native losses, it is clear that the number of immigrants with jobs increased dramatically at the same time as the number of unemployed natives looking for jobs also increased.

Native Nonworkers Increased

The bottom of Table 10.1 shows the number of working-age (18 to 64) natives and immigrants not in the labor force. Between 2000 and 2004, the number of natives not working increased by nearly 4 million, from 30.8 million to 34.8 million. Thus, not only are 500,000 fewer natives working and 2.3 million more unemployed, but 4 million more natives of working age are not in the labor force at all. Of course, many adults choose not to work. But a closer examination of census data shows that changes in childrearing, pursuit of higher education, and a rise in early retirement do not seem to explain the increase in the number of natives

TABLE 10.1. *Immigrant and Native Labor Force Status, 2000 and 2004*

	Immigrant	Natives
Number working 2000[a]	17,463	115,797
Number working 2004[a]	19,742	115,315
Change in number working[a] 2000–2004	2,279	−482
Number unemployed 2000[a]	904	4,812
Number unemployed 2004	1,292	7,085
Change in number unemployed[a] 2000–2004	388	2,273
Number not in labor force 2000[b]	5,883	30,846
Number not in labor force 2004[b]	6,923	34,813
Change in number not in labor force[b] 2000–2004	1,040	3,967

[a] Figures for those working or unemployed are for persons 18 years of age and older.
[b] Figures for those not in the workforce are for persons 18 to 64 years of age. Persons not in the labor force are neither working nor looking for work.
Source: Center for Immigration Studies analyses of March 2000 and March 2004 *Current Population Surveys.*

not in the labor force.[4] It seems almost certain that at least some of the increase is related to economic conditions and perhaps a continued high level of immigration.

Immigrants Are Also Affected by Recession

The figures in Table 10.1 show that immigrants were also adversely impacted by the economic downturn that began in 2000. While Table 10.1 shows that the number of adult immigrants holding jobs increased dramatically, unemployment and nonwork also increased for this population. The rapid growth in the foreign-born population over this time period makes it possible for the number of immigrants holding jobs and the number not working to increase simultaneously. The data show that despite a significant deterioration in unemployment and labor force participation among immigrants, growth in the immigrant population remains at record levels. The overall immigrant population grew by more than four million between March 2000 and March 2004. The continued increase in immigration during an economic slowdown is a clear indication that immigration is not a self-regulating phenomenon that will rise and fall with the state of the economy. Immigration is a complex process driven by a variety of factors, and even a significant economic downturn does not result in significantly lower levels of immigration.

TABLE 10.2. *Immigrant and Native Workers in 2000 and 2004*

	Number Working[a] (2000)	Number Working[a] (2004)	Change in Number Working[a]
All foreign-born	17,463	19,742	2,279
<HS education	5,087	5,778	691
High school only	4,468	4,906	438
>High school	7,908	9,057	1,149
All natives	115,797	115,315	−482
<HS education	9,704	8,341	−1,363
High school only	37,953	35,794	−2,159
>High school	68,139	71,180	3,041

[a] Figures are for workers 18 years of age and older.

Source: Center for Immigration Studies analyses of March 2000 and March 2004 *Current Population Surveys.*

GAINS THROUGHOUT THE LABOR MARKET

Less-Educated Workers

Contrary to the perceptions of some, most of the net increase in immigrant employment was not at the very bottom of the labor market. Table 10.2 reports the number of persons holding jobs by education level. The table shows that less than 700,000 (only 30 percent) of the net increase in adult immigrant employment was among workers with less than a high school degree. About 20 percent of the net increase in immigrant employment was for those with just a high school degree, and 50 percent of the growth was for those who had an education beyond high school. The table shows that immigrants are not simply taking jobs that require little education, pay relatively little, and are menial in nature. While it is true that a much larger share of immigrant workers than native ones have few or no years of schooling, immigration is increasing the supply of workers throughout the labor force.

Native-Born Dropouts

Turning first to native-born dropouts, Table 10.2 shows that the number holding a job declined by 1.4 million. Table 10.3 reports unemployment rates by education level. It shows that some of this decline is explained by an increase of 217,000 in unemployment among native dropouts. The decline in the number of native dropouts also seems to be related to the retirement of older natives with few years of education. Table 10.4 reports

TABLE 10.3. *Unemployment among Foreign-Born and Native Workers in 2000 and 2004*

	Number Unemployed (2000)	Number Unemployed (2004)	Increase in Number Unemployed
All foreign-born	904	1,292	388
<HS education	483	563	80
High school only	194	287	93
>High school	226	442	216
All natives	4,812	7,085	2,273
<HS education	1,066	1,283	217
High school only	1,898	2,783	885
>High school	1,847	3,019	1,172

Figures are for persons 18 years of age and older looking for a job.
Source: Center for Immigration Studies analyses of March 2000 and March 2004 *Current Population Surveys.*

the number of working-age (18 to 64) people not in the labor force by education level. This table shows that the number of native dropouts not in the labor force went down slightly between 2000 and 2003, indicating that there was not an increase in nonwork for this type of worker. Because American society has become more educated in recent decades, there has been a decline in the number of natives lacking a high school degree.

TABLE 10.4. *Immigrants and Natives Not in the Labor Force in 2000 and 2004*

	Not Working or Not Looking for Work (2000)	Not Working or Not Looking for Work (2004)	Change in Number Not Working
All foreign-born	5,883	6,923	1,040
<HS education	2,279	2,625	346
High school only	1,384	1,738	354
>High school	2,220	2,560	340
All natives	30,846	34,813	3,967
<HS education	6,980	6,785	(195)
High school only	10,681	11,847	1,166
>High school	13,185	16,181	2,996

Figures are for persons 18 to 64 years of age. Persons not in the labor force are neither working nor looking for work.
Source: Center for Immigration Studies analyses of March 2000 and March 2004 *Current Population Surveys.*

Many older native-born dropouts are retiring. On the other hand, the unemployment rate of 13.3 percent and the rate of nonwork for native-born dropouts are dramatically higher for native dropouts than for other workers. By significantly increasing the supply of unskilled workers during the recession, immigration may be making it more difficult for these workers to improve their situation.

While it might be reasonable to describe these jobs as ones that most Americans do not want, clearly there are still millions of unskilled Americans in the labor force. Given the persistently high unemployment rate and low rate of labor force participation among this population, it may make little sense to continually increase the supply of unskilled workers through immigration, especially during an economic downturn.

Immigrant-Heavy Occupations

The impact of immigration can also be examined by looking at occupations. Unfortunately, it is not easy to examine changes in the number of immigrants by occupation because the way the government classifies occupations changed between 2000 and 2004. However, Table 10.5 reports the occupational distribution of immigrant and native workers in 2004. The first column reports the percentage of adult immigrants employed in each occupation. For example, in the farming/fishing/forestry occupational category, 2 percent of immigrants are employed. The second column reports the share of all workers for each of these occupations that are immigrants. Thus, immigrants comprise 36 percent of adult workers in the farming/fishing/forestry category. The third column shows the number of adult natives employed in each occupation. The fourth column shows, for each of these occupations, the number of unemployed natives who indicated that this was their last job. The fifth column shows the number of immigrants who arrived between 2000 and 2004 who are employed in each of these occupations. The last column shows the native unemployment rate.

Table 10.5 ranks occupations based on the percentage of workers that are immigrants. It is often suggested that the kinds of jobs immigrants do are so different from what natives do that the two groups seldom, if ever, compete. But Table 10.5 shows that, at least when looked at by occupation, this does not appear to be the case. Clearly there are jobs where immigrants make up a large share of workers, but there are still millions of natives employed in those same occupations. In the first five occupations listed in the table, immigrants comprise 20 percent or more

TABLE 10.5. *Immigrants and Natives by Occupation in 2004, Ranked by Immigrant Share of Occupation*

Occupation	Share of All Immigrants Who Work in Occupation	Share of Occupation Comprised of Immigrants	Number of Natives Employed	Number of Unemployed Natives[a]	Number of Recently Arrived Immigrants (2000–2004) Employed	Native Unemployed
Construct. and extraction	10%	24%	5,999	874	462	12.7%
Food preparation	8%	23%	5,090	525	380	9.3%
Bldg. cleaning and maintenance	8%	35%	3,054	375	318	10.9%
Production manufacturing	11%	22%	7,249	566	272	7.2%
Sales	9%	12%	13,569	879	204	6.1%
Office and admin. support	9%	10%	17,278	994	162	5.4%
Transportation and moving	7%	16%	6,925	608	150	8.1%
Management	7%	10%	12,969	344	133	2.6%
Educ., training	3%	8%	7,464	101	102	1.3%
Computer and mathematical	3%	19%	2,451	130	95	5.0%
Personal care and service	3%	16%	3,549	218	87	5.8%
Installation and repair	3%	13%	4,296	224	68	5.0%
Health care practitioner	4%	12%	5,932	88	66	1.5%
Farming, fishing, and forestry	2%	36%	540	73	63	11.9%
Health care support	2%	17%	2,342	166	59	6.6%
Business and financial	3%	10%	5,098	172	54	3.3%
Architecture and engineering	2%	15%	2,203	77	45	3.4%
Life, physical, and social science	1%	18%	1,059	48	39	4.3%
Arts, entertain., and media	1%	11%	2,313	145	37	5.9%
Protective service	1%	8%	2,538	134	29	5.0%
Community and social service	1%	9%	1,944	55	23	2.8%
Legal occupations	1%	7%	1,454	40	10	2.7%
TOTALS	100%	15%	115,316	6,836	2,857	5.6%

Figures are for persons 18 years of age and older.

[a] Not all unemployed persons report an occupation.

Source: Center for Immigration Studies analysis of March 2004 *Current Population Survey.*

of all workers. But there are still 21.9 million adult natives employed in these occupational categories. In fact, the vast majority of workers in these heavily immigrant occupations are natives. In the six occupations where immigrants comprise between 15 percent and 19 percent of all workers, we again see that there are 18.5 million adult natives employed in these occupations. If we focus just on the four occupations with the largest number of newly arrived immigrants (construction, food preparation, cleaning and maintenance, and production workers), we again find that there are 21.4 million natives employed in these occupations. In these four occupations, there were 1.4 million newly arrived immigrants, and there were more than two million unemployed natives who have experience or skills related to these occupations. This does not mean that immigrants caused the unemployment of natives, though that is a possibility. But it does mean that the idea that there are no American workers available to fill these lower-skilled jobs is not supported by available data.

It is possible that the occupational categories are so highly aggregated in Table 10.5 that they obscure large differences between immigrants and natives. But it must be remembered that there are 48 million natives in the labor force who have only a high school degree or less. Most of these workers do jobs that require only a modest level of training. Moreover, Table 10.5 makes clear that although they are concentrated in more menial jobs, immigrants are employed throughout the labor market.

New Immigration Explains Growth

Tables 10.1 and 10.2 dealt with the net change in immigrant and native employment between 2000 and 2004. But they do not indicate when the immigrant workers arrived in the United States. In contrast, the fifth column in Table 10.5 reports the number of immigrants holding a job who arrived between 2000 and 2004. While it is possible that the growth in adult immigrant employment over the four years could be the result of young immigrants aging into the labor force or adult immigrants already here in 2000 entering the labor market, this is not the case. Table 10.5 shows that there were 2.9 million immigrant workers in 2004 who said that they arrived in 2000 or later. We know this because the CPS asks immigrants to report what year they came to stay in the United States. The net increase in the number of immigrants holding jobs was 2.3 million. Therefore, all of the net growth in immigrant employment is due to new immigrants arriving from abroad. It should be noted that the reason the number of adult immigrant workers did not grow by 2.9 million is that some immigrants here in 2000 had died, gone home, or left the labor force by 2004. Thus 2.3 million represents the net increase in immigrant employment.

EMPLOYMENT TRENDS

Change in the Years Between 2000 and 2004

Tables 10.1 through 10.4 show snapshots of employment for the years 2000 and 2004. They do not show what happened in the years between 2000 and 2004. Figure 10.1 reports changes in the number of natives and immigrants holding jobs in the intervening years. The figure shows that all of the job losses for adult natives were between 2001 and 2002, when adult natives lost 1.7 million jobs. The job gains natives have made since then have not made up for that loss. In fact, the pace of native job gains seems to have slowed, while the job gains for immigrants have increased. The number of employed adult natives increased by almost 850,000 between 2002 and 2003, but between 2003 and 2004 the number increased by less than 300,000. In fact, in the last year, the gain by adult immigrants was twice that of natives. This is striking because immigrants account for only 15 percent of all adult workers, yet two-thirds of employment gains went to immigrants in the last year. Figure 10.1 makes clear that in every year since 2000, the number of immigrants working held roughly constant or increased substantially. Even though there was a large downturn in native employment from 2001 to 2002, the number of immigrants holding jobs did not decline significantly.

Nonwork Among Natives Continues to Increase

Figure 10.2 shows the number of natives of working age (18 to 64) not in the labor force and the number of immigrants who are in the labor force. Unlike the number of jobs being held by natives shown in Figure 10.1, which at least shows positive growth in recent years, Figure 10.2 shows that the number of working-age natives not in the labor force increased every year during 2000–2004. Figure 10.2 indicates that from 2000 to 2001 the number of working-age natives not in the labor force increased by more than 200,000; from 2001 to 2002 it increased by 1.4 million; from 2002 to 2003 by 1.2 million; and from 2003 to 2004 by another 1.2 million. Over the same time period, the number of immigrants in the labor force increased by a total of 2.7 million. It is very possible that by dramatically increasing the supply of labor, immigration may be discouraging native-born workers from looking for work.

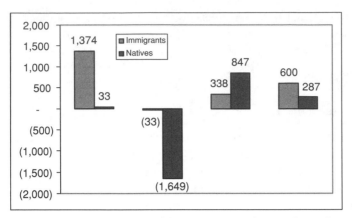

FIGURE 10.1. Immigrant employment gains and native losses by year. Figures are for workers 18 years of age and older. *Source:* Center for Immigration Studies analyses of March 2000 through March 2004 *Current Population Surveys.*

ILLEGAL IMMIGRATION

Illegals in the *CPS*

It is well established that illegal aliens do respond to government surveys such as the decennial census and the *CPS*. While the *CPS* does not ask the foreign-born if they are legal residents of the United States, the Urban

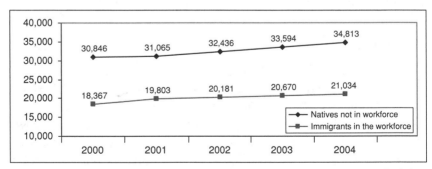

FIGURE 10.2. As immigrants in the labor force have grown, natives not in the labor force have grown. Figures for natives not in the labor force are for persons 18 to 64 years of age. Persons not in the labor force are neither working nor looking for work. Figures for immigrants in the labor force are for persons 18 years of age and older. Persons are in the labor force if they are working or looking for work. *Source:* Center for Immigration Studies analyses of March 2000 through March 2004 *Current Population Surveys.*

Institute, the former Immigration and Naturalization Service (INS), and the Census Bureau have all used sociodemographic characteristics in the data to estimate the size of the illegal population. Preliminary estimates for the March 2004 *CPS* indicate that there were slightly more than 9.1 million illegal aliens in the United States. It must be remembered that this estimate only includes illegal aliens captured by the March *CPS*, not those missed by the survey. This estimate is very similar to those prepared by the Census Bureau, the former INS, and the Urban Institute. Although it should be obvious that there is no definitive means of determining whether a respondent in the survey is an illegal alien, this estimate is consistent with previous research. We estimate that in 2000, based on the March *CPS* from that year, there were between 4.2 million and 4.4 million adult illegal aliens employed in the United States and that this number had grown to between 5.4 million and 5.6 million in the March 2004 *CPS*. These figures are for illegal aliens who are employed. As already indicated, the total number of illegals in the survey was 9.1 million in 2004. This means that about half of the 2.3 million increase in the number of adult immigrants working in the United States was due to illegal immigration.

Why Illegals Are Such a Large Share of Immigrant Employment Growth

The fact that illegals account for half of the overall growth in adult immigrant employment may surprise some, especially because illegal aliens account for slightly more than one-fourth of the total foreign-born population. Research on illegal aliens has shown that they are overwhelmingly of working age. Relatively few illegals come prior to age 18 or after age 50. Because their primary motive for coming is work, it should also not be surprising that our estimates, and other research, find that illegals have a relatively high labor force participation rate. This means that illegals make up a much larger share of both adults in general and adult immigrant workers in particular than they do of the overall population. As a consequence, they also account for a large percentage of the increase in immigrant employment. Another way to understand why illegal immigration must account for such a large share of the employment growth among immigrants is to focus on the Mexican immigrant population. Mexican immigrants are thought to comprise 60 percent to 70 percent of the illegal alien population. Research by the Urban Institute has shown that some 80 percent of recently arrived Mexicans are illegal aliens. In 2004, there were 2.2 million Mexican immigrants in the *CPS* who indicated that they arrived in 2000 or later. (This includes those in and out of the labor force.) It is virtually certain that at least 1.7 million–1.8 million of these individuals are illegal aliens. Just looking at the scale of Mexican immigration makes it clear that illegals comprise a very large share of the net increase in the overall immigrant population and in the number of immigrants holding jobs.

NATIVES DID BETTER IN AREAS WITH LOW IMMIGRANT GROWTH

Top Immigrant-Receiving States

So far, I have considered immigration's impact at only the national level. Table 10.6 reports employment figures for states with the largest numbers of immigrant workers. This table shows that, for the most part, in these top immigrant states it was immigrants who took most of the new jobs where there was a net increase in employment. In Texas, New Jersey, Arizona, Maryland, Virginia, North Carolina, and Georgia, all or almost all of the net increase in jobs went to immigrants. And in California, half of the new jobs went to immigrants. In Illinois, natives lost a large number of jobs, while immigrants made very modest gains. Overall, the figures for these states tend to support the idea that immigrant job gains come at the expense of natives.

While in most of the states in Table 10.6 immigrant employment gains were accompanied by native employment losses, a somewhat different pattern exists in New York, Florida, and Massachusetts. In New York, the number of adult immigrants and natives working both declined. In Massachusetts, it was natives who gained jobs, while the number of immigrants working actually declined. The results for Massachusetts would also tend to support the idea that in order for natives to make employment gains, immigration has to be low. The figure for Florida also buttresses this argument. In Florida, immigrant employment growth was very modest, while native gains were significant. Overall, the numbers in Table 10.6 show that in most of the top immigrant-receiving states, immigrants gained jobs, while natives lost jobs. But in those states where immigrant employment gains were the smallest or nonexistent, natives tended to do better, though not in every case.

What we do not see in Table 10.6 are any states where both groups gained substantial numbers of jobs. Such a situation would tend to undermine the idea that immigrants harm natives. However, it must be pointed out that job losses for both immigrants and natives in states such as New York make it clear that factors other than immigration impact native

TABLE 10.6. *States with the Largest Numbers of Immigrant Workers*

State	Number of Immigrants Working, 2000	Number of Natives Working, 2000	Number of Immigrants Working, 2004	Number of Natives Working, 2004	Change in the Number of Immigrants Working, 2000–2004	Change in the Number of Native Workers, 2000–2004	Shared Employment Growth Going to Immigrants, 2000–2004
Texas	1,534	8,049	1,921	8,114	387	65	86%
North Carolina	217	3,686	410	3,496	193	−190	100%
Maryland	302	2,303	490	2,236	188	−67	100%
Georgia	223	3,787	410	3,644	187	−143	100%
California	5,177	10,385	5,339	10,552	162	167	49%
Arizona	383	1,912	527	1,947	144	35	80%
New Jersey	782	3,326	924	3,199	142	−127	100%
Virginia	337	3,116	455	3,086	118	−31	100%
Florida	1,607	5,691	1,670	6,048	63	357	15%
Illinois	800	5,276	818	5,159	18	−117	No emp. increase
New York	2,162	6,489	2,121	6,329	−41	−160	No emp. increase
Massachusetts	524	2,617	478	2,652	−46	35	0%

Figures are for persons 18 years of age and older.

Source: Center for Immigration Studies analyses of March 2000 and March 2004 *Current Population Surveys.*

employment. Immigration is only one of many factors that can have an impact on labor market outcomes for natives.

States with the Largest Immigrant Employment Gains

Some of the states that saw the largest numerical increases in immigrant employment are not among the states with the largest existing immigrant populations. This situation exists because for some time now immigrants have been spreading out into parts of the country that previously saw little immigration. Thus there are many states with smaller immigrant populations that experienced rapid growth between 2000 and 2004. Table 10.7 ranks the 10 states with the largest numerical increases in immigrant workers between 2000 and 2004. They are also states where the number of immigrant workers increased by 100,000 or more. In contrast to Table 10.6, New York, Massachusetts, Illinois, and Florida are not included, while Pennsylvania and Ohio join the list. The total net change in adult native employment in these 10 states was 336,000, while immigrants gained 1.7 million jobs. It should be remembered that nationally the number of adult natives working decreased by a total of 481,000 during this period. Thus the net job loss in these 10 states was equal to 76 percent of the total native job loss nationally. While many factors impact employment, there is no question that these 10 states account for almost all of the net increase in immigrant employment. It should also be pointed out that, with the possible exception of Ohio, there does not seem to be any state where immigrant employment and native employment both rose significantly. This shows that immigrant gains may tend to come at the expense of natives.

Table 10.8 examines labor force participation and unemployment among natives in the same top 10 states with the largest numerical increases in immigrant workers during 2000–2004. Again, we see that native unemployment or nonwork rose in every one of these states. In fact, with the exception of Georgia and Ohio, unemployment and nonwork together grew in every state. In Georgia, while the number not in the labor force held constant, unemployment grew significantly. Ohio may be the one exception, but even here unemployment increased by 100,000 while nonwork held steady. Although there is no conclusive proof that immigration has adversely impacted native-born workers, the results in Table 10.8 are consistent with the possibility that immigration may have had an adverse impact on native employment during the recent economic downturn.

TABLE 10.7. *States with the Largest Increases in Immigrant Workers, 2000–2004*

State	Number of Immigrants Working, 2000	Number of Natives Working, 2000	Number of Immigrants Working, 2004	Number of Natives Working, 2004	Change in Number of Immigrants Working, 2000–2004	Change in Number of Natives Working, 2000–2004	Growth in Number of Immigrants Working, 2000–2004	Growth in Number of Natives Working, 2000–2004
Texas	1,534	8,049	1,921	8,114	387	65	25%	1%
North Carolina	217	3,686	410	3,496	193	−190	89%	−5%
Maryland	302	2,303	490	2,236	188	−67	62%	−3%
Georgia	223	3,787	410	3,644	187	−143	84%	−4%
California	5,177	10,385	5,339	10,552	162	167	3%	2%
Arizona	383	1,912	527	1,947	144	35	38%	2%
New Jersey	782	3,326	924	3,199	142	−127	18%	−4%
Virginia	337	3,116	455	3,085	118	−31	35%	−1%
Pennsylvania	196	5,500	301	5,364	105	−136	54%	−2%
Ohio	156	5,171	260	5,232	104	61	67%	1%
Totals for top 10 states	9,307	47,235	11,037	46,869	1,730	−366	19%	−1%
Balance of country	8,157	68,562	8,702	68,443	545	−119	7%	−0.2%

Figures are for workers 18 years of age and older.
Source: Center for Immigration Studies analysis of March 2000 and March 2004 *Current Population Surveys.*

TABLE 10.8. *Native Labor Force Status in States with the Largest Increases in Immigrant Workers, 2000–2004*

State	Growth in the Number of Immigrants Working, 2000–2004[a]	Change in the Number of Natives Not in the Labor Force[b]	Change in Native Unemployment[a]
Texas	387	237	104
North Carolina	193	199	53
Maryland	188	102	35
Georgia	187	248	−7
California	162	475	255
Arizona	144	29	32
New Jersey	142	67	62
Virginia	118	232	57
Pennsylvania	105	31	100
Ohio	104	−23	100
Totals for top 10 states	1,730	1,597	791

[a] Figures are for workers 18 years of age and older.
[b] Figures for natives not in the labor force are for persons 18 to 64 years of age and older.
Source: Center for Immigration Studies analyses of March 2000 and March 2004 *Current Population Surveys.*

Comparisons Across All States

Tables 10.6, 10.7, and 10.8 provide some insight into the effect of immigration in states with large or rapidly growing immigrant populations. In order to look for a relationship between immigration and native employment, Figure 10.3 analyzes every state, not just those with large or rapidly increasing immigrant populations. Figure 10.3 reports the proportional relationship between immigrant and native employment using data from every state. The horizontal axis shows the increase in immigrant employment, and the vertical axis reports the change in state employment for adult natives. Figure 10.3 reads as follows. In states where immigrants increased their share of workers by 5 percentage points or more, the number of native workers fell by about 3 percent on average. In states where immigrants increased their share of workers by 3 to 4 percentage points, the number of natives holding jobs declined by 1.1 percent. In states where immigrants increased their share of workers 1 to 2 percentage points, native employment fell by one-tenth of 1 percent. Finally, in states where the immigrant share of workers increased by less than

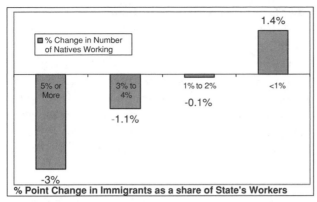

FIGURE 10.3. Percentage change in immigrants as a share of the state's workers. All figures are for workers 18 years of age and older. *Source:* Center for Immigration Studies analyses of March 2000 and March 2004 *Current Population Surveys.*

1 percentage point or actually fell, the number of adult natives holding a job increased by 1.4 percent.[5]

It must be pointed out that states are not necessarily discrete labor markets. Moreover, many factors besides immigration have an impact on employment. Thus, the results do not prove that immigration has adversely impacted natives. But the findings presented here do add support to the idea that immigration has adversely impacted native-born workers. However, more research and analysis are clearly necessary to confirm these results and to arrive at a more definitive conclusion about the relationship between immigration and native employment.

CONCLUSION

The time period 2000–2004 was difficult for many American workers. This chapter shows that all of the employment losses during this period were absorbed by native-born Americans. The number of natives holding jobs in March 2004 was half a million lower than in March 2000, and the number unemployed was 2.3 million higher. Over the same time period, the number of immigrants holding jobs in the United States increased by 2.3 million. About half of the increase in immigrant employment is due to the growth of the illegal alien population. I find little evidence for the argument that immigrants only take jobs natives do not want. Immigrant employment gains have occurred throughout the labor market, with half of the increase among workers with education beyond high school. Moreover, closer inspection of particular occupations shows that there are millions of natives employed in occupations that saw the largest influx of new immigrants.

We find some direct evidence that immigration has adversely impacted natives. Areas of the country with the largest increases in immigrant workers were, in many cases, areas that saw the most significant job losses for natives. Immigrant occupations with the largest immigrant influxes tended to have the highest unemployment rates among natives. This certainly raises the very real possibility that immigration has adversely affected native employment.

The economic downturn earlier this decade was accompanied by record levels of immigration. Given the labor market difficulty of many natives, the dramatic increase in the number of immigrants holding jobs certainly calls into question the wisdom of proposals to increase immigration levels further by granting and instituting a new guestworker program. Instead, actually enforcing immigration laws and reducing the number of illegal aliens in the United States as well as reducing the levels of immigration may be helpful for the job prospects of native-born Americans.

11

Economics of Immigration and the Course of the Debate since 1994

Peter Brimelow

> It ain't what folks don't know that's the problem, it's what they know that ain't so.
>
> Will Rogers[1]

In the early 1990s, I got interested in the economics of immigration, first for a massive cover story for *National Review*,[2] which was then enjoying a last flurry of intellectual independence before regressing to the Beltway Right mean, and later for a book, *Alien Nation: Common Sense About America's Immigration Disaster*,[3] which was published in 1995.

I researched the topic by what turned out to be the radical technique of actually reading the technical literature. This seemed normal to me as a financial journalist. But it was apparently shocking to political journalists and pundits (and politicians, although they, of course, are excused from not participating in such ivory tower debates). They actively resisted it – even (in fact, especially) those working for newspapers nominally concerned with business and economics, particularly the *Wall Street Journal*.[4]

Indeed, to this day, the public debate about the economics of immigration simply does not reflect the professional consensus among labor economists, although this consensus has only strengthened over the last decade.[5] In Will Rogers's words, the problem is not what folks don't know, it's what they know that ain't so.

This is an unusual situation. But it is not completely without parallel. Thus, professional economists in the United Kingdom were actually quite tempered about the benefits to be gained from Britain's entry into the European Union, although it was always publicly justified as an economic panacea. We are looking here at a case of elite enthusiasm – similar to, but less celebrated than, extraordinary popular delusions and the madness of crowds.[6] Oddly, American economists have put in relatively little effort to measure the overall economic benefits of immigration. But the answer is quite clear:

- On balance, current mass immigration contributes essentially nothing to native-born Americans in aggregate.
- In fact, counting transfer payments, mass immigration is probably a loss for the native-born.
- But mass immigration does cause a substantial redistribution of income among the native-born – basically from labor to capital.

In other words, the United States is being transformed for nothing. If anything, Americans are paying to be displaced.

What does economic growth mean anyway? Basically it can be viewed in three ways:

1. *Growth of overall national income* – literally, any increase in the size of a country's output. Of course, if immigration increases the workforce at all, it must cause such an increase, even if it is just one immigrant mowing lawns.
2. *Growth in national income per capita* – increase per head of the population, including the new heads that have just immigrated. This could happen, for example, if all immigrants earned more than the national average, as perhaps they might if they were just those much-publicized PhDs. Immigration of this sort – which government policy could easily arrange – would be an economic luxury.
3. *Growth of national income of native-born Americans* – that is, the Americans already here increase their standard of living because of the presence of immigrants, even if the immigrants themselves do not rise to the same level.

Thus an American lawnowner is happy to pay to have his lawn mowed. The lawnmowing immigrant is happy, too (presumably). And national output will rise by the wages that the immigrant receives. But national income *per capita* will fall because those wages are far below the national average.

Obviously, immigration that results in everyone getting richer on average is the easiest to defend. And immigration that results in native-born Americans getting richer is at least rational in economic terms. But it might be socially disturbing if it led to a racially distinct, lawnmowing servant caste.

Immigration that just results in some (possibly minimal) growth in overall output is the most questionable. But how much growth are we talking about anyway? One mowed lawn's worth? And why should native-born Americans put up with immigration at all if they do not get significant benefits themselves?

Unfortunately, point (1), some (possibly minimal) growth in overall output, is just about the only thing we can be sure that immigration achieves. It does generate instant population growth. The host country cannot achieve instant population growth by other policies. And an instantly larger population can be very useful if you are seizing a continent or fighting a war (at least it could before high-tech weapons).

But, from an economic standpoint, instantly acquiring more people is not so obviously useful. A country's living standard is expressed by its output per capita, not just its sheer output. The economies of Britain and China had about the same output in the early 19th century. But Britannia could afford to rule the waves, while China was starving, because British output was 15 times higher *per capita* than Chinese output.

In short, just acquiring more people is not enough. In an increasingly technical age, what will count is not the quantity of people but their quality – and the quality of their ideas.

How much does current mass immigration benefit native-born Americans? Harvard's Professor George J. Borjas provided the best answer, using a standard applied economics technique called a "Harberger Triangle." It made possible a simple estimate of the growth of national income of native-born Americans through immigration – the additional economic "surplus" generated by immigrants and accruing to native-born Americans.[7]

The surplus generated by immigrants and accruing to native-born Americans was very small: about one- to three-tenths of 1 percent of the total U.S. economic output in 1992, or between $6 billion and $18 billion. That was 0.2 or 0.3 percent in an economy whose long-run average annual growth is about 2 percent anyway. In fact, this surplus was well within the normal margin of error for economic projections – *so it was, for practical purposes, nugatory.* If immigration was indeed causing a net loss to taxpayers of $16 billion through transfer payments – as George Borjas then estimated – that meant its macroeconomic economic effects were negative.

Borjas's calculation also revealed a subtle but ugly implication. The overall economic surplus generated by immigrants and accruing to native-born Americans might be very small – but immigration might still be causing a significant redistribution of income within the native-born American community. This happens because the (arguably small) amount by which immigrants drive down the wages for all American workers, nationwide, adds up to a sizable sum – which goes to American owners of capital. Borjas estimated that in 1992 it amounted to 2 percent of gross national product (GNP), or as much as $120 billion. The ugly implication, of course, is that the American elite's support for immigration may not be a result of their greater enlightenment but a result of self-interest – as a way to prey on their fellow Americans.

Naturally, immigration enthusiasts have trouble accepting this. They are shocked to hear that the net gains from immigration are so trivial – particularly if they live in New York or California, where immigration's gross effects are very visible. "How can it be?" they ask. And they start telling anecdotes about immigrant entrepreneurs.

Well, you can fit a lot of Korean convenience stores, and even Silicon Valley electronics firms, into $6 billion to $18 billion. (Indeed, even if immigrants ran the entire computer industry – software and hardware – that would only account for just over 2 percent of the GNP, some $120 billion annually.) But the real reason is that, because of the uncritical, one-way, pro-immigration nature of contemporary debate, anecdotes about immigrants on welfare, in jail, or in the hospital do not really get equal time. In other words, what is important is not the *gross* economic contribution of immigrants but the *net* contribution – subtracting the cost to the native-born in transfer payments and reduced wages.

In 1995, I was able to quote ironic evidence in support of Borjas's Harberger calculation: a study by two immigration enthusiast economists who argued that, by 1912, immigration since 1790 had generated social savings that had increased the capital stock of the United States by about 13–42 percent, depending on the discount rate used. (The lower is more likely.) Sounds like a lot? They thought so, too. But, *by their own calculation*, it would have taken the U.S. economy only 5 to 18 years more to achieve the same capital stock if there had been no immigration at all. This is a shockingly small increment, given the magnitude of the population movement involved. It is a measure of the emotion affecting even economists in the area of immigration that two professionals presented, and a technical journal published, such an elementary misinterpretation.[8]

The fact is that much of American immigration history probably needs revision – and has, in fact, been revised, but no one has noticed it. For example, Professor Richard A. Easterlin, writing in the *Harvard Encyclopedia of Ethnic Groups*, has argued that the vast immigration into the United States in the 19th century "probably did not alter substantially the growth of output per capita." The innovations that drove American economic growth, such as mass production in manufacturing, Easterlin pointed out, were already celebrated worldwide by 1850, when mass immigration was just getting under way. In the next hundred years, both France and Germany outstripped the United States in per capita output growth.[9]

"*Immigrants built America.*" Well, not quite, as it turns out. The colonial-stock Americans had things rolling along pretty well before mass immigration began.

Why is labor only a small element in economic growth? Audiences always burst out laughing at one apparently gagless scene in the 1986 hit movie *Back to the Future*: the time-transported hero was amazed to see a car drive up to a gas station in the 1950s and an army of uniformed attendants leap forth to pump the gas, clean the windshield, fill the tires, polish the hubcaps, offer maps, and so on. The joke was in the shock of self-recognition. It was only yesterday – and yet completely forgotten, so accustomed is everyone now to self-service.

"*We need immigrants to meet the looming labor shortage and do the dirty work Americans won't do.*" This further item from the immigration enthusiasts' catechism seems to be particularly resonant for American conservatives, deeply influenced by libertarian ideas and open, somewhat, to the concerns of business. But it has always seemed incongruous, given persistent high levels of unemployment among some native-born Americans. These groups obviously eat, after all. Unless they are all criminals, they must be living on government transfer payments. Public policy is subsidizing their choosiness about work and thus artificially stimulating the demand for immigrants.

And *if* there is a looming labor shortage – which is hotly disputed – it could presumably be countered by "natalist" policies. That is, Americans could be encouraged to step up their nation's below-replacement birthrate. But *Back to the Future* makes a more fundamental point about economics: labor is not an absolute. Free economies are infinitely ingenious at finding methods, and machinery, to economize on labor or any other scarce resource.

The implicit assumption behind the popular economic argument for immigration appears to be something like this:

$$\text{labor} \times \text{capital} = \text{economic growth}.$$

So, for any given capital stock, any increase in labor (putting aside the question of its quality) must result in some significant increase in output. This assumption is just wrong. However surprising it may seem to laymen, capital and labor are relatively minor factors of production. For example, the work of Simon Kuznets – such as his *Modern Economic Growth: Rate, Structure and Spread*[10] – has shown that increases in capital and labor together accounted for no more than 10 percent of the West's increase in output over the last two hundred years, and possibly less. The balance was caused by technical innovation – new ideas.

Although it has been ignored in the immigration debate, there is an entire "accounting for growth" industry among applied economists that attempts to isolate and measure the causes of economic growth. Invariably, it finds that *increases in labor and capital together* account for *at most half and often much less of increases in output.* The rest seems to be attributable to changes in organization – to technological progress and ideas. Or:

$$\text{economic growth} = \text{labor} \times \text{capital} \times [???]$$

And [???] is dominant.

Back to the Future illustrates this process in action. On the face of it, gas stations have simply substituted capital (the self-service pumps) for labor (gas jockeys). But what has happened is actually more complex: the cost of making the pumps, and of designing the computer system behind them, is far exceeded by the savings on labor, which extend indefinitely into the future. It is reorganization that has resulted in a permanent increase in productivity.

Or think about that lawnmowing immigrant. If he was not around, maybe local kids would organize lawnmowing services. Maybe better lawnmowers would be invented. Or maybe houseowners would stop demanding their very own putting greens and adopt gardening styles better suited to local conditions – desert flowers in the southwest, for example. It would save on water bills, too.

This has happened before. When British aristocrats began to run short of gardeners in the late 19th century, they substituted perennial flowers for annuals and invented the herbaceous border – now recognized as one of the glories of what Noël Coward hymned as "the Stately Homes of England."

From an economist's standpoint, *the factors of production are not absolutes. They are a fluid series of conditional interacting relationships.* This insight won the University of Maryland's Julian Simon one of the famous debating victories of recent years. In 1980, he bet Paul Ehrlich, the well-known environmentalist commentator and Stanford University entomologist, that several commodities Ehrlich claimed were running out would, in fact, be lower in price in 1990, the economy having adjusted in the meantime. They were, and Ehrlich had to pay up.

But, paradoxically, when it came to immigration, Simon reverted to a classic noneconomic view: labor is good, more labor is better. Until his death in 1998, he was the media's designated immigration enthusiast economist, although his scholarly credentials were not in that field at all.

There's an irony here. Immigrant enthusiasts often boast, "*Most studies show American workers' wages have been driven down only very slightly by competition from immigrants.*" And that was basically true as of 1995. (There is evidence[11] that the impact on wages of the First Great Wave of immigration in 1890–1920 began to show up much more strongly as time passed, stimulating the labor union agitation that helped bring about the legislated immigration cutoff of the 1920s.)

But it was exactly because wages have not been driven down that Borjas's Harberger calculation reported such minimal overall economic benefits. The formal economic logic of immigration is that *only* if wage rates are driven down – meaning that American owners of capital can hire workers more cheaply and make an increased profit for themselves – can the economy derive an overall benefit. That increased profit is the basic way in which native-born Americans are supposed to benefit from immigration. If it cannot be shown to exist, then native-born Americans are just not benefiting at all. In other words, the very wage stability that helped the immigration enthusiasts' political argument also worked to undermine their economic argument. This, of course, is why they have been so anxious not to hear it.

What has happened since 1995? The consensus among professional economists exemplified by George Borjas's work has simply strengthened. If anything, it might be too moderate. These are the key developments:

- The 1997 publication of the National Research Council's *The New Americans: Economic, Demographic, and Fiscal Effects of Immigration*[12]

Intended to establish the consensus among academic economists for the U.S. Commission for Immigration Reform (the "Jordan Commission"), *The New Americans* (1) confirmed that the "immigration surplus" from the current inflow is nugatory – $1 billion–10 billion, maybe 0.1 percent of gross domestic product (GDP); (2) showed significant net fiscal losses – $166–226 annually per native-born family nationwide and $1,174 in California – that outweighed the "immigration surplus"; and (3) showed a small but significant wage depression for native-born workers, maybe 1.2 percent overall, and substantially more for high school dropouts.

The New Americans had absolutely no impact on public debate, in part because of the most mendacious press release I have seen in 30 years in journalism. Immigration appears to be one of those subjects about which people feel lying is morally justified.

• *Increasing evidence that immigration is impacting native-born incomes*

As in the early 1900s, this evidence has simply showed up over time. The difference is visible in George Borjas's two survey books, *Friends or Strangers*[13] in 1990 and *Heaven's Door*[14] in 1999. The former reported little detectable impact; the latter reported significant impact on less-skilled workers.

Subsequently, in a methodological breakthrough, Borjas has shown that immigration is impacting the wages of all native-born workers, including even new native-born college graduates.[15] Recently, he has demonstrated that the impact of immigrant PhD students on the earnings of native-born PhDs is particularly acute.[16]

Of course, depressing native-born incomes means that the "immigration surplus" is larger. But it is distributed among a diminishing number of the native-born at the expense of their fellow countrymen. Accordingly, it will be increasingly hard to make most Americans stand still for it, even with the help of the *Wall Street Journal*.

• *The possibility of much larger losses from immigration*

Using a trade theory approach, two Columbia University economists have estimated[17] the losses to U.S. natives from immigration at 0.8 percent of the GDP – or $96 billion in today's $12 trillion economy. That is an average loss of $833 for each native worker.

These are "big numbers." According to the authors, immigration is about as costly to the United States as all trade protection. Considering the magnitude of the immigration increases proposed by President George W. Bush, research into immigration's macroeconomic impact is still surprisingly minimal. But its message is powerfully negative – and getting more so.

12

Immigration and Future Population Change in America

Charles F. Westoff

Immigration has been a controversial subject periodically in this country throughout much of the past 150 years and has reappeared prominently on the political agenda. Much of the current controversy focuses on illegal immigration, which is at an all-time high. The U.S. Census Bureau estimates their number at 10–11 million. Between 2000 and 2004, there was a net increase of 4.3 million immigrants, close to half of whom are illegal. In broader terms, the controversial political discussions have revolved around competition for jobs, cost of schooling, housing, crime, and so on. A total of 34 million immigrants, both legal and illegal, are now in the United States, the largest number in the history of the country. Some of the legal migrants – about 700,000 a year currently – fill important professional specialties but also bring along immediate family and relatives (about two-thirds of the arrivals).

However one evaluates the net costs and benefits of immigration, it is a major demographic force as well as a political issue in the United States. In Europe, the issue has been pushed to the front of the political agenda as a result of the sustained low level of fertility that is now resulting in actual or imminent population declines along with increasingly aging populations that carry serious implications for retirement pensions and labor force shortages. The situation in the United States is very different from that of Europe both because of the volume of immigration and because the fertility rate of the American population is around the replacement level, where it has stayed for some time now, a level that is 50 percent higher than that of Europe today. The United States has the most rapidly growing population in the developed world.

The remarkable thing about the immigration debates and discussion in the United States is the absence of any reference to immigration's effect on population size and growth. Once in a while, a journalist will note the higher fertility rates of Hispanic migrants or the concentration of immigrant populations in certain locales such as California, Miami, and New York. But, for whatever reason, there never seems to be any attention paid to the implications of immigration for the growth and size of the U.S. population. The subject of population growth, in general, is itself a separate and debatable issue, but it is certainly a dimension of the immigration debate that should not be ignored. The chief difficulty in tying the two together became apparent in one of the few publicized debates on the subject within the Sierra Club, a U.S. group that has been concerned about the environmental consequences of population growth. The Sierra Club's experience illustrates the difficulty of reconciling concerns about population growth with one of its major components – immigration. The debate became both political and acrimonious when some members running for office within the organization who are concerned about the growth implications of immigration and who advocated some controls on immigrant numbers were accused of racism – leading Frederick Meyerson to observe in a review of the Sierra Club infighting: "Playing the race card virtually ensures the end to intelligent debate on immigration (or any other) policy."

More broadly, the concern about population growth in general that was so much in the news in the 1960s and 1970s has largely disappeared from the radar. The reasons for this include the decline of fertility in the West and more recently in many developing countries; the mistaken belief that the spread of AIDS has cancelled population growth; the focus of the environmental movement on technological fixes to improve agricultural productivity; the politics of the abortion issue in the United States; and the U.S. government's mantra that capitalism can cure everything.

An interesting political aspect of the immigration issue is the extremely wide gulf between public opinion and the views of opinion leaders, including members of Congress. This difference, which has been the subject of several studies over time, indicates that 60 percent of the public regards the current level of immigration to be a threat to U.S. interests, in contrast to only 14 percent of the nation's leadership who think likewise. The reasons for this difference certainly include the fact that the public is more concerned than the elite about competition for jobs.

The aim of this chapter is more narrow. Here I show the magnitude of the numerical implications of current rates of immigration for the potential growth and demographic changes of the U.S. population. Whether immigration and its social and economic consequences are good news or bad news involves complex questions beyond the scope of this chapter.

MEASUREMENT

The annual rate of natural increase (births minus deaths) in the United States is 6 per 1,000 population, while the overall rate of population growth is 10 per 1,000. The difference between the two rates is the annual contribution made by net migration, 4 per 1,000. Thus net migration currently accounts for some 40 percent of our annual growth. But this statistic is problematic because it depends on the balance of birth and death rates. As these become closer, the relative importance of migration increases; in a population with equal birth and death rates, such as in many European countries, immigration would account for 100 percent of annual growth.

A more revealing approach to understanding the impact of immigration on the nation's population size is through population projections that include not only the annual numbers of immigrants but their descendants as well. The sharpest contrast is to compare projected populations with and without migration. This is obviously unrealistic, but it serves to illustrate the magnitude of the effect of immigration on the growth of the population. The comparison assumes that current rates of immigration remain unchanged, an assumption that could easily be affected by changes in policy or enforcement of existing policies, or by changes in the economic attractiveness of the United States or the sending countries, or by increases in security concerns. The high volume of immigration in recent years despite periodic slowdowns in the U.S. economy and an increasing unemployment of immigrants suggests that the amount of immigration and economic conditions in the United States are now less correlated than in the past.

The projections are also sensitive to future fertility and mortality assumptions. It is possible that the future fertility of the United States may rise as the proportion of first-generation Hispanics increases. Currently, the fertility rate of the Hispanic population (2.72 births per woman) is 48 percent higher than that of white, non-Hispanic women (1.83) and 32 percent higher than the rate for black, non-Hispanic women (2.05). It is also possible, however, that the fertility of the U.S. native population will decline, following the European track. So, the projections only

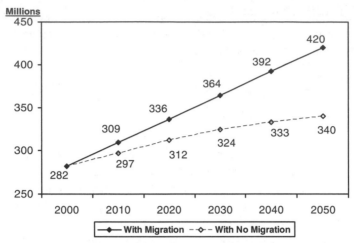

FIGURE 12.1. Projected U.S. population with and without migration.

illuminate future population growth possibilities, assuming that the determinants remain unchanged. For what it is worth, then, here is the picture
of the numerical implications of current rates of immigration.

PROJECTIONS

The most recent Census Bureau population projections (medium series)
show a growth in the U.S. population from 282 million persons in 2000 to
420 million by 2050. With no migration, we estimate a rise to 340 million
by 2050[1] (Figure 12.1), a difference of 80 million persons. This path, if
continued, would increase to a difference of 200 million additional inhabitants by the year 2100, when the population would be one-third larger
than without any migration. But, the reliability of a 50-year projection is
shaky enough without stretching it to 100 years.

So what does one make of an 80-million-person effect over 50 years?
A first reaction is that this is not a trivial number; it is the current population size of Germany and more than twice the population of California.
Second, this projection assumes zero migration, which is clearly not a policy option. An estimate of the numerical effects of a lower net migration
assumption – more or less what might result with only current levels of
legal migration – would be a population of around 400 million by 2050,
a net increase of 60 million rather than 80 million.

A major consideration is that these are all national estimates, whereas
immigration and its consequences are concentrated in certain places,

such as California, New York, Florida, Texas, New Jersey, and Illinois, which together attract nearly three-quarters of all immigrants. Immigrants now comprise 27 percent of the total population of California and 20 percent of the New York state population. Nearly half of the Miami–Dade County population are immigrants and their children.

OTHER DEMOGRAPHIC DIMENSIONS OF IMMIGRATION

There are other demographic dimensions to immigration besides numbers and places. Some have speculated that immigration, because of its more youthful age composition, will ease the retirement burden by improving the ratio of workers to retirees. It is evident that the ratio of persons aged 65+ to the population 15–64 would be lower in 2050 with immigration −34 percent, compared with 39 percent with no immigration.[2] However, this advantage is overwhelmed by the overall aging of the population, due in major part to low fertility, from a ratio of 19 percent in 2000.

Immigration has another economic implication for retirement that relates to illegal migrants. Many of these migrants obtain employment with forged Social Security cards on which their income is taxed. Because these accumulating benefits are not claimed, a substantial amount of money is generated – an estimate from the April 5, 2005, *New York Times* was $6.4 billion from Social Security taxes in 2002. It would of course be a perverse argument to encourage illegal migration in order to buttress future shortfalls of Social Security funds, and there are certainly economic costs of illegal migration involving public schools, welfare, and so on.

There has also been a recent trend toward more female immigrants, who now account for 55 percent of immigrants, and that trend seems to be increasing. This has numerous implications, including increasing the likelihood of more permanent settlement.[3]

Another factor that some believe operates to increase the proportion of illegal migrants that become permanent residents is increasing border surveillance, which makes it more difficult for Mexicans, for example, to "commute" in off-seasons.

Another clear change in immigration to the United States is the shift away from European origins before 1960 to Latin America, which now accounts for about half of all new arrivals, and to Asia, mainly India, China, and the Philippines. Mexico alone accounted for 36 percent of all immigrants to the United States in 2004 according to the March 2004 *Current Population Survey* of the U.S. Bureau of the Census. China is the next largest contributor, with 5 percent of the total. The most recent

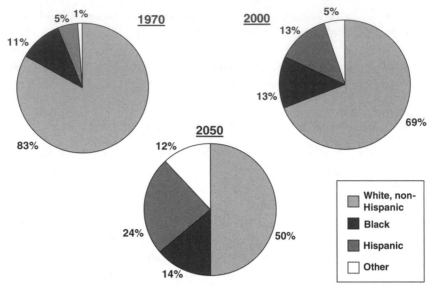

FIGURE 12.2. Changes in ethnic composition. *Source:* U.S. Census Bureau.

Census Bureau projections (Figure 12.2) show a decline in the white, non-Hispanic population from 83 percent of the total in 1970, to 69 percent in 2000, to 50 percent in 2050. By this time, the Hispanic population, assuming no intermarriage, is expected to comprise about one-quarter of the total population. The black population, in contrast, will continue at 13–14 percent of the total.

Immigrants to the United States have probably always been the least educated segments of the population, a difference that persists today. The educational disadvantage of the foreign-born population is of course understandable considering the importance of employment-driven motives and the increasing number of migrants originating in developing countries such as Mexico. Sharp differences in educational attainment as of 2003 are evident in Figure 12.3. The overall difference in the proportion of native-born and foreign-born who at least completed high school is 20 percent; the native-born are at 88 percent, compared with 67 percent of the foreign-born. The extreme difference is for Latin America, at 49 percent (the lowest is 38 percent, mostly from Mexico). The range for college graduates is from 12 percent for Latin America to 50 percent for Asia. The fact that the Latin American influx now exceeds half of all current immigrants sharpens the significance of the low educational achievement of this population.

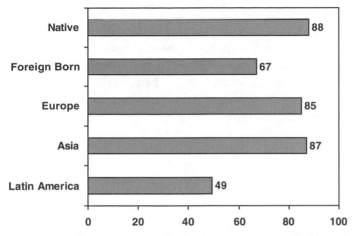

FIGURE 12.3. Percentage of individuals age 25 years and older who have at least a high school education, by region of birth, 2003. *Source:* U.S. Census Bureau.

A similar and related pattern of differences is evident for the proportion of persons living below the poverty level (in 2002). The highest proportion in poverty is observed for the foreign-born originating in Latin America (22 percent) and the lowest proportions for those from Europe (9 percent) and from Asia (11 percent). For the native-born population, 12 percent are below the poverty line.

CONCLUSION

These, then, are some of the demographic aspects of immigration to the United States. How one assesses these trends is a complicated public-policy question; it is one that we will be hearing more and more about over time. It is unlikely that the discussions will even touch on the questions of population growth and size. It is much more likely that the dominating topics will be more immediate economic interests, security issues, humanitarian concerns, and ethnic politics.

If one is concerned about problems associated with continuing population growth in the United States, it is abundantly clear that the high current rate of immigration is the main policy lever. The path to eventual population stabilization will need to involve some reduction of the number of immigrants. One obvious alternative is to reduce illegal migration; another would be the tightening of the family reunification criteria among legal immigrants. In 1972, the Commission on Population Growth and the American Future recommended the restriction of the total number of immigrants to 400,000 annually, significantly below the one million currently arriving. Their recommendation and the reasoning behind it are certainly worth revisiting. At the very least, it is reasonable to raise the question of how many immigrants is ideal. The growth and size of the future population are certainly no less important than the economic and political criteria currently employed.

PART IV

RACE

13

The Congressional Black Caucus and the Impact of Immigration on African American Unemployment

Carol M. Swain

Who speaks for African Americans when it comes to U.S. immigration policy? I contend it is not the Congressional Black Caucus (CBC) who vociferously purport to represent the interests of 34.6 million African Americans.[1] A perusal of the CBC Web site and press releases shows that immigration is not listed among its legislative priorities, nor has the organization, traditionally concerned with jobs and education, acknowledged the negative impact that high immigration has had and is continuing to have on many of its constituents. Because the organization has not taken an official position, despite conditions in black communities and surveys that show black and white Americans in agreement about the need for major reform, African Americans have been left devoid of a strong black voice in Congress on a topic that affects them deeply, given their high unemployment rates and historic struggle to get quality housing, health care, education, and other goods and services.[2]

In this chapter, I discuss black representation before exploring the impact of high levels of immigration on black communities. After presenting data on the employment situation of blacks in high-immigrant areas, I argue that the best representation for African Americans will not necessarily come from the CBC. Instead, it must come from other members of Congress who have taken more decisive leadership roles on this issue. I conclude that black representation emanating from the collective institutional body will always trump dyadic representation between black legislators and black constituents, largely because the self-interest of CBC members prevents them from effectively representing their black constituents. Robert Weisberg has demonstrated that a given representative's failure to represent his or her constituency's interests could be corrected, or canceled out, by the actions of other legislators elected outside the district.[3] In the case of immigration reform, African Americans must look beyond the CBC for effective representation. Ironically, white members of Congress have been more of a voice for working people than the CBC, which sometimes operates out of self-interest and embraces a politics of symbolism. Often the latter is expressed through prayer vigils and grandstanding press conferences rather than working diligently for substantive remedies on difficult issues. For example, D.C. Delegate Eleanor Holmes Norton sponsored a bill to establish a commission on an open society with security (H.R. 1525, April 6, 2005). It causes one to wonder where the bills designed to protect the working man are.

WHAT DOES IT MEAN TO REPRESENT BLACKS?

Hanna F. Pitkin argues that representing means "acting in the interest of the represented, in a manner responsive to them."[4] By examining objective conditions and standards, one can gauge the quality of black representation on the issue. When one considers the socioeconomic situation of black communities, with their high rates of poverty, crime, unemployment, and disease, their need for effective political representation takes on an added sense of urgency. Black representatives are widely perceived as being more likely than white representatives to discern and act in the interests of African Americans.[5] This might be true on some issues, especially if we equate representation with position taking and rhetoric on issues such as jobs, education, health care, housing, social justice, and denouncements of racism. However, if we move beyond rhetoric and position-taking to efforts to actively shape debates on issues such as immigration reform, it becomes clear that a disjuncture exists between the needs and preferences of the people and what CBC members do. This is the same disjuncture that Peter Schuck finds among the public at large (see Chapter 2, this volume). Historically, the CBC has not been out front shaping immigration policy by seeking the procurement of employer sanctions for hiring illegal workers, by developing provisions designed to stem the flood of illegals, or by encouraging illegals to engage in civic education and naturalization at higher rates.[6] When the CBC was more actively involved with the immigration issue during the 1980s and 1990s, it weakened legislation designed to address key aspects of the problem such as stronger employer sanctions.[7]

Whether the topic is education, poverty, housing, health care, or unemployment, blacks remain clustered at the bottom of the ladder in a most desperate situation.[8] Therefore, their need for representation is ongoing – the more vigorous, the better. Members of the CBC bring descriptive representation in the form of shared skin color between the representative and the constituency, but their actions as a collective body do not ensure substantive representation on critical bread-and-butter issues. Substantive representation can only take place when a legislator identifies and actively champions the policy interests and preferences of constituents.[9]

The CBC Web page lists press releases put out by the organization going back to March 2005. While it is easy to spot the numerous documents pertaining to African American unemployment, it is much more difficult to find any mention of immigration. In fact, of the nearly 100 press releases listed on the site, only one, a transcript of a statement by CBC Congressman Jesse Jackson, Jr. (D-IL) on May 5, 2006, even mentions immigration.[10] This brief mention came four days after immigrant protesters staged a nationwide economic boycott called a "Day without Immigrants." The CBC's lack of discussion regarding immigration is especially surprising considering the first line of Jackson's statement, which reads: "Marchers are marching, protesters are protesting, broadcasters are reporting, cable and radio talk shows and Congress are all talking about immigration."[11]

Indeed, in the 109th Congress, a debate over the issue of immigration was raging.[12] A search for the keywords "immigration reform" on the U.S. House of Representatives Web site yielded no fewer than 82 legislative proposals. These bills included ones seeking or opposing amnesty for illegal residents; disqualifying "anchor babies" born on U.S. soil to noncitizens from automatic citizenship; reexamining patterns of chain migration, the importation of foreign workers, and interior enforcement; clarifying designations for refugees and asylum; and the criteria and numbers for visa lotteries.[13]

The main debate in the Congress was centered on two immigration reform bills (see Table 13.1), including an especially restrictionist House bill titled "The Border Security Act of 2005" (H.R. 4437) and a more immigrant-friendly Senate bill titled "The Immigration Reform Act of 2006" (S. 2611). The House bill, sponsored by James Sensenbrenner (R-WI) and 35 co-sponsors, would, among other things, punish institutions such as churches and other nongovernmental organizations that provided services to illegal immigrants. The bill passed the House on

TABLE 13.1. *Comparison of House and Senate Immigration Bills*

Topic	House Bill H.R. 4437	Senate Bill S. 2611
Removal of illegal immigrants	• Illegal presence in the United States is a felony • Increases penalties for illegal entry into the United States • Makes drunken driving a deportable offense	• Removal depends on the length of time the illegal immigrant has been in the United States: if 5 years or more, may remain and become citizens if they pay fines and back taxes; if 2–5 years, must go to a border checkpoint and apply to return; if less than 2 years, must leave the United States
Border enforcement	• 700 miles of new fencing along U.S.-Mexico border • Requires mandatory detention of all non-Mexican immigrants arrested at points of entry • Establishes mandatory sentences for smuggling illegal immigrants and reentering the country after deportation	• 370 miles of new fencing along U.S-Mexico border • Authorizes up to an additional 14,000 Border Patrol agents by 2011 • Authorizes additional detention facilities for illegal immigrants
Penalties for employers	• Makes it a felony to knowingly or unknowingly assist undocumented immigrants in entering the United States illegally • Employers that employ undocumented workers can be fined $15,000 to $40,000	• Employers that employ undocumented workers are fined $20,000
English as official language	• Does not address the issue of English as the official language	• Establishes English as the official language of the United States
Guestworkers	• No guestworker program	• Establishes a temporary guestworker program by enabling noncitizens to obtain H-2C visas, which allow them to work in the United States for a period of 3 years

Sources: "Immigration Bills Compared," *Washington Post*. Available at http://www.washingtonpost.com/wpdyn/content/custom/2006/05/26/CU2006052600148.html; U.S. House of Representatives, 109th Congress, H.R. 4437; U.S. Senate, 109th Congress, S. 2611.

December 17, 2005, by a vote of 239 to 182. Of the CBC's 40 voting members of the House, 39 rightly voted against the bill. Harold Ford (D-TN), running for the Senate in a Republican-leaning state, was the only CBC member to support the proposal. The Senate bill, sponsored by Senator Arlen Specter (R-PA) and co-sponsored by Senators John McCain (R-AZ) and Edward Kennedy (D-MA), among others, contains a provision for a guestworker program for foreign workers that would offer renewable visas and an opportunity for some illegal residents to pay a modest fine and become U.S. citizens. The bill passed the Senate on May 25, 2005, by a vote of 62 to 36. Barack Obama (D-IL), the only CBC member in the Senate, voted for the bill.

The passage of the two diverse immigration bills in the 109th Congress has made immigration reform a highly salient issue. Members of Congress have found themselves in the difficult position of choosing which bill will be effective at combating illegal immigration, while at the same time being humane to illegal immigrants currently living in the United States. As the debate rages on, members of the CBC should be openly discussing the negative impact that illegal immigration is having on black communities and crafting new legislation. However, despite the heightened attention immigration reform is getting from Congress, the CBC still has not listed it as one of its legislative priorities as of August 2006. The legislation sponsored by CBC members does not deal with the difficult issues. Immigration remains unreformed because of the difficulty of reconciling differences between the House and Senate bills.

The following question arises: Why is there not greater substantive representation coming from the CBC? The failure of the CBC to act assertively on immigration reform might relate to how the representative sees his or her constituency. Increasingly, black members of Congress represent districts with growing numbers of Hispanic and Asian residents. In some of these districts, the percentage of blacks and whites is rapidly decreasing relative to the growth rates of other groups, especially as reverse migration takes place and urban and Midwestern blacks return to the South. The new demographic shifts mean that CBC members are confronting new realities and new incentives. Since 2002, Hispanics, a group that includes Cubans, Dominicans, Mexicans, Puerto Ricans, Guatemalans, and Salvadorans, have surpassed African Americans as the nation's largest minority group.[14]

No fewer than 11 CBC members represent districts with a greater than 15 percent Hispanic voting-age population (VAP). The growth in the number of Hispanic residents in CBC member districts[15] has already increased intergroup competition and conflict around a number of issues, including legislative redistricting.[16] The fact that CBC members have large numbers of Hispanic constituents should encourage them to actively work at framing immigration initiatives that will work to the benefit of the district's majority rather than assume a reactionary posture toward proposals advanced by other groups. The organization follows, rather than leads, despite the growing diversity of many CBC districts. Individual members, however, are actively pushing bills that protect and expand the rights of some immigrants. For example, Kendrick Meeks (Florida) and Alcee Hastings (Florida) have sponsored bills protective of Haitian refugees.

Unfortunately, the CBC has offered native black America an inadequate quality of representation on immigration issues that goes back to the Immigration Reform and Control Act of 1986, when it joined with members of the Congressional Hispanic Caucus and other liberal Democrats to gut the employer sanctions provisions of the Simpson-Mazzoli immigration reform bill.[17] Because of the loopholes and concessions in the legislation passed in 1986 and the changes made in the 1990 immigration reform bill, illegal immigration is a greater problem today than it was before the reforms began.[18] Massey (Chapter 9, this volume) points out that the immigration reform bills passed in 1986 and 1990 provided enforcement at specific entry points along the U.S.-Mexico border where large numbers of illegal immigrants entered the United States. However, while this prevented immigrants from entering at those specific points, all the legislation really did was cause immigrants to enter at points along the border where enforcement measures had not been increased. This meant that immigrants crossed into the United States at rural entry points, which in turn meant that they would be less likely to be caught by the Border Patrol. In addition, immigration became a more widespread problem because immigrants found themselves traveling to new parts of the country because of the increased enforcement at traditional entry points.

THE ECONOMIC IMPACT OF IMMIGRATION ON BLACK AND OTHER LOW-SKILLED AMERICANS

The CBC includes job procurement among its most pressing legislative priorities. To draw attention to the issue, it sends out press releases whenever the Labor Department releases its new numbers. As Figure 13.1 shows, African American rates of unemployment are consistently higher than those of other groups. Consider the fluctuation in the unemployment rate

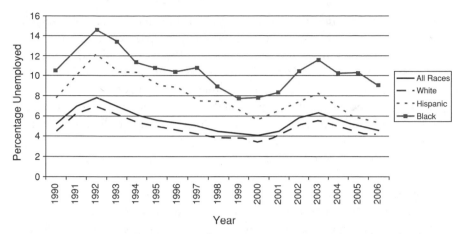

FIGURE 13.1. Unemployment rate by race. *Source:* U.S. Department of Labor, Bureau of Labor Statistics. Available at http://www.bls.gov/data/home.htm. Data taken from June of each year.

between June 2004 and June 2005. In June 2004, the overall unemployment rate was 5.6 percent, with white unemployment at 5.0 percent, black unemployment at 10.2 percent, and Hispanic unemployment at 6.7 percent. By June 2005, the economy as a whole seemed to be improving, as the overall unemployment rate had dropped to 5.0 percent. However, the employment situation for blacks did not improve. In fact, black unemployment actually increased to 10.3 percent, up from 10.2 percent the previous year. So, while white unemployment dropped from 5.0 percent to 4.3 percent and Hispanic unemployment dropped from 6.9 percent to 5.8 percent, blacks saw their unemployment rate actually increase, while members of other races enjoyed substantial job gains. Although most mainstream media accounts focus on the low rates of unemployment for whites, the CBC points out the persistent disparities between the two groups.

Among the black unemployed are a disproportionate percentage of black high school dropouts and graduates. In fact, during the 2003 recession, blacks aged 16–24 were nearly two-and-a-half times more likely to be unemployed than white workers of the same age and, by a slight margin, black high school graduates, constituting 40 percent of the black population, were more adversely affected than members of other groups. When job gains have occurred for blacks, they have been disproportionately in dead-end, low-paying jobs. A study published by the Pew Hispanic

Center found significant employment gains for Hispanics in newly created low-wage jobs, although these gains were offset by reduced earnings for the newer immigrants, who were suffering a two-year decline in wages.[19]

The high black and Hispanic unemployment rates can be partially attributed to the oversupply of low-skilled immigrants who have arrived since 1990, increasing the supply of labor by 25 percent for the kinds of jobs traditionally taken by high school dropouts and graduates.[20] While immigrant workers constitute 15 percent of the U.S. labor force, they are a whopping 40 percent of workers without high school diplomas.[21] Only 12 percent have greater than a high school diploma.[22] The greatest competition, therefore, occurs among people at the margins of society, a multiracial group that includes poorly educated blacks, whites, and Hispanics who compete against each other and against new immigrants for low-wage, low-skill jobs. No wonder it is members of the working classes and not highly educated Americans who are most upset about immigrant labor. Many of the other Americans parrot the refrain that immigrants merely take "unwanted jobs."[23]

The best research on the impact of immigration on native workers has found that immigrant competition for jobs hurts natives by holding down wages and reducing employment opportunities for native workers at different occupational levels.[24] In Los Angeles, for example, immigrants fill more than half of the unskilled, blue-collar jobs but hold no more than one-fifth of the managerial and professional jobs.[25] Central city workers have found it harder and harder to find alternative employment when old jobs have been lost, ostensibly to growing immigrant populations.[26] The availability of cheap labor causes employers focused on the bottom line to neglect the needs of native workers by failing to work at improving their productivity or by offering higher wages. Too often, the big business focus is on increasing the labor supply, which works to the detriment of native workers by depressing their wages.[27] George Borjas has found that when immigration increases the supply of workers in any skill category, the wages of native workers decrease.[28]

Greater immigrant competition for low-wage, low-skill jobs has made it easier for Congress not to address the needs of the working poor. The federal minimum wage has been $5.15 an hour since 1997, with Congress unwilling to raise it any higher, presumably because the number of adults actually earning that rate constitutes only a small percentage of the population. But it is the case, however, that in parts of the South adult men and women work at low-wage, low-skill jobs earning $6.00 to $8.00 per hour, even though most analysts target $10.00 per hour as a living wage.

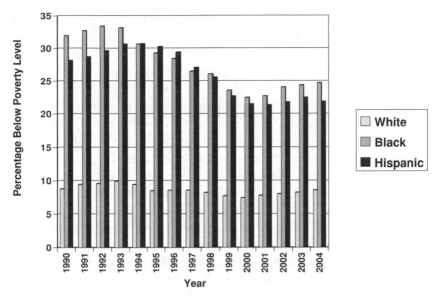

FIGURE 13.2. Poverty statistics by race. *Source:* U.S. Census Bureau. Housing and Household Economic Statistics Division. Available at http://www.census.gov/hhes/www/poverty/histpov/perindex.html.

In some industries and regions of the country, illegal residents are able to command wages of $12.00 to $18.00 an hour for jobs American workers routinely performed in the past and continue to do in places where immigrant competition is weak. This includes jobs within the construction, landscaping, hotel, and restaurant industries.

Figure 13.2 shows poverty rates by race. Since 1990, poverty has been growing in the United States, especially among African Americans and Hispanics. But starting in 2000, the poverty rate for whites also increased. The plight of poor people in the United States is likely to worsen. No one seriously expects illegals to be asked to return home. More people of lower socioeconomic status will compete for fewer opportunities. When Congress gets around to legalizing millions of illegal residents, it will increase the ranks of those eligible to compete for the full range of social welfare programs.

Although education has largely been seen as an equalizer, cuts in governmental programs such as student loans and Pell grants have made it far more difficult for lower-middle-class and inner-city students to get the kinds of support they need to prepare themselves for higher-paying jobs. What is at risk is a permanent disgruntled underclass of people only qualified to work as low-wage service providers. Their situation and that of their children is worsened even more because of the poor quality of public schools in some areas of the United States.

Many African Americans firmly believe that the U.S. government favors newly arrived immigrants over them in the administration of government benefits and opportunities for advancement. Affirmative action issues come into play. Some African American citizens feel threatened by surges of immigrants because of their impact on affirmative action. A source of disjunction between African American civil rights activists and immigration advocates is the preference for opposing roles for government. Civil rights activists seek an expanded regulatory state, while immigration reformers want to dismantle a tight regulatory regime.[29]

Ricky Gaull Silverman, vice-chairman of the Equal Employment Opportunity Commission, labeled immigrant participation in affirmative action as "the ultimate nightmare of affirmative action. It is its Achilles heel."[30] In recent years, tensions have emerged between African Americans and immigrants over its benefits. Historian Hugh D. Graham has stated:

For the Black urban poor, whose lives were largely untouched by affirmative action programs, the economic effects of large-scale immigration have been overwhelmingly negative. On balance, immigrant participation in affirmative action programs has been destabilizing.

Historically, African American leaders, such as Frederick Douglass, Booker Washington, and W. E. B. Du Bois, had opposed importing cheap foreign-born labor to compete with native-born workers. But the 1960s encouraged a new "people of color" solidarity that paid political dividends for a generation. The immigrant success ethos, however, with its emphasis on hard work, merit, and social assimilation, clashed with hard affirmative action's emphasis on historic victimhood, reparations, and racial entitlement. These tensions were underlined in the 1990s.[31]

What is at once puzzling and disconcerting for many black residents is that immigrants often achieve economic success without having to acculturate. These feelings often boil over into antipathy and sometimes lead to black boycotts of immigrant-owned businesses. Sociologist Jennifer Lee has captured this tension between African Americans and immigrant groups in New York and Philadelphia. She found that as Jews moved out of black neighborhoods and other new immigrants moved in, blacks saw these groups as getting ahead of them and achieving the success that eludes so many of them. Seared into many minds is the image of new immigrants invading their communities, taking the businesses, and leaving at night with the community's money.[32] In the case of Hispanics, many of them crowd into the low-income neighborhoods formerly occupied by blacks, creating much resentment and increased acts of ethnic violence among minority groups.

The impact of immigrant competition is now national in scope. The competition was once confined to a few key states such as California, New York, Illinois, and Texas, but it has now spread to more distant southern places such as Georgia, Mississippi, North Carolina, South Carolina, Tennessee, and Virginia, where more than 54 percent of the nation's black population resides. Blacks from urban and rural places, and poor whites, have seen their high-paying, unskilled union jobs (e.g., janitorial services, textiles, meatpacking, and construction) either disappear or be given over to nonunionized immigrants. Although some scholars have argued that immigrants have not had negative economic impacts on particular communities, research by economists George Borjas, Richard Freeman, and Lawrence Katz tells a different story for the nation as a whole.[33] These scholars have found that comparisons by geographical areas *understate* the potential effect that immigration-induced increases in the labor supply have on lowering native wages. When the nation as a whole is examined, there are greater depressant effects than what is found by confining the analysis to single metropolitan geographical areas.[34] The impact is also national because of evidence that high immigrant populations affect internal migration by causing some native-born workers with low skill levels to migrate to other regions of the country in an effort to flee immigrant competition.[35]

Often neglected in discussions of illegal immigration is the impact of the oversupply of labor on the earning capacities of older immigrants and legal residents who find themselves adversely affected by the influx of newcomers. Borjas found that the average wage for legal migrant workers in rural areas is $9.54, compared with illegal residents, who are willing to work for $5.98.[36] Indeed, one of the most strident supporters of tougher immigration laws and more secure borders has been the United Farm Workers union, once led by the great labor activist and Mexican immigrant César Chávez. In 1966, Chávez led a melon worker strike in an attempt to bring wages over $1 an hour, but the company simply hired workers straight from Mexico.[37] The undercutting of immigrant wages by immigrants competing with immigrants may be happening on a much grander scale than imagined. A 1992 Agriculture Department study found roughly one million farmworker jobs and 2.5 million potential farmworkers during the peak season, many of whom were newly arrived immigrants.[38]

The oversupply of labor is not confined to dead-end jobs. It also includes the technology sector, where foreign workers compete with more highly educated Americans. While the number of highly skilled immigrants pales in comparison with the number of unskilled and uneducated ones, the oversupply of labor creates similar problems that lead employers to justify paying lower wages for longer hours. In 2001, one in four research personnel at IBM's Yorktown Heights lab and two in five researchers at Bell Labs were new immigrants brought in on work visas, while many native engineers and programmers were unemployed or underemployed.[39] Some employers openly expressed a preference for immigrant laborers because they were willing to work longer hours for less pay than American workers.[40] U.S. immigration policy provided both a means and an incentive for companies to use the H-1B work visa program to create competition for American technical workers.

In a survey of Chicago area employers, William J. Wilson found that third world immigrants were preferred by many employers because they are willing to tolerate harsher work conditions, lower pay, fewer upward trajectories, and other job-related characteristics that would deter native-born workers.[41] Immigrants were perceived as exhibiting a much better "work ethic" than blacks. In fact, Hitty Calavita quotes former Secretary of Labor Ray Marshall as commenting that undocumented residents were more likely to "work scared and hard."[42] Perhaps as a consequence, African Americans suspect quite correctly that some employers would rather hire new immigrants than give them a chance.

In short, a need exists for aggressive action to address the negative effects on American workers. Steven Camarota argues in favor of two sets of policy options that might address the needs of U.S. workers.[43] One proposal takes aggressive steps to enhance the position of native-borns employed in low-skill jobs by increasing the minimum wage or by expanding the Earned Income Credit. Camarota notes, however, that taking such an action without reducing the levels of illegal immigration would most likely make matters worse for the native-born workers by increasing their unemployment levels. A second proposal actively works at reducing the percentage of unskilled legal and illegal immigrants in the country. As Camarota points out, only 12 percent of legal immigrants are admitted on the basis of their education, skills, and training. Two-thirds of the immigrants are coming for family reunification purposes. Unskilled illegal immigration could be tackled by greater enforcement provisions in the interior of the country. Camarota argues that rather than having the government deport millions of illegal residents, reduction can be achieved by attrition simply through the enforcement of existing laws that would encourage and pressure many illegals to go home voluntarily by self-deportation.

Clearly, there are both moral and ethical issues of social justice involved in how the nation addresses the situation. The voice of the CBC is needed on this issue because immigration affects all low-wage, low-income workers.

THE CBC's MISPLACED PRIORITIES

The CBC decries unemployment. A December 2005 CBC press release states that the "possibility of obtaining a job and developing economic security remains out of reach for too many African Americans and this negatively impacts every aspect of life. Unemployment makes it impossible to have access to health care, widens the opportunity gap in education and makes it impossible for individuals to achieve their full potential."[44] Given the CBC's concern with unemployment and social justice as highlighted on its Web site and in its press release, it would seem reasonable for it to be actively involved in shaping immigration laws. The oversupply of labor hurts blacks more than other groups because of negative stereotypes and other factors surrounding blacks' work habits and perceived dependability and honesty, which even affects an employer's willingness to accept their job referrals.[45]

According to the CBC's Web site, its mission is to

close (and, ultimately, to eliminate) disparities that exist between African Americans and white Americans in every aspect of life. These continuing and troubling disparities make it more difficult, and often make it impossible, for African Americans to reach their full potential. In pursuing the core mission of the CBC, the CBC has been true to its motto that 'the CBC has no permanent friends and no permanent enemies, just permanent interests.'[46]

Consider that the statement above is an especially ambitious goal that the organization is unlikely to achieve given that African Americans surpass every other racial and ethnic group when it comes to poverty, unemployment, crime, and incarceration rates. If the CBC wants to correct disparities, it should begin by identifying achievable goals that encourage the active involvement of its constituents. Whether we examine the

CBC's history on immigration or its votes on other issues that affect low-income people, such as the 2005 bankruptcy reform bill, where 10 CBC members voted in favor of a bill that benefited big business at the expense of working people, we find too many of its members failing to live up to the mantle they have claimed for themselves and for their organization.

Unless something dramatically changes in the CBC, black representation on immigration will not be forthcoming from it. Fortunately, however, a broader conceptualization of representation that focuses on the performance of the institution as a whole offers a possibility for more vigorous representation on the issue coming unexpectedly from the Republican side of the aisle, where a number of legislators have staked out positions conducive to the interests of working people and sensitive to the needs of new immigrants. Because many citizens and legal residents are adversely affected in different ways by the failure of existing immigration policy, it becomes more likely that multiracial and multiethnic coalitions can be formed if enough legislators are willing to bypass narrow self-interests in reelection to focus on the needs of the nation. Although the immigration reform proposals of the past have been dismal failures, it is sometimes possible for Congress to formulate legislation that achieves its stated intent to the benefit of the nation. Because immigration reform affects all Americans, the most beneficial reform approaches will include strategies that make it costlier for employers to discriminate against native-born workers, create incentives for them to train and hire new workers, create a tamper-proof Social Security card, and include concrete plans to protect and expand the gains of members of historically disadvantaged populations such as American Indians, Appalachian whites, legal immigrants, and black descendants of slaves.

14

Hispanic and Asian Immigrants

America's Last Hope

Amitai Etzioni

INTRODUCTION

The claim that large waves of "nonwhite" immigration will have a significant effect on the American creed, identity, and society is not without foundation. Immigration waves have continually changed American society since its earliest days. However, these immigrants have made their mark not by undoing the established creed, thus leaving a normative vacuum and sowing societal dissent, but by *recasting the framework that holds the United States together and often making it the better for it.* This same process of societal reframing is occurring in the current stage of American history. A large number of immigrants, many from Mexico and other South American countries (and to a lesser extent from Asia), are making the United States more communitarian than it has been in recent decades by fostering a stronger commitment to family, community, and nation, as well as respect for authority and moderate religious-moral values. Like other immigrant groups, they have proved themselves to be industrious and achievement-oriented. Furthermore, by virtue of their young age, many of these immigrants will help to protect the United States from the demographic malaise that is diminishing European and Japanese populations. And, least noted but of much importance, these

In drafting this chapter, I drew on several of my previous works, including *The Monochrome Society* (Princeton, NJ: Princeton University Press, 2001), *The New Golden Rule: Community and Morality in a Democratic Society* (New York: Basic Books, 1996), and the Diversity Within Unity platform. Please see www.communitariannetwork.org for additional information on these titles. I am indebted to Jessica Roberts Frazier for research assistance and numerous editorial suggestions.

same immigrants are going to modify American society, changing a country often depicted as divided along immutable racial lines between whites and blacks – a society in which many of the latter continue to see themselves as victims – to an increasingly varied society in which more fluid ethnic groups will play a greater role and in which victimhood will play an ever-smaller role. Their high intermarriage rates serve as but one example of this positive modification, for through intermarriage Hispanic and Asian immigrants help to ensure that the most intimate ties – those of family – will prevent American society from breaking down along ethnic lines.

I do not claim that all of the effects of recent (or previous) immigrants have been salutary. However, most of the troubling effects are temporary and limited, and they pale in comparison with the constructive ones. American society is light-years ahead of most other societies, which have yet to learn how to incorporate large numbers of immigrants without losing their own core values or abusing the immigrants.

ASSIMILATION, MULTICULTURALISM, OR DIVERSITY WITHIN UNITY?

Three Competing Paradigms – Their Definitions and Affiliated Metaphors

Examinations of the effects of immigrants draw implicitly or explicitly on competing paradigms. The paradigm through which a study of immigration is approached in turn affects the findings and conclusions drawn. Regrettably, after centuries of debate on these issues (issues that have been contested since the colonial days), there are still no agreed-upon terms through which one can frame the discussion. Several terms are used to refer to the same phenomena, and the same terms are used to refer to different developments. I follow here those who use the term *assimilation* to refer to the full immersion of immigrants into the existing culture, bleaching out all distinctions. I employ the term *multiculturalism* to indicate the views of those on the other end of the spectrum, who prefer to break up the American framework and have the land occupied by a variety of ethnic and racial groups – each acting as a societal whole, in effect as a nation unto itself. (Some who embrace the multicultural paradigm also refer to the American society as a "multiracial society."[1]) And finally, the *integration* paradigm encompasses the perspectives of those who think immigrants ought to become incorporated into American society but should simultaneously maintain some differences that may benefit both them and the society as a whole. A model that I refer to as "diversity within unity" (DWU) serves as a particular form of the integration paradigm.[2]

Affiliated with each of these paradigms are various metaphors that serve to illustrate further the distinctions among the three approaches. For example, one image frequently associated with the assimilation paradigm is that of the *melting pot* – a cultural caldron in which all groups are stripped of all of their distinctive characteristics and are assimilated into one homogeneous amalgam. Those preferring the paradigm of multiculturalism often invoke a rainbow as their emblem, with the diversely hued bands connoting the various people of different colors "arranged" next to one another in a multicultural America.[3]

The image of a mosaic, if properly understood, well captures the integration approach and more specifically the DWU model to which I earlier referred. A mosaic is enriched by a variety of elements of different shapes and colors, but it is held together by a single framework. Yet to what sociological concepts do these two parts of the mosaic, the individual pieces and the framework, connect, and what is their implication for American society? One can fairly easily conclude that the pieces of the mosaic symbolize the country's diverse populations or communities. Yet selecting the appropriate sociological concept for the shared framework proves a bit more involved. Some call it a "creed," which prejudices the discussion by assuming a tightly and clearly demarcated set of shared beliefs. Others use the term "culture," which brings to mind art and music, as well as values and habits of the heart – a very open-ended term. I refer to the mosaic's framework as a "core of shared values" to stress that there are some values – important, normative ones – we all embrace and to which we adhere, while there are others, not part of the core, on which we may well differ.

Thus, in light of this understanding, the mosaic symbolizes a society in which various communities (the pieces) maintain their cultural particularities, ranging from religious commitments and language to cuisine and dance. But while they are proud and knowledgeable about their specific traditions, these distinct communities also recognize that they are integral parts of a more encompassing whole.

This is not to say, however, that the framework of the mosaic remains static. It can be, and has been throughout American history, both reinforced and recast by immigrants – a point that cannot be stressed enough, as reference is often made only to the enrichment that the addition of pieces brings to the American mosaic (or society) by providing greater diversity through the incorporation of a growing range of cuisine, music, and holidays. Certainly, the mosaic has been made more varied. But of equal importance are the changes made to the framework of the mosaic – to what unites us and makes us Americans.

Which Paradigm Should Guide the Analysis?

The extent to which large waves of immigration, especially if they differ significantly from previous ones, are viewed as straining the American society depends in part on what one considers a sound societal condition. For example, two people might make the same observations about society; however, the person expecting assimilation might find what he or she sees much more troubling than the individual who seeks only to maintain unity in the face of growing diversity. Multiculturalism "solves" the problem by denying unity exists; if there is no one, unified American society and none is desired, then increased cultural and social differences matter not.

Throughout American history, and again recently, alarms have been sounded when immigrants did not seem to assimilate (or do so quickly enough) and continued to maintain subcultural distinctions. As a result, various coercive measures have been advocated both to stop additional immigration and to deal with those immigrants already in the United States. (For example, Hispanic children were prohibited from speaking their native language even on school playgrounds,[4] and laws have been enacted in several states that require all ballots, street signs, and official transactions to be in English only.[5]) But these, to a significant extent, have reflected the alarmists' measuring rod and not the scope of the problem. Generation after generation of immigrants who were first viewed as undermining American society and its core of shared values have become an integral part of it, including Jewish immigrants and immigrants from Catholic countries (especially Ireland and Poland), without giving up their subcultures and ethnic identities.

I join with those who see that there are no compelling reasons, sociological or otherwise, to assimilate immigrants into one indistinguishable American blend. There is no need for Greek Americans, Polish Americans, Mexican Americans, or any other group to see themselves as plain Americans without any particular distinction, history, or subculture. Similarly, Americans can, if they so choose, maintain their separate religions (from Greek Orthodox to Buddhism) and their subcultures (including distinct tastes in music, dance, and cuisine) without constituting a threat to the American whole. Indeed, American culture is richer for having an introduction to jazz and classical music, the jig and polka, Cajun and soul food, and so on. In her essay "What It Means to Be American in the 21st Century," Tamar Jacoby addresses the introduction of these diverse cultural enhancements into the American mainstream of the mid-20th century, writing, "If anything was different, it was the hybrid culture that had evolved through the decades. From African American music to Jewish humor, from the German work ethic to Irish eloquence: more and more of what it meant to be American was something that had been brought here by an outsider and then . . . gradually seeped into the mainstream."[6]

The sociological challenge posed by recent immigrant waves is basically the same as that of previous ones: to maintain the uniquely American societal formations of DWU, which leave considerable room for the enriching particulars of autonomous subcultures and communities, and still sustain the core of shared values and societal bonds.

DIVERSITY WITHIN UNITY: THE KEY ELEMENTS

Diversity Elements

In line with the DWU concept, while immigrants are expected to buy into the shared core of American values, they, like all Americans, are free to diverge on many other values. They are free to differ when it comes to which country of origin they hold especially dear, have a sense of loyalty to, maintain social bonds with, send remittances to, and choose to learn more about and visit more often; which second languages they learn; which religion they adhere to, if any; and which subcultural traditions they uphold, as reflected in preferences for cuisine, music, dance, and holiday rituals.

I turn next to list the key elements of unity, the core of shared values, that immigrants are expected to embrace (i.e., those values that are so essential that a lack of adherence to them by immigrants would pose a serious threat to the American society, polity, and indeed its future as a nation). Several individuals who have previously written about integration of the DWU kind have underscored that it is difficult to specify the elements involved. Others, including Diane Ravitch and Lawrence Fuchs, have provided a rather brief list of the components.[7] I draw here on their work, as well as that of others, to try to draft a fairly specific list of those core American values that must be shared. One may, of course, disagree about one or more of the items, but the merit of having such a

clearly delineated list is that it allows a stronger assessment of the effects
that new waves of immigration have on American society.

Shared Elements

Democracy as a Core Value
Proceduralists view democracy as a mechanism; communitarians see it as
a core value that must be shared. The basic reason is that if democracy
is viewed merely as an arrangement or procedure, it may be abandoned
when it comes into significant conflict with a major interest group or with
the values of one of the major contesting subgroups.

Democracy is not a lifestyle option – a political format adhered to by
some while others prefer to follow rules set by a Qadi, rabbinical courts,
a national authoritarian regime, or some other authority. It is a core value
that all those who seek to join our community and polity must embrace.

There is no indication that Hispanic and Asian immigrants are seeking
a different form of polity. On the contrary, they are actively participating in the democratic process by fielding candidates, voting, and so on.
Certainly, much disagreement exists over the large body of voting data.
Some scholars point to statistics showing lower voting rates for Hispanics and Asians than for other Americans.[8] Other scholars argue that after
accounting for socioeconomic factors, these immigrants vote at largely the
same rate as other Americans. Usually these data do not take into account
what one might call the "newcomer factor," a factor that has been highlighted by Linda Chavez.[9] It refers to the fact that when one compares
an immigrant group that has many members who came to the United
States recently to groups whose number of new immigrant members has
stemmed, the group with many newcomers will look less integrated. A
valid comparison would "deduct" this factor. The result would be a vast
improvement in the voting and other acculturation scores for Hispanics
and Asians.

The Constitution
The Constitution embodies the core values that guide the American polity
and society. It is the embodiment of the shared conceptions about the
ways in which liberty will remain ordered, of the basic individual and
minority rights that hold the government at bay. The Constitution defines
the relationship between the individuals and communities that constitute the society. It does so by drawing a line between the decisions
that individuals and communities can make and those that are framed

by the overarching society. This balance is manifested in the distinction between those numerous matters in which the majority rules and those in which the majority cannot reign because of the need to guarantee minority and individual rights. For instance, no majority (local or otherwise) can vote to allow individuals to be sold as slaves, to be denied the right to vote or speak freely, and so on. On the other hand, the majority is entrusted with deciding the level of taxes that will be exacted, the allocation of these funds among various competing demands, and so on.

Although the line between legitimate majority decisions and those from which the majority is excluded does not *necessarily* parallel the line between community particulars and the societal common (the pieces and the framework of the mosaic), it often does. Most policies concerning education, transportation, and similar issues are set locally in each of the 50 states. The policies that local and state governments pursue often reflect values that particular communities seek to uphold. This is the reason for stricter antidrug policies in Houston, Texas, than in New York City; immigrants are treated more harshly in Southern Californian communities than in those of Maine; and so on. In each of these communities, local or state majorities set their particular course. However, all of these communities must act within the values embodied in the Constitution. This prevents communities from following their particular values in those specified areas in which the society at large has agreed that shared values are to take precedence. Foremost among these values are various freedoms, such as the freedom of speech, association, and assembly, that prevent communities from banning speakers whose views a given community finds offensive, from outlawing troubling books, or from discriminating against a given racial or ethnic group. Here the Constitution, speaking for the shared values of the society at large, upholds universals in the form of limits on local policies. All those who seek to become members of the American community must agree to honor the Constitution, as reflected in the oath they take when they become American citizens.

Some Jewish and Muslim immigrants (as well as some Native Americans) have preferred to deal with matters such as divorce, estates, and conflict resolution through their respective religious institutions. However, there is no evidence that Hispanic or Asian immigrants seek extraconstitutional treatments. Moreover, the Latino National Political Survey conducted in the early 1990s revealed that by and large Hispanic immigrants (of all nationalities) did not believe that immigrants from

their own countries of origin should be given any special legal considerations when it came to immigration law.[10] Most relevantly, no one has
presented systematic data to show that Hispanic and Asian immigrants
and their descendants are less supportive of American constitutional conceptions than other immigrant families who have been established in the
United States for the same period of time and who occupy the same socioeconomic status (income, education, etc.).

Respect for the Law and Universalism

The normative conception that no one is above the law, that all are equal
before the law, and that laws must be respected is a profound part of the
American core of shared values – although these values are not always
respected in the streets and courts of the nation, to put it carefully.

Whether or not immigrants adhere to these values is a particularly key
test for their successful integration into American society because many
immigrants – Hispanics, Asians, and others – come from cultures in which
the government is often corrupt to the point that it cannot be trusted. In
such cultures, working around the law is the norm, and particularistic
loyalties to one's family, friends, and community take precedence over
observing the law. It is particularly important that immigrants from such
countries shed these notions and habits.

There is no evidence that Hispanic and Asian immigrants are slower
to incorporate these values than the waves of other immigrants that came
from traditional, particularistic societies. Indeed, many Hispanic immigrants identify the cronyism, corruption, and favoritism that permeate
the political systems of their countries of origin as the source of many of
the problems facing those countries. For instance, take the overwhelming agreement among Latino National Political Survey interviewees that
corruption within the Mexican government proved responsible for the
majority of that nation's internal quandaries.[11] And results from the same
study also reveal that Hispanic immigrants' greatest concerns are those
illicit activities that deviate from American law and endanger communities, such as drug use and crime.[12]

Societal Values

Trumping Loyalty

To maintain the proper equilibrium between the particular constituting
communities (many of which are ethnic- and immigrant-based) and the
overarching American community (the nation), a *layered loyalty* must

be fostered in which commitment to the overarching community takes precedence in matters concerning political action. The DWU approach is based on a split loyalty, divided between commitment to one's immediate community and to the nation and according priority to the nation on key but select matters.

In recent years, much has been made of the fact that some immigrants (and some American-born citizens) have dual citizenship or dual nationality. Peter Salins takes umbrage with the notion of dual citizenship, warning that such continued loyalty to one's country of origin cheapens the value of American citizenship.[13] Others worry that the loosening of restrictions on citizenship by foreign powers thinly veils these countries' desire to gain access to and power in American politics. Although far from an alarmist, Nathan Glazer does note this possibility: "it [the alteration of the Mexican Constitution to allow for dual nationality] would help Mexican-Americans serve as an interest group in defense of Mexican interests in the United States with respect to trade and immigration."[14]

However, experience and data show that these fears are vastly exaggerated. Actually, dual nationality often merely reflects a matter of convenience, making travel easier. Sometimes it might indicate a mild sentimental attachment to the country of origin and, in some cases, an unresolved conflict of loyalties, largely limited to the first generation.[15]

Drawing on findings from two comprehensive studies, Rodolfo de la Garza concludes that Mexican Americans, like Italian immigrants before them, not only harbor negative sentiments about their homeland's government but also display little interest in following the political machinations of their original homeland. He writes, "Although [Mexican Americans] have positive feelings for Mexico as a nation, their feelings toward the United States are much stronger. More significantly, they have little interest in Mexican politics, and they are extremely critical of the Mexican government."[16]

Mutual Respect

For the American community to be sustained, immigrants need to combine their appreciation of and commitment to their own particular traditions, cultures, and values with respect for those of others.[17] James Hunter argues that the criterion should be tolerance, which does not mean accepting all views as equally valid as one's own but rather learning to live peacefully next to those with whom one disagrees.[18] The term "tolerance," however, implies considerable distancing. It implies that one will put up with such views out of good manners or for the well-being of society, while actually judging them to be inferior. Respecting subcultures other than one's own, so long as what is at issue are particulars and not mores and values that concern the "framework," seems more communitarian. Respect means that one would have no normative objections to others holding values that one would not personally hold.

There appears to be no evidence that Hispanic or Asian immigrants are less tolerant or respectful of others than previous groups of immigrants or American-born citizens. It is true that there have been a few incidences of interethnic conflicts (and even violence) involving Cambodian and Vietnamese immigrants and others. But these have been few and far between. Moreover, all the cases that I could trace concerned first-generation immigrants. By and large, it seems that Hispanic and Asian immigrants overall demonstrate levels of respect at least comparable to those of other groups of immigrants.

Openness

One of the key elements of the American shared framework is the relative unimportance attached to social distinctions. Indeed, American society has few sharp, insurmountable class (let alone caste) lines. And those divisive, largely immutable lines that do exist, especially those between the races, are considered lines that should be overcome rather than valued. It is true that in American society there are very great differences in wealth; however, these are fluid in the sense that the wealthy can end in poverty and the poor can overcome meager beginnings. (At least this is what the creed strongly holds.) Where do Hispanic and Asian immigrants fit into this aspect of the framework?

Although attempts have been made to treat Hispanic Americans as a distinct race ("brown") or as black[19] and to view Asians as a race, they behave much more like ethnic groups and are so treated – a concept underscored in Peter Skerry's work on Mexican Americans.[20] This is most evident in the very high rates of intermarriage for Hispanic (and Asian) immigrants. Indeed, these rates provide strong evidence that these two groups are accepting the core American value of openness and living up to its tenets. When accounting for all generations, data from 1998 show that cross-racial or cross-ethnic marriage reached 16.7 percent for Hispanics and 15 percent for non-Hispanic Asians.[21] Studies that look beyond first-generation Hispanic and Asian immigrants to subsequent generations reveal even higher numbers.

As a result, Hispanic and Asian immigrants will help to encourage a sense of connectedness. Americans will be linked across, not in spite of, ethnic and racial lines, with families consisting of individuals of varied ethnic backgrounds.[22] Not only will this sense of interconnection reinforce America's core values of social and economic mobility and limited social distinctions and decrease racial tensions, but it will also mute fears of tribalism, equally divisive and destructive. As I noted in *The Monochrome Society*, "If one must find a simple image for the future of America, Tiger Woods, or Hawaii, as I see it, seems more appropriate than a view of a country in which Louis Farrakhan and his followers and the Aryan Nation are threatening one another."[23] Nothing refutes the notion that Hispanics will form a separate nation more conclusively than their high rate of intermarriage.

One Shared Language?

Many societies – such as Belgium, Switzerland, Canada, and Israel – debate whether one set language should comprise part of the shared framework or whether several can coexist. In the United States, some have used the commitment to English as the official language (the only one in which government documents can be issued, voter guides published, etc.) as a code word for nativism and anti-immigrant sentiments.[24] Some of these groups have been associated with a movement to keep immigrants out and America white and Aryan.[25] Most recently, it has been suggested that Mexican Americans are slow to learn English, which, it was argued, is one sign that they are refusing to assimilate and are thus endangering the American creed.[26] Some on the Left have used the existence of racist, pro-English groups as proof that to favor English as a core language is an attempt to rob immigrants of their culture.

However, after stripping away such emotive overtones, the following facts stand out. Most immigrants, including Mexican Americans, are keen to learn English and do not view learning English as an attack on their culture or something forced upon them. According to the Latino National Political Survey, more than 60 percent of Mexican Americans agree that both U.S. citizens and residents should acquire English.[27] And Alejandro Portes and Richard Schauffler conclude from their research in South Florida that "[c]hildren raised in the core of the Spanish-speaking community in Miami (those attending bilingual private schools) are actually the most enthusiastic in their preference for the language of the land."[28] Moreover, most second-generation Hispanics have a full command of English, and most third-generation Hispanics know little Spanish.

Most importantly, only an assimilationist viewpoint would suggest that to maintain a distinct subculture, including speaking a distinct secondary language, say Turkish for German Turks, is a sign of trouble. From a DWU perspective, this is completely acceptable.

In light of the foregoing discussion, it may be said that there is every indication that Hispanic (and Asian) immigrants are integrating into American society without altering its framework as a result of their presence. It may be true that integration is slower in areas with an unusually high concentration of immigrants of the same ethnic background, especially if there is a continuous flow of additional immigrants into these areas. However, there is no convincing evidence that even in these parts integration will not take place, although it may occur at a slower pace.

I suggest that Hispanic and Asian immigrants *do better than merely buy into an existing unity-preserving framework*; they *seem to have a rehabilitation effect on the American core of shared values and the institutions embodying them*. This will become evident once this examination is extended to encompass a facet of society not often included in such analyses: the communitarian balance.

CORRECTING A COMMUNITARIAN IMBALANCE: THE REHABILITATION EFFECT

I have argued elsewhere that societies flourish when they maintain a carefully crafted balance between liberty and social order, between individual rights and social responsibilities.[29] There are those who have characterized American society as centered around rights and individualistic values, a Lockean nation. Various historians, including Louis Hartz, J. G. A. Pocock, Isaac Kramnick, and Rogers Smith, have espoused the centrality of this liberal individualism to the American society.[30] In his writings about American "exceptionalism," Seymour Martin Lipset also sees American society's emphasis upon individual rights and liberties as the defining quality of the "civic culture." The values that he perceives as the main components of the American creed are individualism, antistatism, populism, and egalitarianism.[31]

As I see it, this characterization of the core American values is an accurate but only partial one – and one that makes America's core values and character seem much more self-centered, more Lockean, than they actually are. I join with those who see the American society as constantly struggling to balance these values of liberty with commitments to community, to forming a "more perfect union," to advancing the common good, and to shoring up shared values and communal bonds.

The special normative standing accorded to the common good in American society is reflected in the high value historically attributed not only to the nuclear and extended families (common in other societies) but also to communities.[32] Many of these communities are not of the traditional and receding kind (traditional villages and small towns) but modern, voluntary communities (the Tocquevillian elements of America), including prominently those of various ethnic groups and also religious groups.

Throughout American history there has been a continuous struggle between the Lockean and the pro-community elements. Up to the 1960s, the pro-community elements were rarely highlighted, as they were powerful and by and large not contested. Indeed, one may well argue that despite normative commitments to the contrary, Lockean elements came up short. Much of the history of the nation can be depicted as an attempt to scale back authoritarian elements and excessive community controls and to expand the liberties and rights of people without property, of minorities, and of women and other groups, and to free the market forces from excessive interventions by special interests (not necessarily the government). But as communitarians have often pointed out, as of the 1960s, individualism expanded, as reflected first in the expressive individualism of the sexual revolution and the counterculture and then in the 1980s in the instrumental individualism of the Reagan/Thatcher era.[33] As of 1990, communitarians pointed out that this excessive tilt toward individualism had resulted in several dysfunctional effects, including an increase in the neglect of children, withdrawal from other familial commitments, self-centered behavior, white-collar and violent crime, drug abuse, litigiousness, a strong sense of entitlement but a reduced sense of responsibility for the common good, and a rejection of all forms of authority.[34] I hence called for a pro-community correction, which to some extent did take place in the decade and a half that followed.[35]

The values to which most Hispanic and Asian immigrants subscribe are supportive of this rehabilitation of the American society. That is, in matters concerning a restoration of the communitarian balance, these immigrants by and large do not recast the framework, do not modify it, but reinforce one of its cardinal elements: the pro-community element, broadly understood as including a sense of responsibility for children, family, ethnic group, and nation.[36]

Because this thesis has not been subjected to significant amounts of social science research, there seems to be little data to support it. Yet the research that does exist largely supports this view. Hispanic Americans have a relatively low divorce rate. Around 73 percent of "Mexican-origin" immigrants are married – a figure matched only by "whites," who have marriage rates of 80 percent.[37] The number of single-parent homes among Hispanic immigrants remains low, as does the percentage of children born out of wedlock – especially when compared with African Americans.[38] Also, the Latino National Political Survey reports that "[m]ore than half of Mexican and Puerto Rican and 40 percent of Cuban respondents engaged in school-related activities."[39] When I served as the staff director of a commission that investigated nursing homes, we found very few Hispanic and Asian senior citizens in these homes. We were told that these ethnic groups are strongly inclined to take care of their elders in their own homes. Furthermore, these immigrants possess a strong work ethic. According to Harry Pachon and Louis DeSipio's 1994 study, most immigrants of Hispanic descent hold full-time jobs, and most eschew any form of government aid.[40] As Chavez notes, "Family members are expected to help each other in times of financial or other need, which some analysts believe explains why so many Mexican-origin families shun welfare even when their poverty makes them eligible for assistance."[41]

Religion, too, plays a role in the lives of Hispanic and Asian immigrants, with estimates that Hispanics will comprise more than half of the United States's Catholic parishioners in the near future.[42] According to Peggy Levitt, integral spiritual tenets find expression within and beyond the church walls of the Hispanic community in the United States from "lighting candles in a church to establishing private altars within the home."[43]

When all is said and done, to the extent that data allow one to gain a preliminary impression, Hispanic (and Asian) immigrants are reinforcing the weakened communal elements of the American society and are thus helping to rehabilitate it by restoring a communitarian balance.

I do not argue that the communitarian rehabilitation of the American synthesis of communal and individualistic elements, which these immigrants foster, will necessarily result in the perfectly balanced mix. Each element must be examined in its own right, which in turn may point to various desired public education campaigns (for instance, on women's rights). However, as I see it, out of this renewed synthesis, for instance when these immigrants' element of authoritarianism blends with recent American tendencies to be disrespectful of authority and when their strong sense of gender differentiation mixes with current American trends toward de-gendering (if not androgyny), American society will move closer to the desired communitarian balance.

THE NORMALIZATION OF POLITICS

The move from separatism and identity politics to "normal" politics of interest groups, which accepts the basic societal framework, is one important effect of Hispanic (and Asian) immigration not often discussed. This is occurring as a direct result of the increase in Hispanics and the *relative* decline of African Americans in the total demographic and political picture.

The Census Bureau has projected that the African American population, which made up 13 percent of the total U.S. population in the year 2000, will grow to approximately 15 percent in 2050, where it will remain steady until 2100.[44] In contrast, the Hispanic population, which made up approximately 12 percent of the total U.S. population in 2000, is projected to rise to approximately 24 percent of the total U.S. population in 2050 and approximately 33 percent in 2100.[45] Often reference to race relations still evokes the opposition of black and white, while other groups are mentioned only as an afterthought, if at all. This will change in the future as the number of Hispanics continues to grow, along with their political awareness and organization. (The same holds true, although to a lesser extent, for Asian immigrants.)

The current and forthcoming changes in the composition of American society are especially consequential because African Americans have been much slower to intermarry and to be otherwise absorbed into the American society than other minorities. And although some African Americans, particularly middle-class blacks, tend to be politically moderate, on average their leadership has been less moderate and more given to identity politics than the leaders of other minority groups.

One may wonder whether Hispanic leadership may be driven to less-moderate, identity politics. This is hard to predict; however, one notes several factors that agitate against such a development: the strong tendency to intermarry, movement up the economic and social ladders, and the growing Hispanic middle class. The same holds true for Asian Americans. (The fact that members of these ethnic groups act like earlier immigrants and unlike African Americans was reflected in the 2004 elections, when African Americans continued to vote largely for one party – albeit less so than in previous years – while Hispanic and Asian Americans distributed their support more evenly between both parties.)

When all is said and done, one should expect that Hispanic (and Asian) Americans will contribute to the depolarization of American society. They will replace African Americans as the main socially distinct group and will constitute groups that either are not racial (many Hispanics see themselves as white or as an ethnic group and not as a member of a distinct race, black or brown) or are of a race that is less distinct from the white majority (as in the case of Asian Americans). By increasing the proportion of Americans who do not see themselves as victims and who intermarry with others, these immigrants will continue to "normalize" American politics.

RECASTING THE FRAMEWORK

Societies are constantly in flux as the framework that holds them together is recast. Part of maintaining the framework is to uphold the fiction that no changes to it are being made – as continuity, tradition, and following the Founders carry a measure of legitimacy. This tendency to claim that one ought to follow the old and true is particularly highlighted in the treatment of the Constitution (and the shared values ensconced in it) but is also evident in the respect accorded to traditional conceptions of marriage, authority, and the core values. But, actually, instead of rigidly adhering to traditional conceptions that are no longer adaptive as economic, technological, environmental, and international conditions change, one must realize that over time certain modifications to the core values and to the societal institutions that embody them prove a requirement for continued societal stability and adherence to those values. Such modifications, however, should remain within the deeper meaning of the original framework. In that sense, metastability requires low-level change. Thus, allowing people without property to run for office was a change, yet it did not undermine the original concept of democracy but instead deepened it; the same of course holds true for extending voting rights to women and ensuring that African Americans can exercise theirs. And adding the right to privacy to the other rights enumerated in the Constitution modified the Constitution but reflects its core conception that the people need to be protected from excessive intrusion by the government. I am not suggesting that historically every change to American institutions has been in line with America's core values but that alterations can be made to these institutions and to the core values themselves without undermining them.

It is difficult at this point to determine if Hispanic and Asian immigrants will not only reinforce the American framework but also modify it because the large waves of these immigrants have been occurring only recently and because this matter has been so little studied. However, there are some indications that Hispanic and Asian immigrants help to reorient American society's traditional focus on Europe toward a more mindful and informed focus on Asia and, to some extent, on Latin America. Also, Hispanic immigrants make the American character more expressive and less instrumental; in this sense, they join immigrants from Southern Europe in modifying extreme American elements of self-restraint and in providing for greater psychological openness, easier forms of empathy, and maybe a dash of fatalism.[46] This is one of the least studied and arguably less predictive matters concerning Hispanic and Asian immigration.

Further analysis along these lines would require taking into account that both categories, Hispanic and Asian, are convenient simplifications; there are significant and relevant differences within each group – for instance, between Cuban and Mexican Americans and between Japanese and Cambodian Americans. The essence of prejudice is to assume that all the members of one group have the same traits, attributes, views, and feelings or that they all conduct themselves in the same way. However, one simply cannot conduct a study of the issues at hand without noting that statistically speaking many members of the same group conduct themselves in a similar fashion and in a fashion different from that of members of other groups. Keeping these reservations in mind, I hold that when such detailed analyses are conducted of the various ethnic subgroups of immigrants currently lumped together under the terms "Hispanic" or "Asian," they will show that the conduct and values of the overwhelming majority of the members of these groups not only far from undermine the American core of shared values and the institutions based on them but also help to shore them up – albeit not by returning American society to its founding days but to its deeper ideals as adapted to current history.

15

Strange Bedfellows, Unintended Consequences, and the Curious Contours of the Immigration Debate

Jonathan Tilove

I am a reporter with Newhouse News Service. Since 1991, I have been writing stories exclusively about race and immigration. Those stories are then sent to two dozen newspapers across the country owned by the Newhouse family and to an assortment of other subscribing papers, all of which can use the stories as they see fit.

Early in my tenure, prompted by developments in California, I became interested in the question of whether there was a new form of white flight afoot, this time away from the growing diversity in those places receiving the most immigrants. To help find the answer, I entered into what would become a long and continuing collaboration with the demographer William Frey of the Population Studies Center at the University of Michigan. The first fruit of our collaboration was a story that appeared in the summer of 1993. It began as follows: "Unprecedented white flight from the breaking waves of immigration is transforming the American landscape in sweeping ways."[1]

The story reported that while most immigrants in the 1980s were settling in a handful of states, significant numbers of whites in those states were relocating to places then largely untouched by immigration. It was, as the story put it, "recreating on a grand scale the classic pattern of white suburbs ringing minority cities."

In the body of the story I noted that blacks, too, were leaving prime immigrant destinations and relocating to thriving black communities, mostly back south, Atlanta foremost among them. But the emphasis of the story was on this new "white flight," which seemed, journalistically, the headline news.

But, as I was to learn some months later, a reader in Princeton, New Jersey, had taken umbrage.

In a special issue of *Time* magazine on "The New Face of America," in December 1993, Toni Morrison, just before embarking for Sweden to claim her Nobel Prize, authored an essay entitled, "On the Backs of Blacks."[2]

"In race talk the move into mainstream America always means buying into the notion of American blacks as the real aliens. Whatever the ethnicity or nationality of the immigrant, his nemesis is understood to be African American," wrote Morrison.

She continued, "Current attention to immigration has reached levels of panic not seen since the turn of the century. To whip up this panic, modern race talk must be revised downward into obscurity and nonsense if antiblack hostility is to remain the drug of choice, giving headlines their kick. PATTERNS OF IMMIGRATION FOLLOWED BY WHITE FLIGHT, screams the *Star-Ledger* in Newark. The message we are meant to get is that disorderly newcomers are dangerous to stable (white) residents. Stability is white. Disorder is black."

Of course, the story in question was my own. I have read and reread that passage from Morrison's essay many times and have never quite parsed how it fits into the larger logic of her piece, a logic that, as this chapter will indicate, I find compelling. As best I can figure, Morrison's point is that I was waving the bloody flag of "white flight" – itself tattered "on the backs of blacks" – to scaremonger afresh.

Fair enough. White fright. White flight. A slick and sensational little couplet.

But wait.

"White flight" had long since entered the acceptable lexicon of not just journalism but academia and common speech. Pithy and evocative, this phrase communicated well what was going on. Since when was the reporter, academic, policymaker, or man on the street using the phrase assumed to be cheering the phenomenon, laying blame, or taking sides? Was I being held to a higher or different standard by a Nobel laureate who took her race talk very seriously?

Maybe.

But, as I was to find in the years to come, writing about white flight from immigrants elicits a very different reaction than writing about white flight from blacks, for reasons that I think have everything to do with race and, as you pull the thread, help explain the strong support for immigration even when it comes, as Morrison put it, "on the backs of blacks."

White flight from blacks seems perfectly obvious. But white flight from immigrants? Prove it, and prove not only outcome but intent. And what is your motivation in writing about this and giving succor to nativists anyway?

Before continuing to explore reactions to this story, as I continued to follow it in the years to come, let me be clear about where I am headed, about the point that my contribution to this volume will attempt to make. In the course of my years reporting about race and immigration, I have come to believe that indifference to the fate of black America, or in some quarters a passive–aggressive hostility toward African Americans, has become an animating feature of support for a liberal immigration policy and helps to explain the strange bedfellows who have made that policy unstoppable even in the face of lukewarm public support at best.

Part of the hidden appeal of immigration is that it can and will help relieve the United States of its special obligation to black Americans by reducing their relative importance, by drowning out their complaints, and by creating an even larger percentage of the population who, when asked about the legacy of slavery and discrimination, can reply, "I had nothing to do with that," creating, in essence, a growing population of deaf ears. It is an effect that only works because most of the immigrants arriving since the immigration reform of 1965 are neither white nor black.

This sounds counterintuitive. It might seem that the color of skin of immigrants would work to their political disadvantage. They are, after all, eroding the white majority that the United States has always had and that, one might assume, an important number of whites, who still and for a long time to come will exert political power well beyond their numbers, might want to preserve. After all, isn't maintaining a certain comfort level of white majority part of what white flight is all about?

But, in fact, it is more socially acceptable to up and move than it is to bring explicit questions of race, and racial change, into the immigration debate. As it is, immigration restrictionists are commonly assumed to harbor some racial animus or diversity-phobia, however they may couch their arguments. One can imagine that if most immigrants were now, as they were before, white Europeans, the merits of immigration would be more thoroughly and dispassionately debated.

But there is something both bigger and more subtle at work here as well. Were most immigrants white, the various guardians of social justice in academia, in the press, in the realms of government and advocacy, and in the black community itself would be on alert as to how these new arrivals were affecting the fortunes of America's native-born minorities, first and foremost African Americans. But precisely because the immigrants are themselves "minorities," and more especially newer minorities with their own compelling claims for concern, these sentries of justice have been, for the most part, seduced, or at any rate diverted, from their previous laser-like attention to the plight of blacks in America.

But back to my story.

In the summer of 1995, armed with new metro area figures, Frey and I contributed a short piece to the *New York Times* magazine. This time the headline screamed, "Immigrants In, Native Whites Out."[3]

We wrote, "Look collectively at the New York, Chicago, Los Angeles, Houston and Boston metropolitan areas – 5 of the top 11 immigration destinations. In the last half of the 80s, for every 10 immigrants who arrived, 9 residents left for points elsewhere. And most of those leaving were non-Hispanic whites. Of the top immigrant destinations, only metropolitan San Diego was attracting more whites from the rest of the nation than it was losing."

The story also discussed another largely unreported impact of immigration. Again quoting our piece: "Because of immigration, in the 30-odd years since the dawn of affirmative action, blacks have gone from more than two-thirds to less than half of America's minority population. Nationally, black workers, and especially the black middle class, are disproportionately concentrated in government jobs. But with substantial numbers of new immigrants arriving, blacks in these port-of-entry cities find themselves increasingly overrepresented vis-à-vis their shrinking percentage of the minority population. The result: The new minorities' affirmative action claims for fairness can't help but come at the expense of blacks."

This time the reaction came from Frank Sharry. Sharry was and still is executive director of the National Immigration Forum, the dormitory for the strange bedfellows that make the pro-immigration coalition so formidable. Its board of directors includes leaders of the National Restaurant Association and the National Council of La Raza, the National Association of Manufacturers and UNITE-HERE, Piñeros y Campesinos Unidos del Noroeste (an organization of Hispanic farmworkers in Oregon), and the International Franchise Association. National Immigration Forum dinners are events where those who exploit immigrant labor break bread with those who labor against that exploitation.

In Sharry's letter to the *Times* magazine, Frey and I stood accused of "sociological shenanigans," of "substandard research," and of "scapegoating immigrants" for suggesting that there was any cause and effect between the arrival of immigrants in places like California and the departure of native-born whites.[4]

Well, we had begun our piece by describing Marilyn Yarosko, who had moved to the Las Vegas suburb of Henderson, Nevada, after she began to feel out of place in her native Southern California. We wrote, "The Asian population of her hometown of Torrance, just south of L.A., had doubled to 22 percent in the 1980s. The pastor and most of the parishioners at her Roman Catholic church were now Vietnamese. Most of her fellow nurses at Charter Suburban Hospital, she says, were Filipino, super-hardworking and, she thinks, a bit cliquish. Yarosko, whose parents were Canadian and paternal grandparents were from the Ukraine, is not a xenophobe. She is not bitter or looking for someone to blame. 'We took it from the Indians: who are we to complain?' she says. But, she acknowledges, 'I began to feel like an outsider.'"[5]

Hardly a frothing nativist. But Yarosko had moved at least in part because of some very swift demographic changes, changes precipitated by immigrants moving in and accelerated by natives moving out. (Some academics would refer to this process as "invasion and succession," but that kind of language is way too provocative for daily journalism.)

One could argue that the dislocation of folks like Yarosko was the way of the world, part of a natural cycle of change and renewal. But instead, the impulse by Sharry and others was to deny that people like Yarosko existed or mattered and to suggest instead that reporting or scholarship that took them into account was out of bounds. I was learning – white flight from immigrants demanded a higher order of proof than white flight from blacks.

Classic white flight was a given. It was perfectly obvious that for decades whites were moving to deep white spaces in the suburbs and leaving many cities, and especially what came to be known as the inner city, increasingly black. No one doubted that race played a role in this white flight, even if many, probably most, whites made their choice of where to move without ever explicitly thinking about race. The proof of white flight was the changing demography of cities and their suburbs. Period.

To bring the numbers up to the recent past, now consider that Miami has become only 12 percent Anglo, to use the local terminology. Whites are less than 30 percent of the population of Los Angeles – until 1960 the whitest big city in the United States. In 1970, the New York City borough of Queens, the home of Archie Bunker, was 86 percent white, whiter than

Utah is today, whiter than Kansas. Queens is now a third white and nearly half foreign-born.[6]

Those numbers came to pass because a lot of new people were moving in and a lot of other people moving out, and the people moving in were a lot less likely to be white than the people moving out – just like the other white flight. So why the different standard of proof?

My reading of the unspoken, even unconscious thinking at work goes like this: Of course there was white flight from blacks. Who wouldn't run? But white flight from immigrants? Why would someone run away from immigrants? Blacks are scary. Blacks lower property values. Immigrants aren't scary. Immigrants rehabilitate property values. Immigrants have great restaurants. And so on.

Let us push on. In the January/February 1999 issue of the *Columbia Journalism Review*, Joel Millman, a correspondent for the *Wall Street Journal*'s Mexico City bureau and the author of *The Other Americans: How Immigrants Renew Our Country, Our Economy, and Our Values*, wrote a 3,200-word article entitled "Going Nativist: How the Press Paints a False Picture of the Effects of Immigration."[7]

Millman charged that reporters were rationalizing "nativist arguments, even bigotry" in their writing about native-born flight from immigration. There had been quite a few such stories by then, and, one by one, Millman detailed their flaws as he traced them back to their insidious origins in Frey's work and that first story I had written six years earlier.

Again, Sharry was quoted raising the question of "causality." "People were leaving California because the economy tanked," Sharry said. "Now that they're coming back in droves, you don't see [Frey] saying people are moving to be nearer the immigrants."

There are two points here. First, immigrants continued to pour into California even as the economy tanked. And, secondly, between 1990 and 2000, whites went from being 57 percent to less than 47 percent of the California population. Their absolute numbers dropped 1.2 million over the course of the decade. While the exodus is now more broadly diverse in its makeup, according to the state demography unit's latest projections, the number of whites in California will continue to decline by more than 3 million between 2000 and 2050, a half century in which the state's Hispanic population is expected to increase by 18 million and the Asian population by nearly 3 million.[8]

Sometime after his piece in the *Columbia Journalism Review* appeared, I received a voicemail message from Millman, whom I had never met or talked to. He was inviting me to a book party – I presume it was for the paperback edition of *The Other Americans*. He sounded cheery and ended his message by reminding me who he was: "I'm the reporter who thinks immigrants are good."

Wow. I guess that made me the "reporter who thinks immigrants are bad." Now we were getting someplace. Let us deconstruct. The immigrant story *is* uplifting, especially in a post–9/11 world. It makes Americans feel better about America, about themselves. In the era of "why do they hate us?" immigration seems an act of love and reassurance. Here are people willing to risk everything to become us. We are still the envy of the world. And the individual stories are inspiring – tales of harrowing sacrifice and striving. The immigrant story is a powerful one, Horatio Alger in perpetuity, and deeply embedded in the American psyche and self-definition.

I am as sentimental, as affected by this, as anyone. I, too, think immigrants are good, even if, as a journalist, I might choose not to have that sentiment inscribed on my business card. I am also sympathetic with a reporter who likes the people he writes about and attempts to see the world from their point of view. But there are limits.

It never occurred to me that a reporter or academic who wrote about white flight from blacks would stand accused of blaming blacks for the phenomenon. Would a reporter who "likes blacks" be required to have denied that white flight happened as the price of that affection? So why was it that writing about white flight from immigrants was itself taken as an act of belligerence, of bias, of nativism? There was something more at stake here.

It is naturally quite wrong to assume that a reporter for the *Wall Street Journal* in any way shares the political values of its editorial page, a stalwart voice for high immigration as good for capital. But in this case, I think it is fair to say the *Journal*'s editorial page and reporter Millman are very much in sync on why immigrants are so good and high levels of immigration so necessary.[9]

Chapter 2 of Millman's book begins, "America, strictly speaking, is not a nation." "We have no common culture stretching back to caves or to tiny grains of prehistoric corn," he writes. "What's common in America is the now." And so, "If the mother country is not a race or a tribe or a fixed territory, what is it? That's simple. America is an economy. More precisely, it is a market." Very well. One nation under Wal-Mart.

The rest of Millman's book is a very well-researched treatise on why immigrants are indispensable to the health of the market that is America.

"Immigrants are our oldest and most dependable pool of 'riser,' a kind of demographic yeast that guarantees shared prosperity," he writes. "They are the villagers entering and renewing our cities, repeating a pattern of self-cleansing as old as civilization itself. Essentially, we could not be Americans if we were not foreigners first."[10]

Immigrants help everyone, including blacks, Millman argues, by reclaiming ravaged neighborhoods and dying cities from the white flight that left behind black blight. If cities such as Detroit and Newark never fully recover, the blame rests with the immigration restrictionists who succeeded in tamping down immigration from the 1930s to the 1960s and deprived those cities of the immigrants who might otherwise have spared them the devastating impact of white flight.

The lessons of history are clear to Millman: immigrants are the cure for white flight; never the cause of it. The benefits of their presence are everywhere evident.

For example, in his book, Millman credits immigrants with being "arguably the most important" reason for the dramatic drop in crime in New York City in the early 1990s, as the total population of young adult males declined and the proportion of that population who were foreign-born increased. "Thus New York not only shrunk its crime-prone population, it replaced it with a better class of *homo urbanus* ... with their greater propensity than their American-born neighbors to wash dishes and deliver pizza and then hit the books after working their 'dead-end' jobs."[11]

A better class of homo urbanus. That's it. Immigrants are not just good. They are better. Better than who? Better than native-born blacks, or at any rate those still living in poor urban neighborhoods. This, of course, has emerged as the common wisdom on the matter, with important consequences for African Americans.

Sociologist Stephen Steinberg describes what is going on here in his essay "Immigration, African Americans, and Race Discourse," which was published by the journal *New Politics* in the summer of 2005 and represents one of the rare occasions on which a scholar of the Left has taken a serious look at the impact of immigration on blacks.[12] Steinberg writes, "In the popular idiom, the question takes the form 'We made it, why haven't they?' When these comparisons were made between European immigrants and blacks, it was always possible to contend that blacks alone encountered racism. Now that most immigrants are nominally 'people of color,' the question takes a new and pernicious twist: if Asians and Latinos – and now the clincher, if West Indians can make it – why can't

African Americans? Doesn't this prove that racism is not an insurmountable barrier?"

Peter Schuck made the point in 1993 in a prescient piece in *The American Prospect*.[13] African Americans, Schuck wrote, are competing against "the mythology and imagery of immigration" and losing. "Political elites, ordinary citizens, scholars, and journalists, in polite company as well as on radio call-in shows, are increasingly making comparisons between American blacks and immigrant ethnics. Such comparisons often focus on sensitive topics: economic status, attitudes toward work and welfare dependency, family values and stability, crime and violence, school completion, entrepreneurial spirit, and labor force attachment." And, Schuck concluded, "The crucial, incendiary political fact about these comparisons is that they often disfavor American blacks as a group."

The problem here is that while blacks are losing this high-stakes competition, there is very little attention paid to the ways in which the competition is stacked against them. In *The Other Americans*, Millman agrees that "[i]mmigrants, by entering the poorest neighborhoods, confront black America's weakest families and often outcompete them." But, he argues, "[t]he notion that black neighborhoods need to be protected is not only wrong, it is dangerously counterproductive" because immigrant "vitality tends to raise all economic boats together."[14]

Furthermore, Millman contends that many black Americans simply removed themselves from competition for service jobs – "with the rise of black consciousness, service jobs were perceived as servile positions beneath dignity." The result: "While American-born blacks were chafing against jobs cleaning white houses, watching white children, and spongebathing the white infirm, whites were growing uneasy hiring what they saw as angry young blacks."[15]

Or, as Mexican President Vicente Fox put it in the spring of 2005 (as translated from the Spanish), "There is no doubt that Mexicans, filled with dignity, willingness and ability to work, are doing jobs that not even blacks want to do there in the United States." Fox was roundly criticized for this comment, which the Reverend Jesse Jackson characterized as a "spurious comparison" with "ominous racial overtones."[16] Never mind that Fox was saying what everyone from President Bush to the man in the street is suggesting when they say that immigrants do the jobs "Americans won't do."

But, as widely accepted as this aphorism has become, it bears a little scrutiny. Certainly, immigrants, self-selected as they are, bring a drive and ambition that may make them especially attractive workers. Some may be working beneath what was their station in their home country in order to gain a toehold in America, while many come from such places that even the worst job in the United States means a step up for them. These latter folks may be willing to work at a price and under conditions that most native-born Americans would not tolerate. As former Labor Secretary Ray Marshall has put it, they are working "hard and scared," and the more tenuous their legal status, the more scared they are.[17]

For employers, this especially pliant labor force is a good thing, and if that is the point of immigration policy, then it is working. Of course, by this standard, the undocumented worker is to be preferred to the legal immigrant and, a generation later, the newest arrival is to be preferred to the son or daughter of the earlier immigrant, who, one would expect, acculturates to "American" standards and expectations.

And where do you draw the line? Can there be no African Americans ready and willing to work in construction in Washington, D.C., or the booming suburbs of North Carolina? Absent immigration, would construction grind to a halt?

In the meantime, observers marvel at the vitality of the enclave economy, of the niches created by ethnic entrepreneurs in which every last worker is a co-ethnic, and of network hiring, which enables employers to rely on ethnic-specific referrals from existing workers.

But wait. "This is racism, plain and simple!" writes Steinberg.[18] "Ethnic nepotism and racial exclusion are two sides of the same coin." Network hiring is nothing but the "old-boy network" reborn. And yet, because the practitioners of such exclusion are refugees from South Asia or El Salvador, these exclusionary practices are objects not of head-shaking outrage but nodding admiration and acceptance. And employers are off the hook, too, because the notion that immigrant workers are better than blacks has gained the mahogany sheen of a hardwood truth. Blacks no longer even need be considered for jobs, and, because the immigrants who are hired instead are also not white, employers run little risk of running afoul of antidiscrimination laws or their own sense of shame.

"It used to be a truism that blacks were the 'last hired,' and it has taken a good deal of intellectual artifice and obfuscation on the part of immigration scholars to deny the obvious: that filling the hiring queue with millions of immigrants has had adverse consequences for African Americans, particularly during the post-civil-rights era when blacks were poised for progress," writes Steinberg. But, Steinberg laments, "Immigration scholars have stubbornly avoided these conclusions, not out of any animus toward African Americans, but rather out of sympathy with immigrants and their struggles."

Meanwhile, the black niche in the economy – the public sector and the Post Office – is increasingly vulnerable to cries for the "fairness" of more proportional representation. Over time, affirmative action morphed from a form of reparation to the black descendants of slaves to a prospective guarantor of "diversity," in which everyone of color is more or less fungible.

When I wrote about the effect of immigration on affirmative action in 1994, I talked to James Lewis, who was then research director of the Urban League in Chicago. He recalled his previous job, running an employment agency for Cambodian refugees in Chicago: "I was struck by the number of times employers said to me directly, 'We want to phase out our blacks and bring in Asians. It keeps us clear in EEO and gets us better workers.'"[19] Nonetheless, Lewis said minority immigrants ought to qualify for affirmative action because "It's good public policy."

That is typical of what I think is a genuine generosity of spirit on the part of most black leaders. As Schuck notes in Chapter 2 of this volume, black leaders have been "neutralized" on immigration by their liberalism and political alliances. But I also think that support for immigration feels right for many blacks on account of color and their own history of challenging oppression. Just as it is hard for the children or grandchildren of immigrants to support a more restrictive immigration policy, it is hard for many African Americans not to be sympathetic with other non-whites who are struggling.

This effect was poignantly in evidence in a national survey conducted in 1994 by Louis Harris on behalf of the National Conference (formerly the National Conference of Christians and Jews, it is now the National Conference of Communities and Justice). It revealed a circle of unrequited racial affinity. According to the survey, blacks felt they had the most in common with Latinos and the least with whites and Asians, while both Latinos and Asians felt they had the most in common with whites and the least in common with blacks. While blacks were chasing the Rainbow, Hispanics and Asians were chasing whiteness. Whites, meanwhile, said they had the most in common with blacks and the least with Asians.[20]

There are, naturally, occasions of black backlash against immigrants or immigration, some less obvious than others. Lost in the firestorm of criticism that engulfed the school board in Oakland, California, in 1996 when it voted to recognize Ebonics as a language was the fact that this was the genesis of an effort to provide African American children with the same attention and language help provided to the growing number of immigrant children in the community.[21]

At the leadership level, most of the elected and advocacy leadership of minority immigrant communities do stand shoulder to shoulder with the black civil rights leadership. But no one expects the rank and file Hispanic and Asian newcomers to see their destiny as particularly tied to the fate of black Americans. As the balance of power slowly shifts, one can expect blacks to lose clout.

As Xavier Hermosillo, a Latino activist and talk radio host in Los Angeles, summed up the relationship to me back in 1993, "They shall overcome; we shall overwhelm."[22]

Even if blacks remain the most cohesively meaningful group, what Amitai Etzioni, in his book *The Monochrome Society*, refers to as the "dethroning" of blacks as America's pre-eminent minority matters.[23]

As I wrote after the 2000 census showed Hispanics closing in on blacks numerically, "There are only so many Ford Foundation grants, 'Nightline' town meetings and doctoral dissertations to go around, and the consideration of Latino America cannot help but come at least a little bit at the expense of black America."[24]

In 1968, the Kerner Commission concluded that America was "moving toward two societies, one black, one white – separate and unequal." Twenty-four years later, in 1992, Andrew Hacker could write a book, *Two Nations: Black and White, Separate, Hostile, Unequal*, and be taken quite seriously.

Those days are over. When President Bill Clinton named his advisory board on race in 1997, there was an early disagreement between the chairman, historian John Hope Franklin, and a member, Angela Oh, a Korean-American lawyer from Los Angeles, about where the board should place its emphasis.[25]

Said Franklin: "The country cut its eyeteeth on black–white relations."

Said Oh: "We can't undo this part of our heritage. But what we can affect is where we are headed. I want to talk about multiracialism because I think that's where we are headed."

Both were right. Throughout American history, blacks, and the ways America dealt with blacks, have been the central dilemma – studied and worried over. The traction in those times of progress came because of black claims on the American conscience. But with each passing year, that claim is fading because of the passage of time but also because of America's changing complexion.

For many, the great hope now is that immigrant Hispanics and Asians will fracture the black–white dichotomy, blurring and maybe eventually erasing racial and ethnic lines. It is one of the ways that, in Etzioni's view, they can "save America." As Etzioni explains in Chapter 14 of this volume:

When all is said and done, one should expect that the Hispanic (and Asian) Americans will contribute to the depolarization of American society. They will replace African Americans as the main socially distinct group and will constitute groups that either are not racial (many Hispanics see themselves as white or as an ethnic group and not as a member of a distinct race, black or brown) or are of a race that is less distinct from the white majority.... By increasing the proportion of Americans who do not see themselves as victims and who intermarry with others, these immigrants will continue to "normalize" American politics.

In other words, Hispanic and Asian immigrants will "normalize" an American politics that had been distorted by the alien within – blacks. They will help transform a society where, Etzioni notes, many blacks "continue to see themselves as victims."

So much for history. Ultimately, Etzioni and others pin great hopes on intermarriage to mute conflict and "encourage a sense of connectedness." His chapter in this volume adds:

Not only will this sense of interconnection reinforce America's core value of social and economic mobility and limited social distinctions and decrease racial tensions, but it will also mute fears of tribalism, equally divisive and destructive. As I previously noted in *The Monochrome Society*, "If one must find a simple image for the future of America, Tiger Woods, or Hawaii, as I see it, seems more appropriate than a view of a country in which Louis Farrakhan and his followers and the Aryan Nation are threatening one another."

Etzioni may be right, but he may be wrong.

Hispanics and Asians are much more likely to intermarry than blacks. It is at least possible that America's black/white divide will become America's new black/nonblack divide or some variation on that theme, with the black and some brown poor becoming even more isolated from the otherwise increasingly inclusive beige mainstream. One can anticipate scholarship on "How Everybody but Blacks Became White." More than 60 years ago, in *The American Dilemma*, Gunnar Myrdal wrote that "the overwhelming majority of white Americans desire that there be as few Negroes as possible."[26]

There are troubling echoes of that sentiment in Etzioni's vision of an America "saved" because Hispanic and Asian immigrants have helped to marginalize blacks. Wishing for a future that is more Tiger Woods than Louis Farrakhan may sound all right to many whites but I suspect would deeply offend most blacks. It is, I think, akin to suggesting intermarriage as the answer to the "Jewish problem."

Immigration is transforming America, especially racially. The future may be Etzioni's "Hawaii," conjuring images of a multiracial paradise. But, it is also not beyond imagining an America that becomes both more mestizo and more unequal. For commentary on that possibility, I return to Las Vegas and that first "white flight" story from 1993, and a man I met named Stan Godek. Godek, a native Texan who was descended from Polish immigrants and had converted to Judaism to marry his Israeli wife, had crossed the desert from Los Angeles to Las Vegas, where he got a job working in construction on the Luxor, a new hotel-casino being built in the shape of a pyramid. He was earning $26 an hour, three times what he had been making when he left Los Angeles. "All the illegal aliens in L.A. are driving the wages for construction way down. I mean way down," Godek told me. And, he said, he and his wife were ready to leave Los Angeles anyway. "L.A. was just dying for me," he said. "I'm all for the melting pot. But I'm afraid we're going to end up like Mexico, with just the very rich and the very poor."[27]

PART V

COSMOPOLITANISM

16

The Free Economy and the Jacobin State, or How Europe Can Cope with the Coming Immigration Wave

Randall Hansen

Americans and Europeans tell themselves different immigration stories. Although it is in fact exceedingly difficult to migrate legally to the United States, and U.S. immigration policy was shot through with racist intent until the 1960s, immigration is a basic part of the country's founding myths. By contrast, with the partial exception of France, European nation-states did not base their identity on immigration. The point here is conceptual: it was always grating to see scholars, often with undisguised glee at their cleverness, point out the supposed contradiction between Germany's official claim that it was "not a country of immigration" and the reality of substantial migration. There was in fact no contradiction: the statement was about whether Germany derived its identity from immigration and whether immigration was wanted. It did not, and it was not. Neither Germany nor the rest of Europe pursued a policy of encouraging immigration; on the contrary, all European countries pursued until recently the chimerical goal of zero immigration.

This is now changing. Since the late 1990s, all governing parties in several European countries – the United Kingdom, France, Germany, Italy, and Spain – have changed their rhetoric, attitude, and policy toward immigration. They have good reason to do so. If the demographers are right (and they have been spectacularly wrong about most things over the last century, so the "if" is not rhetorical), Europe will need much more immigration to stave off population decline. In the same way that growth is not an unalloyed good (indeed, we thought a few decades ago that it was a great evil), population decline is not singularly bad. It could reduce pressures on the environment, increase per capita wealth in stagnant or slow-growing economies, reduce costs of fixed-stock goods (housing, for instance), and transfer powers from capital to workers (which may or may not be a good thing). But overall population decline seems to create more problems than solutions, particularly in aging societies with generous welfare states. European policymakers have accordingly accepted that some degree of immigration has to be part of the solution.

At the same time that Europe faces a demographic shortfall, the developing world has a massive and growing surplus. By the middle decades of this century, there will be a drastic population imbalance. Stagnant, aging, and declining European populations will stand against large, growing young populations in the developing South. This perfect synthesis of push-and-pull factors will in all likelihood lead to a great migration to Europe.

The question for European countries is how they can cope with these new migrations. It divides into two parts. First, how can Europe ensure the socioeconomic integration of such migrants given its broad failure to economically integrate past waves of migrants? Second, how can Europe ensure that the new migrants embrace the liberal democratic values institutionalized in Europe belatedly and at the cost of so much blood and treasure? To answer these questions, this chapter considers the lessons Europe might learn from the world's oldest countries of immigration: the United States and France. The chapter is divided into three parts. The first provides a brief historical overview of migration history and migration policy in Europe. The second compares the integration experience of migrants on the two continents, attending to both its socioeconomic and cultural aspects. The third – taking inspiration from the United States and France – outlines a series of steps that it behooves Europe to take if it is to succeed as a continent of immigration.

MIGRATION TO EUROPE

Postwar migration to Europe was a market-driven phenomenon: migrants traveled to Europe in response to the needs of the buoyant postwar economy, particularly in the Franco-German core. Migrants arrived in response to this demand through two distinct channels. The first were the guestworker schemes operated by Belgium, France, Germany, Austria, Switzerland, Sweden, Denmark, and Norway. All these countries sought to fill labor shortages with the migrants regarded as least troublesome and most likely to return: Southern Europeans. Large numbers of Italians, Greeks, Spanish, and Portuguese migrated north for work. Once this initial pool of workers had been exhausted, these labor-importing countries had to look outside Western Europe. Austria, Switzerland, and

Germany had no colonies. As a result, they expanded their guestworker programs to include Yugoslavia and Turkey.

It was at this time that the second migration channel emerged. Unable to compete with Swiss and German wages, Britain, France, and the Netherlands found themselves increasingly reliant on colonial migration. The process was a passive one insofar as none of these countries was keen to encourage large-scale, nonwhite colonial migration. Nonetheless, they all maintained citizenship and/or migration schemes that provided privileged access for colonial migrants. The combination of labor market demand and open or relatively open immigration channels could only have one consequence: West Indians and South Asians migrated to Britain, North Africans to France, and Surinamese to the Netherlands. Most of these migrants were young men, and they later brought their wives and had families. The same process presented itself in guestworker countries. Although many guestworkers did return home, enough stayed – 3 million (out of 14 million) in the case of Germany – to ensure that, following family reunification, these countries would have substantial ethnic minority populations. Some half-hearted efforts were made to ensure that guestworkers would return and to limit family reunification once it was clear that they would not, but these were blocked by domestic courts. A defining case was heard in Germany.[1] It involved an Indian national who had entered Germany on a temporary work visa, which he regularly renewed. As the deadline for his departure approached in 1972, he applied for German citizenship. While his application was pending, the authorities withdrew his work permit in 1973 on the (not unreasonable) grounds that he intended to stay in Germany permanently and ordered his departure. The matter went before the Constitutional Court, however, which argued in a landmark 1978 decision that the repeated renewal of the work permit had built up a "reliance interest" on the plaintiff's part. His deportation would thus violate the "protection of legitimate interests" principle of Article 19 of the German Constitution.

In this and other key legal decisions, activist courts, imbued by a postwar, post-Holocaust concern for individual rights against a heavy-handed state, drew on national constitutions and jurisprudence to ensure the guestworkers' stay. For their part, colonial migrants entered mostly as citizens, and they could not be compelled to leave. Many countries introduced incentives for voluntary return, but these programs were limited, symbolic in intention (designed to placate the restrictionist Right), and rarely used except by those migrants who had intended to return anyway. The result, by the mid-1970s, was a large and stable migrant population – numbering in the millions – in the larger Northern European states. When the European economy entered recession in the early 1970s, all the northern receiving countries ended primary migration (migrants who have no familial ties to the destination country) and limited new migration to family reunification.

MIGRATION POLICY IN EUROPE

From the early 1970s to the late 1990s, all European countries pursued zero-immigration policies and, as noted, attempted to reduce their foreign populations through (forced and voluntary) return and through limited family reunification. With the exception of the United Kingdom (where there is no right to family reunification), these policies were blocked by domestic courts on the basis of domestic constitutions.[2] At the same time, all European Union (EU) member states are signatories to the 1951 United Nations convention relating to the status of refugees, and all have developed complex and lengthy legal mechanisms for processing asylum claims.[3] Most individuals who apply for asylum under the 1951 convention do not get it ("recognition rates" are 10–30 percent across the EU), but legal, financial, and moral constraints on deportation mean that they are not returned either. In practice, asylum has been, and is recognized to be by traffickers and migrants, an effective channel for lengthy if not permanent migration to Europe. The result of these two channels (family unification and asylum) was net migration to Europe that ebbed and flowed not in relation to policy change but rather to the strength of Europe's economy (a pull factor) and economic, political, and environmental crises abroad (push factors). Figure 16.1 provides an overview of net migration to Europe since 1970.

The only way in which zero-immigration policies were effective was in blocking the one type of migration in which European states have an undisputed interest: labor migration. Until recently, it was exceptionally difficult for labor migrants without family in Europe to migrate there. In the United Kingdom, employers could apply for a temporary work permit and, after four years, the work permit holder could apply for permanent residence. Work permits were, however, only exceptionally granted and were subject to intrusive Home Office scrutiny. In Germany, post-guestworker, nonethnic immigration was effectively nonexistent. Across Europe, the migration "stop" of the early 1970s meant that there were only two migrant channels open: family reunification and asylum seeking. In Germany during the 1990s, 90 percent of net migration was made up of

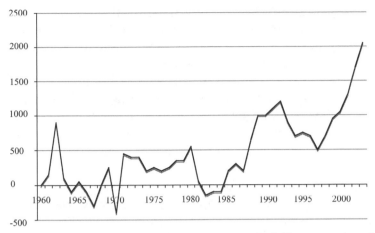

FIGURE 16.1. Net Migration$_1$, EU-15, in 1,000s, including corrections due to population censuses, register counts, and so on which cannot be classified as births, deaths, or migration. *Source: Eurostat Yearbook 2005,* Office for Official Publications of the European Communities.

family migrants (75,000), asylum seekers (100,000), and ethnic Germans (100,000).[4] In France from 1993 to 1999, 78 percent of the migrants arriving annually were family members (37,600) or asylum seekers (23,000).[5] In the United Kingdom in the mid-1990s, 68 percent of arriving migrants were family members (48,400) or asylum seekers (3,700).[6]

EUROPE'S NEW OPENNESS TO IMMIGRATION

In a reversal of their previous zero-immigration policies, the United Kingdom, France, Germany, Spain, and Italy have all opened their doors to new immigration. The change has multiple causes, but they are principally economic and demographic. Starting in 1995, American economic growth accelerated. It appeared for a time that the United States had managed to double its noninflationary growth rate from an average of 2–2.5 percent, common to most OECD (Organization for Economic Cooperation and Development) countries post-OPEC, to (albeit briefly) 4–5 percent. The source of the new growth potential was said to be a productivity increase occasioned by new applications of information technology (IT).

The competition from the United States had two effects on Europe. First, the major European economies faced labor shortages in the IT sector; during the 2000 IT boom, Germany reported 75,000 unfilled vacancies. Second, policymakers saw in the labor shortage one clear source of European sluggishness vis-à-vis the United States: the latter's immigration policy on H-1B visas for high-skilled workers, through which Indians, Koreans, Chinese, and (even) brain-drained Europeans had worked in the United States. The American shadow stood behind Germany's first attempt to attract skilled immigration: its policy of issuing 20,000 visas for high-skilled, high-wage jobs paying more than 51,129 euros (100,000 DM) per year, which was dubbed misleadingly (because of its five-year contractual limit) the "green card" program. Importantly, Germany announced this policy during a time of high unemployment and continued opposition to new immigration.

This policy is also designed to address a demographic time bomb. In virtually all European countries, birthrates are below replacement levels: Italy's and Germany's rates are especially low, at approximately 1.2 and 1.3 births per woman, respectively. Certainly, migration alone will not address Europe's reproductive shortfall. If the number of births remains constant, then Germany would actually require a net total of 600,000–700,000 migrants per year to make up the difference. By any measure, this figure is beyond Germany's integration capacity. But immigration can have the effect of rendering the depopulation process less difficult and can affect the age structure in a manner that might cushion – particularly in the context of later retirement ages – government programs under pressure because of an aging population.

ECONOMIC INTEGRATION

Whether this new openness to migration will pay dividends for Europe and Europeans will depend on how those new migrants are incorporated. Recent European history and current policy are not encouraging. In the area of economic integration, the contrast between the United States and Europe could not be sharper: whereas the United States integrates migrants into work, Europe integrates them into welfare.[7] Table 16.1 provides data on ethnic minority/migrant unemployment rates on the two continents.

The results are striking. In continental Europe, unemployment rates among immigrants are at best double that of the national average and at worst more than three times the national average. In North America, the gap is at most 1.3 percent. What's more, the lines move in opposite directions over time: the longer migrants remain in Canada or the United States, the less likely they are to claim welfare benefits, whereas in Europe the reverse is true. Thus, the relative unemployment rate for foreigners in

TABLE 16.1. *Relative Unemployment as a Percentage of the Labor Force by Origin, 1995*

| Country | Unemployment of Labor Force in % | | | Relative Unemployment Born Overseas/Born in the Country |
	Born in the Country	Born Overseas	Total	
Belgium	8.3	19.5	9.3	2.3
Canada[a]	10.1	10.2	10.2	1.0
Denmark	6.7	14.6	7.0	2.2
France	11.1	17.5	11.9	1.6
Germany[b]	7.5	15.0	8.2	2.0
Netherlands	6.0	19.6	7.2	3.3
Sweden	7.1	21.7	8.1	3.0
United Kingdom	8.4	12.6	8.7	1.5
United States[c]	6.2	7.8	6.3	1.3

[a] Data for Canada are from 1991.
[b] For Germany, data are not divided by place of birth but rather as "citizen" and "noncitizen."
[c] Data for the United States are from 1990.
Source: International Migration Data, OECD.

Europe – which includes both recent immigrants and long-term residents (and sometimes their children) – ranges from 2.2 percent in Germany and the United Kingdom to 5.4 percent in the Netherlands and Sweden.[8]

What explains this difference? Europeans suggest – often with an envious nod to Canada – that the migrants to North America have higher skills and more education. The data do not support this interpretation. Although there is a marked difference between the educational achievements of migrants to Canada and migrants to Europe (which is unsurprising given that Canada's system is geared toward attracting skilled immigrants), the difference between migrants to the United States and those to Europe is small (Table 16.2).

Thus, more immigrants to the United States have completed postsecondary education than immigrants to *some* European countries (France, Belgium, or Germany), but there are also more immigrants (twice as many as Sweden) who have not finished high school. Migrant educational levels between the United States and Europe are roughly similar.

The political Left would argue that higher levels of social exclusion, racism, and Islamophobia in Europe prevent migrants from entering the labor market. Racism no doubt plays a role, but it cannot explain why certain ethnic minorities – such as the Indians and the Chinese in the United

TABLE 16.2. *Relative Level of Education of the Labor Force, 1995*

Country		Relative Level of Education			
		Less than First Level of Secondary Education	Completed Secondary Education	Completed Tertiary Education	Other
Belgium	Born in country	33.2%	36.5%	30.3%	–
	Born overseas	41.2%	32.1%	26.7%	–
Canada[a]	Born in country	3.3%	34.6%	62.1%	–
	Born overseas	7.1%	27.3%	65.6%	–
Denmark	Born in country	14.7%	54.5%	30.8%	–
	Born overseas	22.2%	39.1%	38.7%	–
France	Born in country	30.5%	47.8%	21.7%	–
	Born overseas	47.4%	30.9%	21.7%	–
Germany[b]	Born in country	9.9%	60.4%	26.1%	3.6%
	Born overseas	39.5%	39.8%	15.0%	5.8%
Netherlands	Born in country	13.6%	60.0%	26.0%	0.4%
	Born overseas	27.6%	50.2%	21.1%	1.0%
Sweden	Born in country	20.3%	49.3%	30.3%	–
	Born overseas	22.9%	42.5%	33.8%	–
United Kingdom	Born in country	40.5%	34.2%	25.1%	0.2%
	Born overseas	51.8%	19.9%	28.1%	–
United States[c]	Born in country	23.0%	31.1%	45.9%	–
	Born overseas	41.2%	19.6%	39.2%	–

[a] Data for Canada are from 1991.
[b] For Germany, data are not divided by place of birth but rather as "citizen" and "noncitizen."
[c] Data for the United States are from 1990 and calculations are based on figures for the population rather than labor force.
Source: International Migration Data, OECD.

Kingdom – do as well as, if not better than, the overall population. Racists are unlikely to distinguish between different groups of Asians. The same point applies to the currently fashionable concept of "Islamophobia"; it is doubtful that racists could differentiate Indian or Pakistani Hindus and Muslims in theory or that they would want to do so in practice.

A more plausible explanation concerns the incentive structure faced by migrants and their children. Although the pro-migrant lobby – Proasyl in Germany, No One Is Illegal in the United Kingdom – often speak as if migrants are invariably hapless victims, they are in most cases willful and determined actors. Migrating is not easy; it requires considerable resources – financial and personal – and more often than not guile. Migrating individuals have to leave friends and family, educate themselves on the legal (or illegal) entry points to developed countries, and raise funds for travel or, in the case of most illegal migrants, for traffickers. They are, in short, rational actors who will respond to the incentives they face on arrival. In the United States, arriving migrants receive little or no social support and have to rely on their own initiative and the support of their communities. In Europe, legal migrants are granted the full range of benefits – housing, health care, and subsistence-level social support – available to permanent residents and citizens. Much the same is true of illegal migrants. If they claim asylum, as any rational migrant will do, they are entitled to extensive, if not overly generous, social support, health care, and housing.

The result is that a legal migrant arriving in Europe will face the choice between, on the one hand, seeking a job in an often less-than-buoyant market and (because her qualifications will likely not be recognized) accepting a poorly paid and unrewarding position and, on the other, accepting comfortable, clean social housing and sufficient monthly support to eke out a living. The choice should be clear. In the United States, a legal migrant will face the choice between work and starvation. The choice should be equally clear, and it is borne out by the data discussed earlier. Despite broadly similar educational levels, migrants to the United States work and migrants to Europe do not. During the 2005 riots in Paris's suburbs and elsewhere, much was made of the social deprivation affecting these areas. What was not mentioned was that the standard of housing, welfare benefits, and public safety were all at a level far above that of American urban ghettos; what was as bad, if not worse, was unemployment, often reaching 40 percent.

Academic studies support this line of argument. One study of Europe[9] found that, controlling for personal characteristics and ethnicity (that is, comparing the same ethnic groups), the probability of employment among immigrants varied inversely with the generosity of the social safety net. Others have reached similar findings.[10] A recent study of Canada and Australia showed that recent immigrants to Australia had higher unemployment than new immigrants to Canada or the United States because of Australia's higher unemployment benefits.[11] Higher levels of social support depress employment, and they do so to a greater degree among immigrants than among native citizens.

Given this, the obvious solution for Europe is a bit of tough love: reduce or remove welfare benefits for migrants, and make it clear to them that they are welcome but that their welcome is contingent on their willingness to enter the labor market. Achieving this will not be easy. Many Europeans view with repugnance the idea that migrants should be told to work or starve. More importantly, courts' jurisprudence in Europe allows very little room for distinguishing between citizens and residents,[12] and any effort to strip legal residents of social rights enjoyed by citizens would not likely survive a court challenge. What this means is that a European government intent on rolling back migrant rights to social entitlements would likely have to embed this in a general rollback of welfare state provision. Such a reform effort would naturally face substantial social opposition.

This leaves Europe in a bind, but some hope lies in the fact that other pressures are pushing in this direction anyway. In France, Germany, and the United Kingdom, which collectively constitute almost two-thirds of Europe's total gross domestic product (GDP), the pressures of international competition have led (in the United Kingdom) or are leading (in Germany and, to a lesser degree, France) to a loosening of the labor market and a reduction of social provision. The United Kingdom went down this road long ago; Germany has recently followed. In France, there is support for such reform within the conservative parties, but their opponents' ability to clog Paris's already narrow streets in reaction to any whiff of change makes it difficult to enact even modest reforms. If these countries do succeed, they may be better prepared to cope with the sort of immigration levels viewed as normal in the United States. The corollary of this is, of course, that Europe may look, in matters of social solidarity and economic inequality, more like the United States.

COMMON VALUES AND A COMMON IDENTITY

The second aspect of integration is cultural, by which I mean the incorporation of migrants into liberal democratic values. In the past, such concerns have been expressed about many groups of people – Poles in Germany, Jews in England – but today the focus of these worries is Muslims. It has become a mantra that Muslims do not present any greater integration difficulties than past migrant groups. This might be true, but Muslims do present more difficulties than any other groups at present. These take two forms: violence and values divergence. Although many liberal academics would wish it away, the majority of terrorists in Europe are Muslims, and a substantial portion of them – as July 7, 2005, and August 10, 2006, made clear – are EU nationals from stable, established, and relatively affluent communities. At the same time, a substantial minority of Muslims reject values that are embraced by the broader European population. The Pew Research Center on Global Attitudes published a study on attitudes of Muslims and non-Muslims in 13 countries.[13]

The good news was that attitudes among European Muslims toward non-Muslims were notably better than they are in Muslim-majority countries. With the exception of the United Kingdom, Muslims in Europe generally hold positive views of their non-Muslim countrymen. European liberal democracy and institutions are ensuring the cultural integration of many, and in some instances most, Muslims. The bad news is that the evidence showed a marked values gap between Muslim and non-Muslim Europeans.

Clear majorities of Muslims and non-Muslims in Europe view the relationship between the two groups as "generally bad" and they blame each other. Substantial minorities of Muslims in Europe hold views that can only be viewed as delusional and/or antithetical to liberalism. Between 35 percent (Spain) and 56 percent (Britain) of Muslims believe that Arabs were not responsible for the 9/11 attacks on the United States. Between 5 percent (France) and 16 percent (Spain) of Muslims express "some" or "a lot" of confidence in Osama bin Laden. When asked about the relationship between Islam and modernity, between 25 percent and 50 percent of Muslims living in Europe believe that there is a basic conflict between being a devout Muslim and living in a modern society. Finally, 15 percent of British and 16 percent of Spanish and French Muslims think that the use of suicide bombers against civilian targets is "sometimes justified" or "often justified" in order to defend Islam against its enemies. In Germany, the figure was notably lower at 7 percent. Put another way, 800,000 Muslims in France and 240,000 Muslims in the United Kingdom believe that it is acceptable to blow oneself up in a crowded market in the name of Islam. Muslims are being integrated in Europe, but far from perfectly.

The variances in the attitudes expressed are as important as the common patterns, and they provide a wedge into questions of integration. Two patterns emerge from the data. The first is that Germans hold an unreciprocated set of negative attitudes toward their Muslim co-citizens. Only 36 percent of Germans express favorable opinions of Muslims. On the question of Islam and modernity, fully 70 percent of the general German population think there is a natural conflict (the highest in the West), whereas only 36 percent of German Muslims agree. Interestingly, 37 percent of the general German population also think that there is a basic conflict between being a devout Christian and living in a modern society, which was also the highest percentage in Europe. These figures suggest that Germans are particularly suspicious of religion and that the Turkish community's poor cultural integration – a problem to which non-Turkish Germans devote endless numbers of column inches – is exaggerated.

The second pattern, and the more important of the two, concerns the Franco-British contrast. British policymakers used to congratulate themselves on their more relaxed approach to integration and multiculturalism relative to the French. "Our diversity is our strength" became a common refrain. Following France's 2004 ban on the wearing of "ostentatious" symbols in schools (the hijab, kippa, and large crosses), the left-wing mayor of London, Ken Livingstone, speaking to a packed city hall, delivered the following line: "The French ban is the most reactionary proposal to be considered by any parliament in Europe since the Second World War." He continued, "I am determined London's Muslims should never face similar restrictions. It marks a move towards religious intolerance which we in Europe swore never to repeat, having witnessed the devastating effects of the Holocaust." (Not long after, it might be noted, he refused to apologize to a Jewish journalist or Holocaust survivors after comparing the journalist to a concentration camp guard.) More recently, Tariq Modood, a noted scholar of Muslims in Europe, claimed that the refusal of British newspapers to republish caricatures of Mohammed first published in Denmark reflected the fact that the United Kingdom "came to this fork in the road with the *Satanic Verses* affair. While we could not be said to have made a decisive choice there is greater understanding in Britain about anti-Muslim racism and about the vilification-integration contradiction than in some other European countries."

There might be. The British are tied with the French for the most positive attitudes toward Muslims and the most optimistic view of the prospects for Muslim integration. If so, British Muslims do not show much gratitude. Across almost all categories, attitudes among U.K. Muslims are more hostile and pessimistic than anywhere else in Europe. Clear majorities of British Muslims viewed non-Muslim Britons as selfish, arrogant, violent, greedy, and immoral, and a substantial minority viewed them as fanatical (44 percent). Only a minority of British Muslims viewed their fellow citizens as respectful of women, tolerant, honest, or devout. The one bright spot was generosity: a majority (56 percent) thought that non-Muslim Britons were generous. By contrast, a majority of German, Spanish, and French Muslims viewed non-Muslims in these countries as respectful of women, generous, tolerant, and honest (but not devout), and only a minority viewed them as arrogant, violent, greedy, immoral, or fanatical. Fully 47 percent of British Muslims thought there was a natural conflict between being a good Muslim and living in a modern society. Elsewhere, the percentage was between 25 percent (Spain) and 36 percent (Germany). One-half of British Muslims believe that they cannot live harmoniously in their country while being a devout Muslim.

The European country that, overall, produces the most encouraging results is France. French non-Muslim attitudes toward Muslims are (along with those of the British) the most positive in Europe. The majority of French non-Muslims view Muslims as generous and honest, and a substantial minority (45 percent) view them as tolerant. The sentiment is reciprocated: French Muslims are the most positively predisposed toward their countrymen. They are also the most self-critical: 21 percent, by far the highest percentage in Europe, blame Muslims for the breakdown in trust between Muslims and non-Muslims.

According to every measure, the contrast with Britain is striking. Whereas 47 percent of British Muslims have unfavorable attitudes toward Jews (compared with 7 percent of the overall population), only 28 percent of French Muslims do (compared with 13 percent of the general population). Whereas 71 percent of British Muslims have a favorable view of Christians, 91 percent of French Muslims do (a figure higher than the average for the general population in the two countries – 87 percent and 88 percent, respectively). Whereas 59 percent of British Muslims believe that democracy would work well in Muslim countries, 76 percent of French Muslims hold this view. Finally, whereas almost half of British Muslims believe that there is a natural conflict between Islam and modernity, only 25 percent of French Muslims take this pessimistic view. Culturally, French Muslims are better integrated than British Muslims according to any measure, and they are viewed as positively by the overall population as are Muslims in the United Kingdom.

How can one explain this? As always, many factors are at work, but most of the factors that might distinguish between the two countries – poverty, social exclusion, provenance, experience of discrimination – are common to both. French Muslims suffer high unemployment and low wages, and they are spatially segregated. France's economy offers fewer job opportunities than Britain's. Racism in France is as common as it is in the United Kingdom. Muslims from Pakistan and Algeria originate from different parts of the world, but there is no obvious reason why the Pakistanis should be more radicalized than the Algerians. Finally, both have reason to feel aggrieved by foreign policy. The French stayed out of the current Iraq War, but they have consistently interfered in Algerian politics.

The only obvious difference between the French and the British with regard to migrants is their attitude toward integration. The British have been more laissez-faire than the French in ensuring the incorporation of migrants. French integration is addressed in Paris; in Britain, it is left to the localities. The British have more willingly adopted multicultural policies on school dress and religious schools. France has been famously uncompromising in its suspicion of claims for religious or cultural differences in public institutions. Its hijab/kippa/cross ban was fully consistent with its republican framework and its overriding belief that difference belongs in the private sphere. The Anglo-American chattering classes were furious in their denunciations. It would inflame moderate Muslim opinion and pander to racism. It has done neither.

Evidence from France and the United States provides a clear, if perhaps not popular, message. Large-scale immigration policies work when migrants are channelled into work and kept out of welfare, and integration works when the receiving countries have a clear integration framework reflecting values they confidently hold. This should not be surprising. If we cannot be confident of our values and the society that supports them, how can we expect others to view them as objects of emulation? In different ways, France and the United States have got it right. If Europe is to cope with a new century of immigration, it needs labor market policies à l'américaine and integration policies à la française.

17

The Politics of Immigration and Citizenship in Europe

Marc Morjé Howard

In historical and comparative perspective, immigration and citizenship have been viewed as two of the main features that distinguish the United States from the countries of Europe. The United States, along with Australia and Canada, has typically been considered a "settler" country, with very open and generous policies for the admittance and integration of immigrants. Most European countries, in contrast, have been very conflicted about having immigrants in their midst, and their policies have been relatively restrictive in comparison with those of the United States. But in the postwar period, the growing need for unskilled labor brought about unprecedented levels of immigration in much of Europe, leading to two distinct types of national strategies: former colonial powers (such as the United Kingdom, France, and the Netherlands) began to allow large and increasing numbers of people from their former colonies to immigrate and become citizens, while other countries (such as Germany or Austria) implemented "guestworker" models, through which many ostensibly temporary workers were imported in the 1950s and 1960s without being encouraged to integrate, bring their families, or "settle" into their host societies.[1]

While this two-type categorization of European immigration responses did fit much of the second half of the 20th century quite well, it has considerably less utility today. Indeed, almost all of the 15 "older" countries of the European Union (EU) – regardless of their earlier model – are confronting a new reality, namely that their societies include significant minorities (usually 5–10 percent of the population, and much higher

This chapter draws upon Marc Morjé Howard, "Comparative Citizenship: An Agenda for Cross-National Research," *Perspectives on Politics* 4, No. 3 (2006): 443–455.

percentages in cities) of immigrant origin, who have the intention, and the right, as enshrined in national and European law, to stay permanently. As a result, just as has been the case in the United States for many decades, European policymakers are beginning to distinguish more closely between their policies on *immigration* and *integration*.

In a sense, immigration and integration are two sides of the same coin: the former involves the entry of foreigners into a country, while the latter has to do with what happens when they stay. In terms of immigration, even though the raw numbers and proportions are often very different from one country to the next, most advanced industrialized countries have come to a common conclusion: they need to restrict and better control immigration levels. As a result, ferocious debates have emerged in both the United States and Europe about how countries can accommodate a complex set of contradictory imperatives, including *demographic* pressures to hire more workers in order to keep pension systems afloat, the *economic* need of both businesses and consumers for low-skilled menial and/or high-skilled technical labor, and the *political* risk of either pandering to or fueling the xenophobia and anti-immigrant populism that are often seething below the surface.

Whereas the immigration policies of the United States and Europe now largely share common features and similar goals, their integration strategies have remained very different from one another, with a tremendous amount of variation within Europe itself. The most widely accepted indicator of whether immigrants become incorporated into their new society is the extent to which a country allows them to become citizens. This is not a perfect measure, of course – and the July 2005 terrorist attacks in London and November 2005 riots in many parts of France provide a vivid reminder that even citizens of immigrant origin may not feel loyal or welcome – but it is certainly the best available way of making comparisons across countries. And a closer analysis of citizenship policies shows that national traditions and responses have generally remained enduring and distinct – even in the EU.

The United States has long stood out as having one of the most liberal and generous policies on the granting of citizenship: ever since the 14th Amendment was passed, any child born on U.S. soil – even if the parents were undocumented – has automatically received U.S. citizenship;[2] moreover, naturalization procedures are relatively transparent and automatic; and dual (or multiple) citizenship is openly tolerated. Whereas many other countries in the world offer variants on each of these components of citizenship policy,[3] few if any are so free and open. In the past few years, however, this generous American citizenship policy has come into question – a trend that may continue in the future, especially if illegal immigration continues and if the perception that Hispanic minorities are not integrating continues to grow.[4] Debates over citizenship have also been occurring in many European countries. Over the past decade or two, most EU member-states have been rewriting or revising their citizenship laws, often very quietly but sometimes to great fanfare. How these laws and policies are written and enforced across countries will have enormous consequences for the shape and character of European society in the coming decades.

While recognizing the importance of studying immigration policy itself, this chapter focuses on the integration side of the coin, as it seeks to analyze and compare citizenship policies among the countries of the EU. The goal of this focused comparison is to reach more general conclusions that will help to elucidate some of the vexing problems and contradictions in political debates about immigration and citizenship – in Europe, the United States, and elsewhere.

The chapter starts with a discussion of the concept of citizenship and how I apply it, followed by a defense of the importance of *national* citizenship, even in the age of globalization. Then it turns to an empirical exploration of the historical and contemporary variation in citizenship policies in the "EU-15," focusing in particular on an explanation of continuity or change. In doing so, I develop an argument about the importance of the *politics* of citizenship, showing that while various international and domestic pressures have led to liberalization in a number of countries, these usually occurred in the absence of public discussion and involvement. In contrast, when public opinion became mobilized and engaged – usually by a well-organized Far-Right party but also sometimes by a referendum or petition campaign – on issues related to citizenship reform, liberalization was usually blocked or further restrictions were introduced. The chapter concludes by raising some paradoxical and troubling general questions about the connection between democratic processes and liberal policy outcomes.

WHAT IS CITIZENSHIP?

What exactly is citizenship, and what does it entail? At the most basic level, citizenship bestows upon individuals membership in a national political community. In liberal democracies, it gives them the right to vote, to run for office, and to participate freely in public activities, while also requiring the obligation of paying taxes and possibly serving in the military. In terms of the larger international community, citizenship serves as what Rogers Brubaker calls "a powerful instrument of social closure"[5] in two respects. First, the boundary of citizenship allows rich states to draw a line that separates their citizens from potential immigrants from poor countries. Second, it allows states to create internal boundaries that separate citizens from foreign residents by associating certain rights and privileges with national citizenship.

Citizenship therefore evokes a fundamental paradox within liberal democracies, namely what Seyla Benhabib calls "the paradox of democratic legitimacy."[6] Liberal democracies are based on the universal language of fundamental human rights, along with free association and participation of "the people," yet they also delineate clear and enforceable borders and boundaries. This refers not only to territorial borders but also to the boundaries of political membership. Determining who is included in the concept of "the people" also implies at least an implicit understanding of who is excluded. In essence, the paradox is that liberal democracies are "internally inclusive" while remaining "externally exclusive."[7]

In other words, my understanding and use of citizenship here is as a *legal category* rather than as a feature of civil society, social capital, or state–society relations more generally, although of course this category has tremendous social ramifications. I focus on the rights that formal citizenship entails, and especially the formal legal requirements for having access to those rights, rather than on the beliefs or practices of citizens. Although this may deviate somewhat from some contemporary discussions that use the term citizenship as a synonym for civic engagement and related concepts, it provides a more focused and grounded definition, while staying true to the theoretical and empirical debates that started with Aristotle.

In a major contribution – one that is both theoretical and empirical – to the study of citizenship, T. H. Marshall developed a model of citizenship based on the experience of industrialization and the emergence of democracy, and his work raises questions that are still relevant for contemporary debates about the future of citizenship.[8] Marshall argued that the extension of rights and benefits goes in a specific historical sequence as democracy develops and expands, starting with basic *civil rights* (freedom of conscience, protection of property, and some associational liberties), leading eventually to *political rights* (to vote, hold office, and to speak and associate freely), and finally culminating in *social rights* (to form labor unions and eventually to receive the many social benefits that welfare states provide). The argument is compelling, and it fits the historical experience of the United Kingdom – and to some extent Western Europe in general – quite well.

In recent decades, however, the development and establishment of the welfare state has created a new logic that is quite different from Marshall's historical account. In most liberal democracies today, wide-ranging civil as well as social rights are extended to almost all workers and legal residents, even if they are not citizens and therefore do not have political rights. In other words, political rights are no longer a prerequisite for social rights. Moreover, in an increasing number of places in both Western Europe and North America, noncitizens are being granted local or regional (but not national) voting rights.[9] At the same time as this *sub*national political participation has been expanding, citizens of countries that are members of the *supra*national EU can now choose to vote in European elections in their EU country of residence rather than their country of origin.

While Marshall's historical progression may no longer apply to the contemporary situation, many scholars agree with his normative conclusions concerning social rights as the ultimate priority and objective. But this has, in turn, led some scholars to declare the current or impending empirical irrelevance of citizenship in the nation-state. According to this argument, because social rights can now be achieved without political rights and an increasing number of political rights are now available on the subnational and supranational levels, national citizenship no longer matters. As one proponent of this view argues, "when it comes to social services (education, health insurance, welfare, unemployment benefits) citizenship status is of minor importance in the United States and in Western Europe."[10] In short, this type of argument places great emphasis on the recent emergence of transnational and "postnational" norms based on individual human rights, which undermine the previously dominant system of nation-states.[11]

WHY NATIONAL CITIZENSHIP MATTERS

For a number of reasons, however, it is far too early to dismiss the relevance of the nation-state and national citizenship. And this is true even in the case of the EU – where the broader umbrella of "European citizenship" entitles citizens of any EU member-state to have a vast set of rights and privileges across the territory of the Union – because EU citizenship itself is strictly derivative of national citizenship. As a result, "third-country nationals" (people who are not citizens of an EU country) still face limitations on their rights and opportunities, and the citizen versus noncitizen distinction therefore remains very important to them and to the society in which they live.

First, the right to vote and run for office in national elections is still extremely consequential in all countries. Noncitizens, even if they are permanent residents and long-time workers, have no opportunity to participate in the democratic process on the national level. And because citizenship, immigration, and asylum policies are generally implemented on the national level, this means that noncitizens are excluded from taking part in decisions that may directly affect their own lives.

Second, despite exaggerated claims that social rights are guaranteed to all, regardless of national citizenship, in many countries noncitizens are still excluded from significant social benefits. For example, five of the nine provinces in Austria do not provide their social assistance programs to people who are not citizens of Austria or another EU country. Many other countries place significant restrictions on the rights granted to new immigrants, particularly third-country nationals, who often receive lower benefits and in many cases are barred from noncontributory social programs for a certain number of years after arrival.[12] In short, while the modern welfare state undoubtedly provides greater benefits to immigrants than did nation-states at earlier points in history, noncitizens still receive significantly fewer social rights than do people with national citizenship. For that reason, the citizenship distinction really matters in people's lives.

Third, although citizenship is generally less relevant for most private-sector employment, it is still very important in the allocation of public-sector jobs. For example, France only accepts French or EU citizens in railway, postal, and hospital jobs; in Germany, government service employment positions in such areas as public transportation and education are restricted to German or EU citizens; and in the United States, the government can restrict such postings as public school teachers, state troopers, and probation officers to U.S. citizens.[13] Within the EU itself, it should be added, while citizens of an EU country automatically have the right to live and work in another EU country, third-country nationals can generally only reside and work in the country into which they have immigrated. In other words, noncitizens face de facto restrictions on their labor mobility that EU citizens do not.

A fourth reason why national citizenship is still quite significant has to do with the eventual integration of immigrants into the host society. Many scholars have argued that immigrants who become naturalized citizens are likely to become much more integrated into their new country than those who remain noncitizen residents, or "denizens."[14] Although more empirical research on these questions is still needed, it is logical to assume that naturalized citizens will tend to have better command of the national language, to experience more loyalty to the new country, to be relatively accepted by their fellow citizens, and of course to enjoy some protections that are only available to citizens, such as the right not to be deported. In other words, while there is considerable variability across groups and countries, citizenship acquisition can serve as a rough measure of integration, and the different possibilities to acquire citizenship will have lasting implications for the long-term integration of immigrants.

A final, and much more practical and policy-oriented, dilemma facing the advanced industrialized world – and EU countries in particular – has to do with demographics. European countries have among the lowest birthrates in the world, and they desperately need more workers in order to prevent their pension systems from collapsing over the coming two decades.[15] One obvious (though partial) solution to this problem, which has been recognized by scholars and political elites for years, involves increasing levels of immigration and naturalization. Yet the resistance and outright hostility to immigrants has increased noticeably over the past decade, whether measured by public-opinion surveys, support for Extreme Right parties and candidates, or criminal attacks against foreigners. These two countervailing pressures – the need to incorporate more immigrant workers within a context of an often xenophobic public opposition – will have to be resolved, in one form or another, over time. And political elites will struggle with these contradictory demands, though politicians tend to be more responsive to the short-term nature of the electoral process. The demographic problem, however, is a longer-term one, and a key part of its eventual resolution will depend on how these countries define and enforce their citizenship policies.

In short, whether in terms of politics and elections, welfare state benefits, public-sector employment, social integration, or demographics and pension systems, national citizenship remains an essential and enduring feature of modern life – even in the "supranational" EU.

HISTORICAL VARIATION

Having established the importance of studying citizenship, we can now turn to some important empirical and theoretical questions related to historical variation and relative change over time in the citizenship policies of the 15 established EU members. I focus in particular on the "EU-15" for two main reasons. First, most obviously, the EU-15 have become de facto countries of immigration, with tremendous pressures from would-be immigrants from around the world who would like to benefit from Europe's high standard of living, protection of social rights, and need for more labor. In other words, the stakes surrounding citizenship in the EU-15 are extremely high, much more so than would be the case in less industrialized countries with few pressures for immigration and citizenship. Second, from a methodological perspective, the EU-15 constitute a relatively coherent entity, consisting of countries that face similar pressures of immigration and globalization within the common framework of the EU and its institutional and juridical "harmonization." The EU therefore forms a useful "laboratory" for analysis because it spans a range of variation as wide as the entire industrialized world: some countries have been among the most liberal (comparable to Australia, for example), and others have remained staunchly restrictive (along the lines of Japan). In short, a careful examination of the EU-15 provides an analytically useful contrast and variation within a relatively similar set of cases with tremendous real-world importance as highly desired destinations, thus allowing for more systematic comparisons than would be possible if one were to look at the entire world or the European continent.

Unlike many extensively studied topics in comparative politics that contain ready-made empirical puzzles to be explained, we first need to establish an "empirical baseline" of citizenship policies across the countries of the EU. Only then can we address the related theoretical questions. This section explores the "varieties of citizenship" in historical perspective, while the following section focuses on the extent of change (and potential convergence) in citizenship policies that has appeared over the last two decades of EU integration. My goal is not necessarily to provide definitive evidence but to present some suggestive findings that could spark debate on important questions that have so far escaped rigorous comparative analysis.

In order to make broad cross-national comparisons, and through them draw general theoretical conclusions, it is necessary to move beyond the complex legal and technical specifics of each case and thereby reach a better understanding of the variation in citizenship policies across countries *on aggregate*. Such an aggregation procedure will allow us to distinguish among countries that can be considered "liberal," "medium," or "restrictive" in their granting of citizenship.[16] I have therefore developed a coding scheme that classifies and scores the citizenship policies of the 15 EU countries based on three main components: (1) whether the country grants *jus soli* (i.e., whether children of noncitizens who are born in a country's territory can acquire that country's citizenship); (2) the minimum length of its *residency requirement* for naturalization; and (3) whether *naturalized immigrants* are allowed to hold dual citizenship.[17] In my view, these are the most important general elements of a country's citizenship policy, even though there are of course many other features, conditions, and exceptions in each country's laws.[18] They capture the two main modes of citizenship acquisition (by birth and by naturalization), as well as the primary deterrent that can potentially discourage immigrants from naturalizing even if they are eligible (dual citizenship).

Based on a detailed analysis of the citizenship laws that were in place in the 1980s,[19] Table 17.1 presents an aggregate Citizenship Policy Index (CPI) consisting of a 0–6 scale, with scores derived from a simple coding scheme registering scores of two points for each of the three components.[20] In most cases, the laws in the 1980s were identical to, or closely in line with, the historical origins of each country's laws,[21] and in this sense they can serve as a general proxy for previous laws and traditions, thus allowing us to measure historical variation. The table shows considerable variation in national citizenship policies in the 1980s, with six countries grouped into a restrictive category, five in the medium group, and four in the liberal group.

Space constraints preclude a more thorough explanation of this historical variation, but the answer, in brief, involves two main (and overlapping) *historical* factors that I argue help to explain the trajectories that have developed in each country. The first is whether a country is a former colonial power – on a large scale, outside of Europe, and over a sustained time period. The second, related factor revolves around whether a country was democratic in the 19th century. What matters most is whether a country had *both* a prior experience as a colonial power *and* was an early democratizer, not just one of the two, and it is in these countries that one tends to find the most liberal citizenship policies.[22]

RECENT CONTINUITY AND CHANGE

Over the past several decades, the EU has been integrating and "harmonizing" in just about every area – from economic to judicial to social issues. But has a similar development taken place in the realm of citizenship policy? How have countries changed their policies, and to what extent have they converged?

TABLE 17.1. *Citizenship Policy Index for the EU-15 in the 1980s*

Category	Country	Score
Restrictive (0–1)	Austria	0
	Spain	0
	Germany	0
	Luxembourg	0
	Denmark	1
	Finland	1
Medium (2–4)	Greece	2
	Italy	2
	Sweden	2
	Netherlands	4
	Portugal	4
Liberal (5–6)	Belgium	6
	France	6
	Ireland	6
	United Kingdom	6

Note: For a detailed breakdown of the various components and scoring of citizenship policies, see Howard, "Variation in Dual Citizenship Policies" (see note 20 for full citation).

In order to answer these empirical questions, Table 17.2 compares the CPI scores of the 1980s to the current index and then highlights any change that may have occurred. The results show that 10 countries did not change at all; but the 5 countries that have changed all moved in the positive direction on the scale, toward increasing liberalization.[23] More specifically, the most common change was when countries began to accept dual citizenship for naturalized immigrants, as in Finland (in 2003), the Netherlands (over the course of the 1990s),[24] and Sweden (in 2001); in all of these cases, this was a departure from previous policies. Germany (in 2000) and Luxembourg (in 2001) reduced their residency requirements (from 15 to 8 years and from 10 to 5 years, respectively), resulting in a liberalizing change in their scores. Of all the countries, Germany liberalized the most, as the new law not only reduced the residency requirement but also now allows for a form of *jus soli*, representing an important change from Germany's notorious 1913 law.[25]

Overall, this empirical analysis of change since the 1980s shows that some, but certainly not all, of the more restrictive countries have changed their citizenship policies significantly. And the cross-national differences are not quite as vast as they were a few decades ago, although they are still very wide.[26] In short, there does appear to be a *relative* convergence taking

TABLE 17.2. *Changes in the Citizenship Policy Index Between the 1980s and the Current Period*

Country	CPI Score in the 1980s	CPI Score Today	Change
Austria	0	0	None
Germany	0	3	+3
Luxembourg	0	2	+2
Spain	0	0	None
Denmark	1	1	None
Finland	1	3	+2
Greece	2	2	None
Italy	2	2	None
Sweden	2	4	+2
Netherlands	4	6	+2
Portugal	4	4	None
Belgium	6	6	None
France	6	6	None
Ireland	6	6	None
United Kingdom	6	6	None

Note: For a detailed breakdown of the various components and scoring of citizenship policies, see Howard, "Variation in Dual Citizenship Policies" (see note 20 for full citation).

place (i.e., countries are closer to one another than they used to be rather than more distant), but it is far from the level of *absolute* convergence (or "institutional harmonization") occurring in many other areas and sectors of EU integration, and there is clearly no common EU policy today, or – especially after the major setbacks to the EU Constitution – even on the horizon.[27] This lasting variation reinforces the point about the importance of earlier national historical legacies, which still seem to matter a great deal, even in the era of globalization and Europeanization.

But we still need to explain why change has or has not occurred across the countries of the EU. Why have some countries liberalized while others have resisted the pressures of liberalization and remained quite restrictive? Can one identify common patterns that apply across countries, despite the national idiosyncrasies that inevitably apply to policymaking? In each case, the decisive actors who determine citizenship policy are, of course, domestic political elites and political parties, but they do not act without constraints. What, then, are the factors that have influenced them, and how?

The existing literature on immigration and citizenship is much stronger on providing theoretical reasons for liberalization than for restrictiveness.

Indeed, several arguments have been developed to explain increasing liberalization, with some emphasizing global causes and others stressing domestic factors. On the global level, scholars have stressed economic globalization,[28] neo-functional economic cooperation,[29] and new norms of "postnational" human rights[30] to explain liberalization. And on the domestic level, scholars who focus on immigration have pointed out the role of interest group politics, whereby organized groups and businesses often quietly exert influence on policymakers to expand immigration,[31] or of domestic courts and the judicial system in general, which have often sided with immigrants, thereby putting added pressure on political elites to adjust the policies themselves.[32] Despite the quite different points of emphasis, each of these theoretical arguments expects increased liberalization across the countries of the EU.

The findings shown in Table 17.2 certainly provide support for these arguments because the five countries that changed all moved in a liberal direction. But what about the countries that did *not* liberalize? What explains the resistance to liberalization, and how does it play itself out politically? These questions have been inadequately explored in a literature that primarily focuses on (and predicts) liberalization.

Several plausible arguments could be presented, but most do not work out empirically. Structural factors such as rates of economic growth, unemployment, or immigration levels do not shed any light on the puzzle regarding why, among the nine most restrictive countries with citizenship index scores in the 0–2 range in the 1980s, Finland, Germany, Luxembourg, and Sweden liberalized, but Austria, Denmark, Greece, Italy, and Spain did not. Nor do more cultural factors, such as the level of racism or xenophobia, hostility to immigrants, or general discontent with the EU – at least as measured by such public opinion surveys as the Eurobarometer or the European Social Survey – help to establish any connection to the liberalization of national citizenship policies.[33] And differences in political institutions, such as whether countries have parliamentary, presidential, or mixed electoral systems, different minimal percentage requirements to enter Parliament, or various electoral rules and practices, explain very little as well.[34]

What is missing from these structural, cultural, and institutional explanations is the actual *politics* of citizenship. How have political actors navigated the potentially treacherous waters of this volatile issue? How have they dealt with the various pressures from interest groups, social movements, and public opinion? How have they made choices and attempted to implement them politically into new laws and policies? While it is possible that lack of change simply represents a form of institutional inertia – where the old policies continue to persist simply because they already existed – it is also quite likely that elites have pursued conscious strategies and fought open battles, and that these contingent political factors were decisive.

An in-depth analysis of the politics of citizenship across the EU-15 exceeds the bounds of this chapter, but even a rudimentary examination of the political dynamics within countries will help to explain why some of the restrictive countries liberalized but others did not. And it allows us to draw some more general conclusions about the mobilization of public opinion on issues connected to immigration and citizenship, which generally results in the prevention of liberalization.

One way of exploring the liberalization differential between countries is to consider whether political parties of the Left or Right were in power. As Christian Joppke has argued, left-of-center governments are typically in favor of increasing the citizenship rights of immigrants (what Joppke calls "de-ethnicization"), whereas right-of-center governments want to resist such impulses while simultaneously expanding the country's connections to its émigrés (what Joppke calls "re-ethnicization).[35] This argument certainly applies to Germany, where the 2000 citizenship law clearly resulted from the installation of a new Social Democratic–Green coalition government in 1998, and Joppke also applies it effectively to France, Spain, and Italy. Finland and Sweden also had Social Democratic governments when their citizenship laws were changed, though they had been in power for significant periods prior to this liberalization. Luxembourg, however, had a right-of-center government at the time its new citizenship law was proposed and passed, so it cannot simply be a matter of whether the Left is in power. Moreover, several of the countries that did *not* liberalize their laws also had left-of-center governments at one point or another that clearly did not result in the expected change. In short, the Left or Right orientation of the government does seem to be related to the liberalization of citizenship laws, but having a leftist government only accounts for part of the liberalization.

My own interpretation builds on Joppke's Left–Right dichotomy, but I argue that the political orientation of the Right is even more important than the constellation of forces on the Left. And the issue is not simply whether a right-of-center government is in power but whether it is *mobilized* on the issue of immigration and citizenship reform. Thus, if we accept that the liberalizing pressures mentioned earlier are influential in the EU-15, the question is what can counteract those forces. My answer is the mobilization of public opinion – which once again has been latently hostile to immigrants throughout the EU – either in the form of a successful Far Right party, a popular movement, or a referendum of some kind on the issue of immigration or citizenship. In other words, the mobilization of anti-immigrant sentiment essentially "trumps" the liberalizing pressures that other scholars have identified.

It may seem counterintuitive to focus on mobilization in the context of European politics because public involvement has certainly not been a significant feature of EU integration, which has been widely characterized as having a "democratic deficit." But as more and more elements of domestic policymaking have moved to the EU level, anti-EU sentiments and actors have been emboldened in their resistance and opposition to EU-level policymaking. And perhaps because they touch on raw nerves that are most closely connected to a country's identity and sovereignty, no issue has been more sensitive, explosive, or politically effective than immigration and citizenship.

How does this argument play out empirically in the EU countries? The mobilization of anti-immigrant sentiment is very difficult to measure because it can take on different forms. The most obvious and common form is the emergence of a Far Right party whose main platform emphasizes immigration and national citizenship issues. Figure 17.1 therefore presents a 2×2 matrix showing the nine most restrictive countries from the 1980s and distinguishing between the strength of Far Right parties and whether citizenship liberalization occurred. In order to measure the strength of the Far Right, I incorporate a measure of the average electoral support for Far Right parties between 1992 and 2003.

As expected, of the four restrictive countries that liberalized their citizenship laws, all are located in Quadrant II, leaving Quadrant I empty. In other words, liberalization only occurred in the absence of a significant Far Right party or movement. Among the five restrictive countries that did not liberalize their laws at all, the argument about the importance of the Far Right has some success as well. Also as expected, in Austria, Denmark, and Italy, which have had strong Far Right movements for well over a decade, the pressures for liberalization were effectively blocked by their influential Far Right parties. But Greece and Spain had virtually nonexistent Far Right movements, yet they also did not liberalize. What explains these exceptions? This question cannot be answered definitively, but I would speculate that the potential for change is still there and that there is certainly a much greater chance for liberalization in Spain and Greece than there is in Austria, Denmark, or Italy, at least with the current constellation of political forces. In other words, the fact that

FIGURE 17.1. The strength of the Far Right and its effect on citizenship liberalization in the nine most restrictive EU countries. The percentages refer to the average Far Right support for all national elections between 1992 and 2003. *Source:* Data provided by Christopher Wendt, who has compiled Far Right party results from various sources.

these countries have not changed yet does not mean that they will never do so.

Moreover, if we were to consider the six relatively liberal countries in this analysis, Belgium, France, and the Netherlands – all three of which have fairly strong Far Right movements, with 1992–2003 average Far Right returns in national elections of 11.7, 13, and 6.4 percent, respectively – have seen immigration and citizenship emerge as highly polarizing political issues, and they either have experienced (in the case of France in the mid-1990s) or are currently experiencing (in the case of Belgium and the Netherlands) some tinkering with their citizenship laws as a result of the pressures exerted by the Far Right. Ireland does not have an organized Far Right movement, but proponents of restrictions on citizenship acquisition succeeded in implementing a controversial referendum, which passed overwhelmingly (with 80 percent support) in June 2004, to limit the *jus soli* rights of the children of noncitizens so that children born on Irish soil can only receive Irish citizenship if at least one of their parents has resided in Ireland or the United Kingdom for three of the previous four years.[36] This remarkable development shows the tremendous salience of this issue when it becomes publicly mobilized – and the result is almost always change in the direction of restrictiveness.[37] Finally, Portugal and the United Kingdom have much weaker Far Right movements, and their citizenship policies have not changed much in the recent past.

Although this measure of the mobilization of anti-immigrant sentiment is probably the best single indicator available, it only captures part of the larger political story. The reaction of more mainstream conservative parties to the challenge of the Far Right's message can be just as effective in blocking liberalization. And public referenda and other forms of social mobilization, which are not captured by the Far Right measure, can in some ways result in more rapid and decisive restrictions than the standard process of elite and party politics.

In other words, while my argument about the impact of the Far Right helps account for variation in the type of change that has or has not occurred, it certainly does not provide the final word on the topic of citizenship policies and how they have adjusted to new pressures and circumstances.[38]

CONCLUSION

Over the past few decades, almost every country in the EU-15 has revisited – though not necessarily revised – its citizenship law. And while the international and domestic pressures to liberalize have been significant, and sometimes decisive, they have sometimes been held in check by the countervailing pressure of a mobilized public opinion that is latently hostile to immigrants. In fact, as the evidence in this chapter suggests, it appears that when public opinion gets activated politically, with a concrete sponsor or means of expression, liberalization is usually stopped or an existing law becomes even more restrictive. This was the case in Austria, Denmark, and Italy, where the Far Right parties have played leading roles; in Ireland, where a restrictive referendum passed overwhelmingly; and in Germany, where an unprecedented petition campaign rapidly stopped the momentum of liberalization. But if, on the other hand, elites manage to pass reforms without significant public involvement – as occurred in Finland, Luxembourg, and Sweden – then liberalization will most likely be the outcome.

This brings us to a larger paradox, if not a serious normative problem: in terms of issues dealing with immigration and citizenship, a

nondemocratic, elite-driven process may lead to more liberal policy outcomes, whereas genuine popular involvement can result in more restrictive
laws and institutions. In other words, proponents of liberal, inclusive policies should give more thought to the role of democracy – both representative democracy that results in the inclusion of Far Right parties in governments and policymaking and direct democracy that takes the form of
referenda and initiatives – on issues that are prone to populism, xenophobia, and racism.[39] The trend is clear, as countries are increasingly relying
on referenda and popular initiatives, which advocates of the Far Right
view as being the ultimate expression of "true democracy." The great
challenge, therefore – particularly in the EU but also in the United States,
where reliance on popular initiatives is increasing rapidly and where public opinion may also have strong, if still latent, anti-immigrant tendencies –
will be for elites to surmount the much criticized "democratic deficit" in
shaping immigration policy while simultaneously avoiding the trap of
populism.

PART VI

CONCLUSION

18

Concluding Observations

Nathan Glazer

Not much has changed in immigration thinking since I edited *Clamor at the Gates* more than 25 years ago. During this period, we have been living through the most recent – and by now the most extended – wave of immigration in U.S. history. We have had some excellent research, particularly on the economic effects of recent immigration – although, to be sure, we do not all agree on the conclusions of this research. We have also had a good deal of research, by its nature more difficult to conduct, on the various dimensions of the assimilation and integration of immigrants into American society, and the conclusions of this research are also disputed. We have had extended debate and a good deal of legislation on what is universally considered the most serious issue in current immigration, the huge scale of illegal or undocumented immigration. But as we struggle with this issue in the first decade of the 21st century – just as we struggled with it in the 1980s and 1990s – it is clear that we have come to no generally accepted and politically realizable conclusions as to what, if anything, can and should be done.

This volume on the politics of the contemporary immigration debate tells us some familiar things about current immigration and brings to our attention some of the recent research, particularly on immigration's economic effects, but its true value lies in the new questions it raises. And in view of how difficult it has been to resolve disputes over immigration in the past 25 years, some new thoughts and ideas may well be just what we need. While every individual chapter has something helpful to tell us, I would point to three issues that are brought to our attention in these chapters, if not for the first time (what, after all, is absolutely new in political and social discussion?), with unprecedented forcefulness.

The first of what I consider these new thoughts is the consideration in two of the chapters of the ethical and moral bases that should guide our immigration policy. One point of view that is particularly significant for American politics today, that of evangelical Protestants, generally enters political discussion in the form of demands from one side and denunciations on the other, and almost never appears in reasoned policy discussion. But here it warrants an interesting and important essay: What is the biblical point of view, insofar as it can be drawn from the Christian Bible? This perspective is developed by James R. Edwards, Jr. It is supplemented by a sophisticated essay by Stephen Macedo, in which recent thinking in moral philosophy, particularly the influential work of John Rawls and Michael Walzer, is brought to bear on the immigration issue. I will develop my reasons for thinking that moral and ethical issues are beginning to, and will continue to, play an increasingly larger role in discussions of immigration.

A second of these new thoughts to my mind is developed by Noah Pickus and Peter Skerry. They attack what has become politically the central issue in the immigration debate, the distinction between legal and illegal immigration. They ask: Is this really the problem? Aren't many of immigration's consequences that concern us – consequences affecting the economic interests of various groups, for example – the result of *legal* immigration, which, after all, accounts for a much greater part of immigration than *illegal* immigration? Isn't much of what we applaud and approve among immigrants evident among illegal immigrants, too? It is time to rethink the distinction and explore what light this may throw on immigration issues.

Clearly the moral issues raised by Edwards and Macedo are relevant here, too. We find, I believe, that ideas of natural justice, and moral and ethical concerns generally, play an increasing role in political thinking and in international affairs. Such a development has to throw some doubt on the significance of the difference between legal and illegal immigrants: both come for the same reasons, are escaping the same countries, and are attracted similarly to the realm of free countries with greater opportunities. Can we be so absolute in erecting a wall between them, with rights for those on one side and no rights at all for those on the other?

The third issue to which I would point is spelled out by Peter Schuck, and it is the sharp disconnect between what the American public says it desires in immigration policy – preferably less immigration, and certainly not more – and what the politically decisive forces give us in the way of immigration policy. We see the same issue addressed by Rogers Smith. The issue here is not that the public is right and the politically effective agents are wrong, or the reverse. It is rather that this disconnect raises a problem for democracy whose resolution may well be very disturbing. How long can what the majority claims it wants be ignored, and with what consequences?

It is this chapter, more than most of the others, that suggests to us that a look back at the history of immigration in the United States may be helpful. It will remind us that there are possibilities in immigration policy that are not evident on the horizon today. History reminds us of one thing: the mantra that this is and has always been an immigration society and always will be is as much ideology – the ideology of the past half-century in particular – as a proper evaluation of the actual role of immigration in American society.

We should recall that during large stretches of U.S. history – and indeed in some of the country's most formative periods – immigration was low and not much considered a central and shaping element in its history and society. I would point to two such periods in particular. Consider the 60 years from the time of the American Revolution to the 1840s. Revolution and war played a major role in keeping immigration low during much of this period. The Napoleonic Wars did not end until 1815, but even after the return to peace, immigration remained low. During this entire period, and for a few decades thereafter, there was no national legislation on immigration; as Elizabeth Cohen reminds us, immigration was then a matter for the states, and few bothered to exercise their rights on the subject. Tocqueville, traveling through the United States in the 1830s, did not think of it as a country being shaped by immigration. To him, it was a country of Anglo-Americans, and he did not expect that to change. He was happy to make contact with French immigrants, but they were few. The problematic minorities – to use current terminology – in the U.S. population were Native Americans and blacks, not immigrants.

Consider another lengthy period, from the 1920s to the 1960s, covering the prosperity of the 1920s, the Great Depression, the four terms of FDR and World War II, and postwar prosperity. During that entire period, immigration was low, kept that way by depression and war, and by law if these did not suffice. National sentiment, as expressed in Congress, was strongly anti-immigration. Even efforts to bring in threatened Jewish children, or concentration camp survivors who could find no home in Europe, were met with fierce political resistance. Indeed, when immigration law was finally changed in 1965, it was only because no one expected that immigration would rise much. A degree of family reunification for some Europeans was expected and made possible, and a bow to the antiracism that we had formally espoused in the war against Hitler permitted the elimination of the ban on Asians. But not many of them were expected.

The United States has changed since then, and one of the chief ways in which it has changed is in our acknowledgment, to some degree, of responsibilities and duties to the entire world – an example of the role of ethical and moral concerns to which I earlier alluded. Such an acknowledgment has to raise the question of what kind of claim people in poor or war-ravaged countries, or in countries brutalized by dictators, have to the assistance of richer and more fortunate countries in escaping from terrible conditions. We have seen the emergence of an international ethic according to which it has become an obligation of rich countries to provide aid to poor countries, even to those for whose poverty they bear no particular responsibility. The idea of aid to poor countries as an obligation of the richer ones was certainly no part of international thinking before World War II. The idea may have arisen with decolonization after World War II, but it has become a general obligation. For various poor countries, there is a club of donors, most of whom have no previous colonial relation to the countries in question. The United States is a willing participant in these clubs.

The United States, despite its prickly insistence on untrammeled sovereignty, does accept international obligations set by international organizations, such as the right to asylum, under which many immigrants come. Initially this was sharply circumscribed: we accepted asylum seekers insofar as they furthered our Cold War with Russia, or insofar as their desperate condition was in part a consequence of U.S. policies, or specifically to the failure of U.S. foreign and military policy, such as in Vietnam. But the obligation has become more general over time.

Yet another oddity of our immigration policy illustrates the increasing hold of the idea of international obligation on this proud and independent country. Consider the "diversity" provision in immigration law. We know why it came into effect; the immigration law of 1965, which favored relatives of citizens, also disfavored countries from which immigrants had come a long time ago and no longer maintained close family relations with potential immigrants, and this affected Ireland particularly. The "diversity" provision, permitting persons in countries that provided few immigrants to apply for visas in an international lottery, was designed to make it possible for more Irish to come: its effect over time has been to make it possible for more Bangladeshis, Nigerians, and other Africans and Asians to come. This was no part of its intention, but the law has not been changed or abandoned as a result. It has become an emblem of the idea that all peoples have a claim on entry to the United States and on becoming part of the country, a claim that cannot be limited by differences of religion or race, or lack of connection to the ethnic and religious groups that have played the central role in the making of the United States.

These disparate policies and changes bear the common characteristic that we increasingly accept the idea that we have an obligation to the poorest of the globe and that we are bound by an emerging moral and ethical code in dealing with the peoples of the world. Discussing how this actually works itself out in policy would take us far afield, and many find the expression of this commitment to universal ethical and moral standards and international human rights hypocritical, but the fact remains that the words expressing such a responsibility are pronounced by the most authoritative voices representing America. This has to be reflected in our immigration policy, and thus we and other democratic and free countries of the developed world are increasingly abandoning the right to choose immigrants for the purpose of molding or controlling the racial and ethnic character of the country. This is a surprising development indeed.

The increasing weight of a regime of international human rights, designed for all people whatever their legal status or citizenship, must also affect our thinking about the difference between legal and illegal immigrants, the issue raised in the chapter by Pickus and Skerry. Our two chapters on moral and ethical aspects of immigration both agree that a limited political community with its own defined rules, and a fundamental obligation to its own members, is a morally and ethically legitimate social form, not simply a means of selfishly excluding others outside it. But as Pickus and Skerry indicate, it is hard to consider the overwhelming majority of illegal immigrants – who come to seek work in industries and areas eager to employ them, to provide sustenance to families back home, and to escape difficult economic and political conditions, and so many of whom establish families and in effect become good citizens, even without the status of citizenship – as criminals and lawbreakers, and even those specifically employed to enforce the law and control the borders do not often so consider them.

Consider another change that both bears on the issue of the steady expansion of moral and ethical concerns and also affects our thinking ıt illegal immigrants. We have seen in the last few decades a surprising ınge in our conception of and in the legal status of citizenship. We .ink properly of U.S. citizenship as a treasured and exclusive status. The oath of citizenship specifically gives up all previous allegiances. Yet we increasingly recognize the status of dual citizenship, not only the dual citizenship that is the result of being born in the United States to immigrant parents whose native countries grant citizenship to the children of its nationals born abroad but also the dual citizenship of mature individuals who have maintained their citizenship in their native country even after becoming U.S. citizens and taking the exclusionary oath. Many states allow their citizens to maintain citizenship even when they become citizens of the United States.

In effect, we recognize today not only the sentimental and familial ties that inevitably bind immigrants to their native countries but also – if their native countries permit it – the legal status of citizenship in a foreign country, even when an individual has become a citizen of the United States. Depending on the country, such citizenship may permit voting in its elections, even though that dual citizen also votes in elections in the United States, and running for and occupying office in the native country.

This development is often a subject of outrage, and indeed, were these possibilities of dual citizenship embodied in legislation, it is hard to believe Congress would accept them. The expansion of the status of dual citizenship, and the ability to take up duties of citizenship in a foreign nation (serving it in elected or appointed positions, serving in its armed forces, voting in its elections, etc.) without danger to American naturalization, is the result of Supreme Court decisions that have rejected the harsher and more exclusive version of U.S. citizenship – decisions that Congress has not seen it necessary to overrule, as it probably could.

I mention this development and its possible bearing on our thinking about the difference between legal and illegal immigrants because it reflects, to my mind, the ascendancy of more complex ideas of people and their mixed allegiances than we find in the stark contrast of legal versus illegal immigration. Among illegal immigrants, there is certainly some criminality aside from the specific fact of breaking the laws on entry into or remaining in the United States, and that should and does concern us. Whether this criminality is more or less than among legal immigrants is not a question I have seen addressed. But many illegal immigrants we know are visitors who have overstayed the legal period of their stay, students who are not in the specific status of studenthood that makes them legal, or persons caught in the complexities of immigration law. Many of those who apply for the immigration lottery are in residence in the United States in some status short of legal residency and apply for the lottery with the distant hope that they may win and legalize their status. (If they are so lucky, I believe the previous condition of illegality does not affect them as winners entitled to legal residency.)

Of course, the major impact on our thinking about illegality comes from disappointment about the hopes of the 1986 Immigration Reform and Control Act (IRCA). We thought that granting amnesty to the existing illegal immigrants and imposing restrictions on the employment of further illegal immigrants would dry up the supply and bring the problem to an end. It turned out that our amnesty was restricted and our restrictions on the employment of illegal immigrants were full of holes. Employers benefiting from the labor power of illegal immigrants had enough influence to prevent really effective restrictions on their employment. And did the rest of us – the American people – really want such restrictions? Did we not benefit from these immigrants who worked for us as gardeners, painters, roofers, handymen, nannies, and the like? Is it not clear that the only solution to the illegal immigrant problem, if there is any, is in effect to legalize the illegal?

I believe our more tolerant society will not deport 10 million illegals, or any substantial part of them, many of whom are the parents and husbands and wives of U.S. citizens. I believe we will not accept the costs – in the form of a huge increase in the number of border police and a huge increase in inconvenience for the millions of citizens, immigrants, and visitors crossing the borders daily – that a really serious effort to effectively seal the borders would require. We once did deport hundreds of thousands, but our sense of the proper and legitimate behavior for government has changed, and I believe we will not accept, as a people, either the inevitable cruelty and heartlessness that the physical removal of the illegals would entail or the economic losses and inconvenience that such a radical reduction in the labor force working the fields, hotels, restaurants, homes, and factories would cause.

Or would we? This brings me to the third interesting thought in these chapters I have signaled: Peter Schuck's discussion of the disconnect between what Americans say they want in immigration (less) and the political process that regularly produces a different result (more). What do Americans really want in immigration? The ideology – see the inscription on the Statue of Liberty – that welcomes the unfortunate and the striving says "more." The pragmatic judgment as to personal self-interest generally says, for most of us, "more." But there are strong forces that say "less" when we consider the impact of immigrants on any neighborhood, the inevitable conflict between the known, the stable, and the expected, and the changes that immigration brings. This leaves aside the still powerful, even if minority and somewhat underground, point of view that the United States should remain a white man's country and that its ethnic and racial composition should not undergo radical change.

In Schuck's view, the conflict is, in strictly comprehensible political science terms, between those with a strong interest in more immigrants (for economic reasons, for reasons of familial sentiment, or group attachment) and a more diffuse general feeling that the United States has enough immigrants and that fewer would be better. In such a situation, the specific and powerfully motivated interests overwhelm the diffuse opposition. But this balance may change. One reason it may change – and indeed is already changing to some degree – is the sharp rise in fears of terrorist attacks since 9/11. The impact of this quantum jump in security concerns is discussed by Rogers Smith. But it has already affected one important stream that is often a source of immigrants, the number of students coming from abroad to study in the United States. As a result of the greater difficulty in getting visas to study here, the number of students coming to the United States has shown the first substantial drop since World War II. Security concerns have also reduced the number of visitors – some part of whom overstay to become illegal immigrants, and some part of whom become immigrants – because of the increased difficulty in getting visas. Muslims, coming from many countries, are under specific suspicion, but less understandably our immigration authorities are not very good at making distinctions, and a turbaned Sikh or a Canadian Parsi author of Indian origin, and indeed almost anyone seeking to enter the United States today, is likely to have as much difficulty as a potential Egyptian or Saudi student.

The balance between pro- and anti-immigration forces is delicate and shifting. In the 1990s, we saw some sharp legislation affecting the public benefits immigrants could receive. Many thought that this signaled a new anti-immigration phase, but it did not – neither immigration nor illegal immigration dropped. I believe the changes to which I have referred, in the form of the greater power in international affairs of concern for the poor and the abused, the expansion of rights even for those not part of a specific polity, and the greater tolerance and the reduction of racist attitudes within the United States, are permanent changes, with a permanent impact on our immigration policies. But they do not mean the ebb and flow of attitudes affecting immigration policy has ceased. Public attitudes will respond to large events, such as an increase in terrorism and an awareness of the dangers of extremism among some part of immigrants, or to large changes in the economy. We see this conflict in attitudes not only between different groups and interests but even among the same people – the homeowner who is happy to find immigrant workers who will paint his house for less will also be annoyed at the group of day laborers in the center of town waiting for those who would employ them for the day. The American who favors the deportation of illegal immigrants in general will also resist the deportation of the illegal immigrant who comes to clean the house or to take care of the children. This matter will play itself out and will be influenced by changes in our sense of security and in our economy, but as it does I think we will continue to be affected by a long change in attitudes that is reducing the boundaries between "us" and "them," those within the polity and those outside it, those deserving rights to decent human treatment and those to whom we owe no obligation.

When we speak of those "inside" and those "outside" our polity and society, and how that boundary is changing, we cannot help but think of the one great subject of inclusion or exclusion over which Americans still struggle. This book, unlike much of the discussion of immigration over the years, pays a significant amount of attention to race and ethnicity, devoting an entire section to it, particularly to the question of how the issue of immigration interacts with the place and fate of black Americans as demonstrated in chapters by Carol Swain and Jonathan Tilove. Tilove's chapter makes it central. Having innocently used the term "white flight" to describe movement away from immigrant areas, he aroused outrage from a leading black intellectual. Once again, she asked, was he not placing the black in the position of the true alien, more alien than the immigrant? Ignore the logic, or illogic, of the outrage. The controversy in the wake of Hurricane Katrina in 2005, and the evacuation of the population of New Orleans, parallels Tilove's account of how the term "white flight" might be seen quite differently by whites and blacks. Those who had no resources to flee New Orleans before the storm were mostly black. When they escaped to whatever place of relative safety was available, these internally displaced people were referred to in the media as "refugees." There was an outraged response in the black community. Refugees? Refugees are people forced from their country – how did the black inhabitants of New Orleans come to be called and considered refugees? This outrage exhibited both the legitimate insistence by blacks that they are also Americans – as authentic as any, more authentic than many – and the fear that they were considered in some way outsiders. The interaction between immigration and the condition of African Americans is enormously complex. On the one hand, there is the obvious impact on the jobs blacks hold: it is evident everywhere, from agricultural fields to the office buildings of the great cities, that blacks have been replaced by immigrants. Perhaps some of these jobs are ones from which blacks have graduated, the ones they no longer want. But then, are these not still jobs that some of them need, and for which they see immigrants – many of them true "refugees" – being given preference? But then, if African Americans call for restriction of immigration, are they not allying themselves with the prejudiced, with those who would exclude them as well as immigrants? Certainly one of the issues that must concern us, particularly as we consider the ethical and moral implications of immigration and consider our sense of widening responsibility to people in all parts of the globe, is our initial responsibility to the one group in American society that has suffered from the fullest exclusion and that has found greater difficulty than most immigrants in being fully accepted into American society.

Earlier this year (2006), the strange disconnect between public opinion, which favored fewer immigrants, and the balance of political forces, which generally added up to policies that meant more immigrants, was bridged, and a powerful movement to restrict illegal immigration and make life harder for illegals already here became a major public issue as Congress debated new immigration restriction laws. How the current political storm around these issues will be resolved is unclear at this writing, but I believe the major forces I have identified here, in particular the increasing role in public opinion and politics of the idea that all people have rights and deserve consideration, will continue to work to limit an extreme response to the problem of illegal immigration. (One may argue that an extreme response is already evident in the increasing number of illegals who die in the deserts they are forced to endure in order to make entry into the United States. But our very concern over this matter will have some effect on what we do.) Arizona law

I commented earlier on the ethical and moral considerations that increasingly affect our dealings with peoples outside our borders and our increasing tolerance for mixed and nonexclusive identities. There have been some interesting recent examples of these forces at play. Note the recent quantum jump in the scale of American philanthropy, the greater part of it addressed to problems that afflict the poorer and less-educated populations of the world more than they do Americans – fighting AIDS, developing new and cheaper vaccines and medicines and creating new mechanisms for distributing them, and the like. Perhaps we have heard a few grumbles that a relatively small part of the Gates and Buffet billions are going to aid poor, troubled, and sick Americans. But we more or less accept the idea that we have an obligation to the rest of the world and that the billions created by American enterprise should quite properly deal with problems beyond our borders. The connection to immigration policy may be remote, but this strong demonstration of the idea that we have obligations to heal the ills of the world reflects a tide of opinion that will affect how we think about immigration.

Consider the recent development of law regarding the rights of non-citizens. This has come about because of the ambiguities in the case of terrorists, or those suspected of terrorism, such as those who have been held at Guantanamo, and whether or not these persons should be treated under U.S. law. In effect, the Supreme Court has ruled that one cannot divide rights such that U.S. citizens have all of them and those who are not have none. Indeed, this distinction had become difficult to maintain, as so many Americans turned out to be citizens of two countries. Could the accident of American birth mean that one potential terrorist had to be treated with more consideration of his rights than another?

I note currently (2006) the evacuation of "Americans," and others, from war-afflicted Lebanon. But almost all of these people are also Lebanese, as well as British, or French, or some other nationality. This increasing looseness – for the more advanced part of the world – of the status of citizenship must also, though not in any direct fashion, affect how we think about immigrants in general and illegal immigrants.

The result of the conflict between the simple and clear notion of no illegal immigrants and the continuing shift in public opinion that empha-sizes our obligations to the poorer and less advantaged of the world will moderate how we legislate on immigration. And if it does not moderate the legislation, it will moderate how we enforce it. I do not see how the United States – and Europe, in this respect much like the United States – will simply turn its back on an enormous world of poorer people, living under harsh economic, social, and political conditions, who press on the borders of the part of the world that has found its way to a much greater degree of wealth, stability, and opportunity.

Enormous hardships accompany this effort of the poor of the world to enter its more fortunate parts. But the overall pattern, in Europe and in the United States, remains the same – despite the hardships, more are successfully entering the prosperous world and transforming it. Law can play only a limited role in controlling this monumental process of migration and social change. Indeed, so limited are our successes in stemming this migration that we might do well to consider how we can guide it rather than staunch it. Perhaps that will be the next stage in the development of our immigration policies.

Notes

1. Introduction

1. Nathan Glazer, ed., *Clamor at the Gates* (New York: ICS Press, 1985), 11.
2. For more information about the history of U.S. immigration policy, see Roger Daniels, *Guarding the Golden Door: American Immigration Policy Since 1882* (New York: Hill and Wang, 2004); Hugh Davis Graham, *Collision Course: The Strange Convergence of Affirmative Action and Immigration Policy in America* (New York: Oxford University Press, 2002); Daniel J. Tichenor, *Dividing Lines: The Politics of Immigration Control in America* (Princeton, NJ: Princeton University Press, 2002).
3. Congress has been dealing with the issue of immigration and naturalized citizenship since 1790, when it established rules for naturalization using Article 1, Section 8, of the Constitution, restricting citizenship to free white persons. Other legislative acts include the Chinese Exclusion Act of 1882; the Immigration Act of 1924, which established racial quotas for certain nations; the adoption of a national origin formula in 1929; and the Immigration and Naturalization Act of 1952 (McCarran-Walter Act).
4. IRCA included four main provisions designed to address illegal immigration. It instituted employer sanctions on those who hire illegals, it legalized long-term undocumented residents, it legalized special agricultural workers, and it protected U.S. citizens and permanent residents against discrimination that might come from employers seeking to avoid sanctions.
5. The 1990 Immigration Act raised the immigration ceiling to 700,000 and created preferences for relatives of U.S. residents or citizens and foreigners with specialized skills.
6. IIRIRA made it much easier to deport illegal residents by restricting the judicial review of administrative removal orders and by limiting appeal processes.
7. See also Douglas S. Massey, Jorge Durand, and Nolan J. Malone, *Beyond Smoke and Mirrors: Immigration Policy and Global Economic Integration* (New York: The Russell Sage Foundation, 2002).

8. Legislation passed after September 11, 2001, expanded the grounds for inadmissibility and deportation, allowed for the detention of suspected terrorists or people coming from areas of the country known to harbor terrorists, allowed nationality to play a larger role in decision making, imposed more restrictions on foreign visitors, imposed new limits and barriers on refugees, restricted public access to removal hearings, and expanded the law enforcement role of states and localities.

9. Eric Lipton, "U.S. Crackdown Set Over Hiring of Immigrants," *New York Times*, September 21, 2006, 1.

10. The Pew Research Center, "No Consensus on Immigration Problem or Proposed Fixes: America's Immigration Quandary" (Washington, DC: Pew Research Center, March 30, 2006).

11. Ibid., ii.

12. Mark Potok, "The Year in Hate, 2005," *Intelligence Report* 121 (Spring 2006).

13. "Immigration Bills Compared," *Washington Post*, available online at http://washingtonpost.com/wp-dyn/content/custom/2006/05/26/CU2006052600148.html; U.S. House of Representatives, 109th Congress, H.R. 4437; U.S. Senate, 109th Congress, S. 2611.

14. See the Secure Fence Act of 2006, P.L. 109–369 (H.R. 6061), October 26, 2006.

2. The Disconnect between Public Attitudes and Policy Outcomes in Immigration

1. In general, it will suffice here to discuss the quantitative dimension of immigration policy (the number of immigrants admitted each year). This is why I can describe a policy so simply as "restrictive" and "expansive." Clearly, however, immigration policy's qualitative and temporal dimensions (the categorical bases for selecting particular immigrants and the periods during which they are permitted to remain or must wait to apply for citizenship) are in some respects more important. Where pertinent to the discussion, I shall mention them.

2. This understanding of "policy," which is fairly standard in the policy studies field, is roughly analogous to the long-standing distinction between the law on the books and the law in action. I have suggested elsewhere, in the context of immigration policy, that "[o]fficial behavior that appears on its face to be ineffective may actually serve a deeper, more latent social function (to use Robert Merton's phrase). It may help us to maintain certain cherished myths in the face of contradictory facts we are reluctant to recognize. To put it another way, we may prefer to think that we have certain goals and have failed to achieve them than to acknowledge the possibility that these are not really our goals or, worse still, that the goals were not worth striving for in the first place." See Peter H. Schuck, "Law and the Study of Migration," in *Migration Theory: Talking Across Disciplines*, ed. C. Brettell and J. Hollifield (New York: Routledge, 2000), 196–197.

3. In a 2006 Gallup poll, 55 percent of Hispanics, compared with 48 percent of all Americans, agreed that there are too many immigrants entering from Latin America. See Karlyn H. Bowman, "Pessimism About the Middle East Is Growing," *Roll Call*, July 26, 2006, 8.

4. Available at http://www.pollingreport.com/immigration.htm. A Pew Research Center report in 2006 revealed a similar, though not identical, pattern. See "America's Immigration Quandary" (Washington, DC: Pew Research Center, March 30, 2006), 24.

5. I leave to one side the question of how well informed they are about what the current levels of immigration actually are and what they were historically. I suspect that most Americans have little grasp of the statistics on immigration and are greatly influenced, as in many other areas of public policy, by anecdotal evidence and media accounts.

6. Federation for American Immigration Reform (FAIR) is a Washington-based lobbying group led by activists in the labor, English-language, population control, and environmental movements who seek to limit restriction to levels far below those now prevailing.

7. Even public attitudes toward hot-button, stereotype-driven policy issues concerning race appear to be notably responsive to counterargument. See Paul Sniderman and Thomas Piazza, *The Scar of Race* (Cambridge, MA: Harvard University Press, 1993).

8. I develop this point in Peter H. Schuck, "Law and the Study of Migration," in *Migration Theory: Talking Across Disciplines*, 2nd ed. ed. C. Brettell and J. Hollifield (New York: Routledge, 2007), which draws upon unpublished remarks by Professor Robert Kagan.

9. In contrast, the Illegal Immigration Reform and Immigrant Responsibility Act of 1996 dealt largely with the system for removing illegal entrants, out-of-status immigrants, and criminals.

10. Peter H. Schuck, "The Politics of Rapid Legal Change: Immigration Policy 1980–1990," in *Citizens, Strangers, and In-Betweens: Essays on Immigration and Citizenship*, ed. Peter H. Schuck (Boulder, CO: Westview, 1998), Chapter 4.

11. Kelly Jeffreys and Nancy Rytina, "U.S. Legal Permanent Residents: 2005," Annual Flow Report (Washington, DC: U.S. Department of Homeland Security, April 2006).

12. For a historical account and severe critique of this program, see Peter H. Schuck, *Diversity in America: Keeping Government at a Safe Distance* (Cambridge, MA: Belknap, 2003), 123–131.

13. Ibid., 127.

14. See Peter H. Schuck and John Williams, "Removing Criminal Aliens: The Pitfalls and Promises of Federalism," 22 *Harvard Journal of Law and Public Policy* 367 (1999).

15. See Schuck, *Citizens, Strangers, and In-Betweens*, Chapter 6.

16. Miriam Jordan, "States and Towns Attempt to Draw the Line on Illegal Immigration," *Wall Street Journal,* July 12, 2006, A1. In contrast, some localities have rejected these laws. See, for example, Abby Goodnough, "Florida City Rejects Stringent Law on Migrants," *New York Times*, July 25, 2006, A17.

17. For a legal analysis, see Schuck, *Citizens, Strangers, and In-Betweens*, Chapter 6, especially 151–154.

18. Ibid., 114.

19. The government estimates that almost half are visa violators; the remainder entered illegally.

20. Tamar Jacoby, who makes a strong case for supporting the proposal, contends that it is not really an "amnesty" because of the demanding requirements that the workers will have to meet. See Tamar Jacoby, "Getting Beyond the 'A-Word,'" *Wall Street Journal*, June 20, 2005, A15. Those who observed the notoriously loose administration of the special agricultural worker (SAW) legalization program in the years after IRCA have some reason to be skeptical of this distinction. As Heather MacDonald notes, many immigrant advocates resent the term "amnesty," insisting that despite violations of the immigration laws, "no person is illegal." See Heather MacDonald, "The Illegal-Alien Crime Wave," 14 *City Journal* 46 (Winter 2004).

21. This very rough estimate was prepared for budget planning purposes. Most of those entries would be short-term stays in county/local facilities. E-mail to author dated July 8, 2005, from John Bjerke, statistician, Office of Detention and Removal, Department of Homeland Security.

22. The Department of Homeland Security, Office of Immigration Statistics, Annual Report, Immigration Enforcement Actions: 2005 (November 2006), 1.

23. For discussions of how this dichotomy has been used in past immigration policy and legal debates, see T. Alexander Aleinikoff, "Good Aliens, Bad Aliens, and the Supreme Court," in 9 *In Defense of the Alien*, ed. L. Tomasi (New York: Center for Migration Studies, 1987), 46, 51; Peter H. Schuck, "The Supreme Court and Immigration Law in the 1980's: Some Impressions," in Tomasi, 9 *In Defense of the Alien*, 34–45.

24. I put it this way in recognition of the obvious fact that many nonacademic or nonspecialist commentators favor some form of restriction. Examples include Samuel P. Huntington, *Who Are We? The Challenges to America's National Identity* (New York: Simon and Schuster, 2004); Peter Brimelow, *Alien Nation: Common Sense About America's Immigration Disaster* (New York: Harper Perennial, 1995); George J. Borjas, *Heaven's Door: Immigration Policy and the American Economy* (Princeton, NJ: Princeton University Press, 1999); and the U.S. Commission on Immigration Reform, *Becoming an American: Immigration and Immigrant Policy* 62 (Washington, DC: U.S. Commission on Immigration Reform, 1997).

25. I and a co-author have supported this (see Schuck and Williams, "Removing Criminal Aliens," 460–463), as has Professor Kris Kobach, principal adviser to Attorney General John Ashcroft on immigration issues after 9/11. See Kris W. Kobach, "The Quintessential Force Multiplier: The Inherent Authority of Local Police to Make Immigration Arrests," 69 *Albany Law Review* 179 (2005).

26. For a limited exception, see David A. Martin, "Two Cheers for Expedited Removal in the New Immigration Laws," 40 *Virginia Journal of International Law* 673 (2000). Professor Martin, who has extensive experience as the agency's general counsel, may favor some of these measures.

27. For some novel approaches to reducing unnecessary detention, see Peter H. Schuck, "INS Detention and Removal: A White Paper," 11 *Georgetown Immigration Law Journal* 667 (1997); Christopher Stone, "Supervised Release as an Alternative to Detention in Removal Proceedings: Some Promising Results of a Demonstration Project," 14 *Georgetown Immigration Law Journal* 376 (2000); Margaret H. Taylor, "Dangerous by Decree: Detention Without Bond in Immigration Proceedings," 50 *Loyola Law Review* 149 (2005).

28. I was a co-founder and early chair of this section and have attended most of its programs and try to monitor the rest.

29. James Buchanan and Gordon Tullock, *The Calculus of Consent: Logical Foundations for Constitutional Democracy* (Ann Arbor: University of Michigan Press, 1962); James Q. Wilson, ed., *The Politics of Regulation* (New York: Basic Books, 1980), Chapter 10. See also Peter H. Schuck, "The Politics of Regulation," 90 *Yale Law Journal* 702 (1981) (reviewing Wilson book).

30. See, for example, Michael J. Trebilcock and Matthew Sudak, "The Political Economy of Emigration and Immigration," 81 *New York University Law Review* 234 (2006), for a review of the studies. As the authors indicate, there is much disagreement about the magnitude of these costs and benefits.

31. See, for example, Charlemagne, "Talking of Immigrants," *The Economist*, June 3, 2006, 50.

32. Pew Research Center, "America's Immigration Quandary," 11.

33. I believe that limiting immigrants' access to welfare benefits in the 1996 welfare reform law, far from evincing hostility to immigration per se, may have had the effect of strengthening the argument in favor of immigration – or at least weakening a major argument against it. Indeed, one leading immigration policy analyst bases his own expansionist proposal on the assurance that immigrants would not claim nonemergency welfare benefits. See Michael J. Trebilcock, "The Law and Economics of Immigration Policy," 5 *American Law and Economy Review* 271 (2003). The situation is somewhat analogous to the possibility of increased voter support for social programs such as cash assistance (Temporary Assistance to Needy Families), Food Stamps, and the Earned Income Tax Credit once officials remove "bad apples" from those programs. This possibility is explored in Peter H. Schuck and Richard J. Zeckhauser, *Targeting in Social Programs: Avoiding Bad Bets, Removing Bad Apples* (Washington, DC: Brookings Institution Press, 2006).

34. Americans have always exhibited this ambivalence. See Peter H. Schuck, "Immigration," in *Understanding America: Unique Institutions, Distinctive Policies*, ed. Peter H. Schuck and James Q. Wilson (forthcoming 2007).

35. After many years of intense debate over immigration policy, the public – or at least an important subset of it – may be arriving at a more balanced, sophisticated view about what is realistically possible with respect to immigration enforcement. In October 2005, the Manhattan Institute for Policy Research released a new poll of 800 registered "likely" Republican voters (see the press release from Manhattan Institute for Policy Research, October 17, 2005). According to the findings, 72 percent of these voters favored an earned legalization proposal combined with tougher border

security and employer sanctions, and an even higher share (84 percent) agreed with the proposition that it is not possible to deport all illegal aliens. (On the other hand, this proposition is so obviously true that one might have hoped for 100 percent agreement!)

36. See note 10.

37. In this special sense, the relation between preferences and policy must be unreasonable. This, of course, is the teaching of the impossibility theorem and of the immense literature that it has spawned. See Kenneth Arrow, *Social Choice and Individual Values* (New Haven, CT: Yale University Press, 1951).

38. *League of United Latin American Citizens v. Wilson*, 908 *F.Supp.* 755 (C.D. Cal. 1995). Proposition 200 may well suffer the same fate in the courts.

3. Carved from the Inside Out

1. This has led scholars of immigration to study countries such as France and Germany as archetypes of immigration and nonimmigration states, respectively. See Rogers Brubaker, *Immigration and Citizenship in France and Germany* (Cambridge, MA: Harvard University Press, 1989).

2. K. A. Appiah and H. L. Gates, Jr., *Identities* (Chicago: University of Chicago Press, 1995).

3. Patrick Weil, "Access to Citizenship: A Comparison of Twenty-Five Nationality Laws," in *Citizenship Today: Global Perspectives and Practices*, ed. T. A. Aleinikoff and Douglas Klusmeyer (Washington, DC: Carnegie Endowment for International Peace, 2001), 17–35.

4. Appiah and Gates, *Identities*. Also see W. A. V. Clark, *Immigrants and the American Dream: Remaking the Middle Class* (New York: Guilford, 2003).

5. Louis Hartz, *The Liberal Tradition in America: An Interpretation of American Political Thought Since the Revolution* (New York: Harcourt, Brace and World, 1955).

6. Gunnar Myrdal, *An American Dilemma: The Negro Problem and Modern Democracy* (London: Transaction, 1996).

7. Judith Shklar, *American Citizenship – The Quest for Inclusion; The Tanner Lecture on Human Values* (Cambridge, MA: Harvard University Press, 1991), 4–5.

8. I say systematic philosophical scrutiny because, as has been made abundantly clear during recent congressional debates, plenty of empirical data about immigration and immigrants exist. Yet, as has also been made clear by the vast gulf that exists between the bills produced by the House and the Senate, there is little consensus on what the purpose of immigration ought to be and which immigrants are entitled to a permanent place in American society.

9. Aristide R. Zolberg, *A Nation by Design: Immigration Policy in the Fashioning of America* (Cambridge, MA: Harvard University Press, 2006) (on the Passenger Act, see 110–111). Zolberg's larger thesis is that immigration in the United States has been regulated more than is usually acknowledged and that the regulation of immigration was part of a larger project of nation-building.

While much of what he says is true in that the states did regulate immigration and that zealous support for nativist restrictions has surfaced periodically throughout American history, even his detailed history of immigration regulation in the United States identifies no consistent set of political or cultural goals that constitute the nation-building mission he claims to support.

10. Daniel J. Tichenor, *Dividing Lines: The Politics of Immigration Control in America* (Princeton, NJ: Princeton University Press, 2002).

11. Perhaps Patrick Buchanan's short-lived candidacy most closely approximates an anti-immigrant politics; however, the brevity of his run muted much of his influence and further underscored the degree to which Americans have avoided making immigration central to electoral politics.

12. I would like to reiterate that this is a limited claim: there have been racist and nativist politicians who have had a broad and deep influence on American politics. I seek only to state that none has succeeded in forcing the issue of border control.

13. T. A. Aleinikoff, *Semblances of Sovereignty: The Constitution, the State, and American Citizenship* (Cambridge, MA: Harvard University Press, 2002).

14. Tichenor, *Dividing Lines*.

15. Ibid.

16. Linda Bosniak takes up this topic in Chapter 6 of this volume.

17. Rogers Smith, *Civic Ideals: Conflicting Visions of Citizenship in U.S. History* (New Haven, CT: Yale University Press, 1997).

18. Peter Schuck and Rogers Smith, *Citizenship Without Consent* (New Haven, CT: Yale University Press, 1985).

19. James Kettner, *The Development of American Citizenship, 1608–1870* (Chapel Hill: University of North Carolina Press, 1978).

20. Samuel Huntington, *Who Are We? The Challenges to America's National Identity* (New York: Simon and Schuster, 2004), 114.

21. Kettner, *Development of American Citizenship*, 41.

22. Indeed, references to the partial citizenship of various groups within American society can be found in a range of judicial opinions issued well into the 19th century (see Smith, *Civic Ideals*). The idea of multiple partial citizenships is one that democratic states eschew but find themselves unable to avoid instantiating (see Elizabeth F. Cohen, "The Myth of Full Citizenship," PhD dissertation, Yale University, 2003).

4. A Biblical Perspective on Immigration Policy

1. Biblical citations throughout this chapter are from the New International Version.

2. G. I. Williamson, *The Westminster Confession of Faith* (Philadelphia, PA: Presbyterian and Reformed Publishing, 1964), 242.

3. Williamson, *Westminster*, 240. See Williamson's entire commentary on this chapter of the Westminster Confession. Another excellent source of great value in my research was Matthew Henry's six-volume *A Commentary on the Holy Bible* (Chicago: W.P. Blessing, undated).

4. The term "theocracy" as used in this chapter means the unique, covenantal relationship between Jehovah and ancient Israel. It does not mean direct political rule by God in a given nation, and it especially does not mean the fear-mongering implications intended by antireligious political interests who invoke the term today as a rhetorical fragmentation grenade. See Chapter 4 of Paul Marshall's *God and the Constitution: Christianity and American Politics* (Lanham, MD: Rowman and Littlefield, 2002), particularly 65–70. Marshall's discussion notes that even "theocracy" in ancient Israel included human leaders chosen by the people to carry out the day-to-day functions of civil government.

5. Williamson, *Westminster*, 141–143.

6. Quoted in Marshall, *God and the Constitution*, 92.

7. Marshall, *God and the Constitution*, 96.

8. Religious organizations and denominational groups, in addition to faithful individuals, have throughout American history voiced moral views in the public political discourse. That role, in relation to how certain religious groups have dealt with immigration, is discussed in James C. Russell, *Breach of Faith: American Churches and the Immigration Crisis* (Raleigh, NC: Representative Government Press, 2004). For an in-depth discussion of religion's role in American public affairs, there are plenty of sources available. Recent new contributions to this subject include Daniel L. Dreisbach, *Thomas Jefferson and the Wall of Separation Between Church and State* (New York: New York University Press, 2002), and the edited volume by Dreisbach, Mark D. Hall, and Jeffry H. Morrison, *The Founders on God and Government* (Lanham, MD: Rowman and Littlefield, 2004), to both of which I have referred. In addition, there is the classic by Richard John Neuhaus, *The Naked Public Square* (Grand Rapids, MI: William B. Eerdmans, 1984).

9. See the Westminster Confession, Chapter 23, paragraph 4, which may be found in Williamson, *Westminster*, 240.

10. Although many sources informed this section, Russell Kirk's *The Roots of American Order*, 3rd ed. (Washington, DC: Regnery Gateway, 1991) was one of the most significant, as were Francis Schaeffer's *How Should We Then Live?* and *A Christian Manifesto*, contained in the five-volume edition of Schaeffer's *Complete Works* (Wheaton, IL: Crossway Books, 1982).

11. See Schaeffer, *A Christian Manifesto*, for a fuller discussion of this subject.

12. Schaeffer has expounded on this subject. Of note, Alister McGrath's *The Twilight of Atheism* (New York: Doubleday, 2004) describes some of the Enlightenment's consequences in the West via the French Revolution (Chapter 2) and beyond.

13. Os Guinness, *The American Hour: A Time of Reckoning and the Once and Future Role of Faith* (New York: Free Press, 1993), 339.

14. Schaeffer, *A Christian Manifesto*, 427–428.

15. See, for example, Schaeffer, *A Christian Manifesto*, especially Chapter 2, and Jeffry H. Morrison, "John Witherspoon's Revolutionary Religion," in Dreisbach, Hall, and Morrison, *Founders*, 117–146.

16. Henry, *Commentary*, 2:457.

17. Interestingly, Rahab was an ancestor of both King David and Jesus; see Matthew 1:5.

18. See Marilyn C. Baseler, *Asylum for Mankind: America* (Ithaca, NY: Cornell University Press, 1998), 1607–1800; and James R. Edwards, Jr., "Public Charge Doctrine: A Fundamental Principle of American Immigration Policy," Center for Immigration Studies Backgrounder, May 2001 (available at http://www.cis.org/articles/2001/back701.html).

19. See, for example, Otis L. Graham, Jr., *Unguarded Gates: A History of America's Immigration Crisis* (Lanham, MD: Rowman and Littlefield, 2003); Baseler, *Asylum for Mankind*; and Bernadette Maguire, *Immigration: Public Legislation and Private Bills* (Lanham, MD: University Press of America, 1997).

20. Marshall, *God and the Constitution*, 141–142.

21. Stanley Weintraub, *Silent Night: The Story of the World War I Christmas Truce* (New York: The Free Press, 2001).

22. Nolan Malone, Kaari F. Baluja, Joseph M. Costanzo, and Cynthia J. Davis, "The Foreign-Born Population: 2000," Census 2000 Brief (Washington, DC: U.S. Census Bureau, U.S. Department of Commerce), 2. Also see Office of Immigration Statistics, *2003 Yearbook of Immigration Statistics* (Washington, DC: U.S. Department of Homeland Security, 2004); Steven A. Camarota, "Economy Slowed, But Immigration Didn't: The Foreign-Born Population, 2000–2004," Center for Immigration Studies Backgrounder, November 2004 (available at http://www.cis.org/articles/2004/back1204.html); and James G. Gimpel and James R. Edwards, Jr., *The Congressional Politics of Immigration Reform* (Boston: Allyn and Bacon, 1999), 5–6.

23. See Roy Beck, *The Case Against Immigration: The Moral, Economic, Social, and Environmental Reasons for Reducing U.S. Immigration Back to Traditional Levels* (New York: W.W. Norton, 1996), 38–42.

24. See especially George J. Borjas, *Heaven's Door: Immigration Policy and the American Economy* (Princeton, NJ: Princeton University Press, 1999); James P. Smith and Barry Edmonston, eds., *The New Americans: Economic, Demographic, and Fiscal Effects of Immigration* (Washington, DC: National Academy Press, 1997); Beck, *The Case Against Immigration*; and Graham, *Unguarded Gates*, for a fuller elaboration.

25. See Borjas's work, particularly *Heaven's Door*. Other important sources include Smith and Edmonston, *The New Americans*; and Roy Beck, "'Occupation Collapse' and Poverty Wages: Consequences of Large Guestworker Programs," Testimony before the U.S. House Judiciary Subcommittee on Immigration, Border Security, and Claims, March 24, 2004.

26. While a number of sources illustrate the risks and range of adverse effects immigration has had on the United States, Borjas's *Heaven's Door*, Beck's *The Case Against Immigration*, Arthur M. Schlesinger, Jr.'s *The Disuniting of America: Reflections on a Multicultural Society* (New York: W.W. Norton, 1998), and Graham's *Unguarded Gates* rank among the best.

27. See Beck, *The Case Against Immigration*, Chapters 5, 8, and 9; and Borjas, *Heaven's Door*. Borjas gives many sobering examples of the adverse impact that mass immigration has on vulnerable Americans, but two sufficiently

illustrate the point: "In an $8 trillion economy, native earnings [lost due to immigrants' redistribution of wealth] would drop by about $152 billion" (91) and "It turns out that African Americans are likely to lose from immigration ... [b]ecause blacks own a relatively small proportion of the capital stock of the United States ... [and] because post-1965 immigrants tend to be disproportionately less skilled, they are much more likely to compete with black workers than with white workers" (93).

28. Polls have consistently shown that at least a plurality – and often a majority – of the American public favors reductions in the levels of immigration, including legal immigration. Only a bare minority – usually in single digits – supports increasing immigration levels. For instance, a 1986 CBS News/*New York Times* poll found 52 percent of respondents favored cutting immigration and just 11 percent favored raising it; more than 65 percent wanted immigration cuts in 1994, the American National Election Study reported, with a mere 5 percent favoring immigration increases. This pattern has held firmly for at least two decades. A Westhill Partners/Hotline poll in February 2005 said 37 percent favored keeping legal immigration at its present level, 39 percent wanted it cut, and 14 percent were in favor of increasing it (available at http://www.westhillhotlinepoll.com/WHP_HotlinePoll_February.pdf). See also Gimpel and Edwards, *Congressional Politics*, Chapter 2.

5. The Moral Dilemma of U.S. Immigration Policy

1. Walzer and Rawls are discussed later in the chapter. See also Thomas Nagel, "The Problem of Global Justice," *Philosophy and Public Affairs* 33 (2005): 113–147; and David Miller, *On Nationality* (Oxford: Oxford University Press, 1975).
2. See Jennifer L. Hochschild and Nathan Seovronick, *The American Dream and the Public Schools* (New York: Oxford University Press, 2003), 9–11.
3. Nearly all data are from George J. Borjas, *Heaven's Door: Immigration Policy and the American Economy* (Princeton, NJ: Princeton University Press, 1999), 8–11. The final statistic, on first-generation newcomers, is from the U.S. Census Bureau, Profile of the Foreign Born Population in the United States: 2000. Current Population Reports, Special Studies. U.S. Census Bureau (document P23-206) (Washington, DC: U.S. Government Printing Office, December 2001).
4. George J. Borjas, "The U.S. Takes the Wrong Immigrants," *Wall Street Journal*, April 5, 1990, A18. The quotation continues, "75% of legal immigrants in 1987 were granted entry because they were related to an American citizen or resident, while only 4% were admitted because they possessed useful skills."
5. The basic statistics here are from Borjas.
6. See Chapter 10, this volume. I discuss Borjas later.
7. The report does not emphasize the causal role of immigration, but see Michael A. Stoll, "Taking Stock of the Employment Opportunities of Less-Educated African American Men," Center for Policy Analysis and Research, June 2006.

8. Sec Douglas S. Massey, Jorge Durand, and Nolan J. Malone, *Beyond Smoke and Mirrors: Mexican Immigration in an Era of Economic Integration* (New York: Russell Sage, 2003), 150–151; conceding the wage effects discussed earlier, see 154.

9. Borjas, *Heaven's Gate*, 11, and 22–38, 82–86, 103–104. For an update, see George Borjas, "The Labor Demand Curve Is Downward Sloping: Reexamining the Impact of Immigration on the Labor Market," *Quarterly Journal of Economics* 118, No. 4 (2003): 1335–1374. See also Borjas's Center for Immigration Studies Backgrounder "Increasing the Supply of Labor Through Immigration: Measuring the Impact on Native-Born Workers," which argues that immigration between 1980 and 2000, by increasing the labor supply, reduced the wages of native-born men by 4 percent. Among natives without a high school education (roughly the bottom 10 percent), he estimates the reduction at 7.4 percent. The impact on blacks and Hispanics is especially great because they form a disproportionately large share of high school dropouts. Finally, the effect holds regardless of whether immigration is legal or illegal.

10. Borjas, *Heaven's Gate*, 176–177.

11. See Howard F. Chang, "Public Benefits and Federal Authorization for Alienage Discrimination by the States," *New York University Annual Survey of American Law* 58 (2002): 357–570.

12. Nolan McCarty, Keith T. Poole, and Howard Rosenthal, *Polarized America: The Dance of Ideology and Unequal Riches* (Walras-Pareto Lectures) (Cambridge, MA: MIT Press, 2006), Chapter 4.

13. See Miller, *On Nationality*.

14. See A. Alesina, R. Baquir, and W. Easterley, "Public Goods and Ethnic Divisions," *Quarterly Journal of Economics* 114 (1999): 1243–1284.

15. Of course, there are important debates about whether foreign aid is efficacious. For skeptical views, see William Easterley, *The White Man's Burden: Why the West's Efforts to Aid the Rest Have Done So Much Ill and So Little Good* (New York: Penguin, 2006).

16. Michael Walzer, *Spheres of Justice: A Defense of Pluralism and Equality* (New York: Basic Books, 1983); see Chapter 2, "Membership."

17. Walzer has developed this argument in a number of places, perhaps most pointedly in his "Philosophy and Democracy," *Political Theory* 9 (1981): 379–399; this essay complements the approach of his *Spheres of Justice*.

18. Miller, *On Nationality*, 96.

19. Wendy M. Rahn discusses evidence suggesting that it is harder to sustain mutual trust in ethnically and racially diverse communities. See her "Globalization, the Decline of Civic Commitments, and the Future of Democracy," unpublished paper, available at http://www.polisci.umn.edu/faculty/wrahn/Globalization_the_Decline.pdf.

20. Similarly, Philip Pettit argues that if we are to speak of "peoples" – understood as collective agents capable of making decisions that bind all their members – then we must suppose that the persons who compose these societies "must subscribe as a matter of common awareness to certain ideas about how their affairs should be ordered. They must treat these ideas as common

reasons that constitute the only currency in which it is ultimately legitimate to justify the way things are done in the collective organizing of their affairs." See Philip Pettit, "Rawls's Peoples," in *Rawls's Law of Peoples: A Realistic Utopia*, ed. Rex Martin and David Reidy (Oxford: Blackwell, 2006).

21. I paraphrase here the general approach of John Rawls, *A Theory of Justice* (Cambridge, MA: Harvard, 1971).

22. John Rawls, *Political Liberalism* (New York: Columbia University Press, 1993), 5–6. See also Rawls, *Theory of Justice*.

23. John Rawls, *The Law of Peoples* (Cambridge, MA: Harvard University Press, 1999), 18. Rawls also emphasizes that principles of justice among peoples should take seriously an international duty of toleration.

24. Some misread Rawls's *Political Liberalism* as insisting that principles of justice are limited to matters about which we can achieve an "overlapping consensus." If so, it would then seem obvious that, since in the international arena we encounter more diversity, principles of global justice will therefore need to be thin. However, this misreads Rawls's idea of political liberalism: the idea of an "overlapping consensus" is an account of how principles of justice can be stable given a plurality of conflicting "comprehensive" philosophical and religious views, not an argument that the only justified principles are those that secure a consensus.

25. The account that follows draws on my "What Self-Governing Peoples Owe to One Another: Universalism, Diversity, and The Law of Peoples," *Fordham Law Review* 72 (2004): 1721–1738 (Symposium Issue on Rawls and the Law). I am also indebted to various others, including Donald Moon's excellent unpublished paper "Rawls's Law of Peoples"; Michael I. Blake's "Distributive Justice, State Coercion, and Autonomy," *Philosophy and Public Affairs* 30 (Summer 2001): 257–296; and Thomas Nagel's "The Problem of Global Justice," *Philosophy and Public Affairs* 33, No. 2 (2005): 113–147.

26. See Blake, "Distributive Justice, State Coercion, and Autonomy."

27. See Henry S. Richardson, *Democratic Autonomy: Public Reasoning About the Ends of Policy* (New York: Oxford University Press, 2002).

28. Of course, illegitimate governments – tyrannical states – are *not* recognized by subjects as being capable of making decisions that bind all: some citizens do not recognize the authority of government to bind them. We obviously need some account of the conditions under which collective agency and responsibility can be said to exist, but it is often widely recognized that citizens are collectively bound and obligated by the actions of their governments even when they oppose those governments. We could (not?) ask who is responsible for paying reparations for misguided policies that many opposed; all are obligated when the government is legitimate. See Richardson, ibid. See also Philip Pettit, "Collective Persons and Powers," *Legal Theory* 8 (2002): 38–56, available at SSRN: http://ssrn.com/abstract=347280.

29. Blake rightly emphasizes the central role of the mutual imposition of coercive law, though I do not think that coercion is the only important consideration here. It is important that we are bound by the law we make together, but citizens who share a system of law share a great deal. Much governance is not coercive. In addition, we are prepared to coerce outsiders, including those who try to get in illegally.

30. The U.N. Charter and the Universal Declaration of Human Rights are instruments created by "the peoples of the United Nations" or "Member States." See http://www.un.org/aboutun/charter/. Contrast the phrasing "We the peoples of the United Nations" and "We the people of the United States," which open the preambles to the U.N. Charter and the U.S. Constitution. The U.N. Charter closes, "IN FAITH WHEREOF the representatives of the Governments of the United Nations have signed the present Charter." These matters cannot of course be resolved by these textual or historical facts alone. Provinces and states within nations, autonomous territories, and plural or consociational regimes raise additional issues not covered here.

31. See the Report of the International Commission on Intervention and State Sovereignty, "The Responsibility to Protect," available at http://www.iciss.ca/report-en.asp.

32. See Thomas Pogge, *World Poverty and Human Rights: Cosmopolitan Responsibilities and Reforms* (Cambridge: Polity Press, 2002).

33. Howard F. Chang, "The Immigration Paradox: Poverty, Distributive Justice, and Liberal Egalitarianism," *DePaul Law Review* 52 (2003): 759–776, available at http://ssrn.com/abstract=414561.

34. Massey et al., *Beyond Smoke and Mirrors*, 41–45.

35. Ibid., 54–70.

36. Massey et al., *Beyond Smoke and Mirrors*, 158; *1999 Statistical Yearbook of the Immigration and Naturalization Service* (Washington, DC: U.S. Government Printing Office, 2000).

37. See http://www.house.gov/hunter/TRUE.security.html.

38. Such policies were advocated in the 1970s, and pale versions were enacted in the 1980s. See Cheryl Shanks, *Immigration and the Politics of American Sovereignty* (Ann Arbor: University of Michigan Press, 2001), 224. Congressman Peter Rodino and others pushed for such measures, but the requirement actually enacted – that employers fill out a two-identification affidavit – was not effective.

39. Such policies would lessen the need for immigration restrictions and border security.

40. Massey et al., *Beyond Smoke and Mirrors*, 157–163.

41. Is it possible to combine elements of both approaches? One way to combine policies would be to limit the scope of the work done by guestworkers. There may be sectors of the economy in which poorer Americans really prefer not to work, such as agricultural labor. Such work is far from where most poorer Americans live, and the seasonal nature of this work seems appropriate to a guestworker program. Perhaps it would be possible to devise a guestworker program confined to the agricultural sector. We would, however, need to be very careful that confining guestworkers in this way does not promote their exploitation, something we must surely avoid. For a useful discussion, see Michael Blake, "Discretionary Immigration," *Philosophical Topics* 30, No. 2 (Fall 2002): 273–289.

42. See the report by Oxfam, "Like Machines in the Fields: Workers Without Rights in American Agriculture" (2004), available at http://www.oxfamamerica.org/newsandpublications/publications/research_reports/

art7011.html; and also the report by Foodfirst, available at http://www.
foodfirst.org/node/45.

43. I am grateful to Ronald Dworkin for raising this question and also for sup-
plying part of the answer.

6. The Undocumented Immigrant

1. Despite the extensive immigration enforcement authority enjoyed by the government, border enforcement practices have been subject to certain formal
   limits. See Linda S. Bosniak, "Membership, Equality, and the Difference that
   Alienage Makes," *NYU Law Review* 69 (1994): 1047–1149. It should be
   noted, however, that these limitations are currently far fewer than those that
   prevailed before the draconian curtailments of the last decade.
2. Bosniak, "Membership, Equality, and the Difference that Alienage Makes."
3. The cities of New York, San Francisco, and Seattle, the state of Maine, and
   scores of other localities are among those that have enacted such policies.
4. The recent decision by the Treasury Department to allow banks to honor the
   "matricula consular" – a form of identification issued by the Mexican government – could be described as facilitating noncooperation as well. Critics
   charge that permitting use of the "matricula consular" is "a kind of 'stealth'
   amnesty that grants undocumented immigrants unfair access to mainstream
   American society." See Tessie Borden, "Illegal Migration Foes Target ID's,"
   Arizona Republic, August 30, 2003.
5. Michael Walzer, *Spheres of Justice* (New York: Basic Books, 1983), 58.
6. Benjamin Smith, "INS Offering Reassurance to Illegals on 9/11 Cash," *New
   York Sun*, June 18, 2002. This guarantee applied to employers of undocumented immigrants as well.
7. *Daily Hegemonist*, "What to make of the fact that they're so eager to disburse
   funds that they're perfectly willing to hand over large sums of public money
   to the families of illegal aliens – illegal aliens themselves – while, incredi-
   bly, making promises not to enforce the immigration statutes with regards
   to same (some victims, as members of protected classes, apparently being
   above the law of the land)?" September 1, 2003, http://www.hegemonist.com/
   hegemony/2003/09/blood_money.html.
8. In fact, other laws, in the mode of nonreporting regulations, will sometimes
   penalize employers for reporting the status of an undocumented immigrant to
   the immigration authorities. For example, an employer who reports undocumented immigrants to the former INS, now DHS, in response to her participation in a union organizing drive may be deemed to have violated the
   National Labor Relations Act. On the other hand, even if such a violation is
   found, the remedy available to the employee is drastically limited by virtue
   of her unauthorized immigration status.
9. Under the original language of the initiative, the provision would have swept
   further, but Arizona's attorney general narrowly interpreted the measure
   before ordering implementation in order (apparently) to insulate it from court
   invalidation. The interpretation limits the benefits at issue to those that are

not federally mandated (i.e., to state welfare assistance). Affected programs include general assistance, sight conservation for the visually impaired, utility repair and assistance, and adult foster care. The Federation for American Immigration Reform has sued the state on grounds that the attorney general impermissibly restricted the definition of "public benefit" and seeks to expand the scope of Proposition 200 to include many additional benefits, such as housing, food assistance, college education, and employment benefits.

10. Defenders of Proposition 200 will likely argue that in the 1996 Personal Responsibility and Work Opportunity Reconciliation Act, Congress affirmatively authorized the states to deny most benefits to the undocumented thereby implicitly "consenting" to state enforcement of immigration-related law. In this theory, Congress has devolved some of its immigration power (which, recall, has been deemed to be largely unreviewable by the courts) to the states. Opponents will counter that the immigration power is an inherently and necessarily nondevolvable federal power, "reserved by the architecture and animating principles of the Constitution to Congress and the President." See Michael J. Wishnie, "Laboratories of Bigotry? Devolution of the Immigration Power, Equal Protection and Federalism," *NYU Law Review* 76 (2001): 493, 499. Opponents will also raise due process arguments in relation to the criminal penalties imposed.

11. The agency is deemed to "know," however, only under limited circumstances, and is specifically not authorized to "ask."

12. The Undocumented Alien Emergency Medical Assistance Amendments to the Medicare Act of 2003 (H.R. 3722, Rohrabacher) was defeated in April 2004. However, the Department of Health and Human Services has implemented regulations that require hospitals to verify the immigration status of patients and to keep that information on record for potential federal audit as a condition of emergency care reimbursement.

13. Maldef press release.

14. Id.

15. For an extremely useful discussion of recent policy developments and criticisms thereof, see Michael J. Wishnie, "State and Local Police Enforcement of Immigration Laws," *University of Pennsylvania Journal of Constitutional Law* 6 (2004): 1084.

16. CLEAR Act (Clear Law Enforcement for Criminal Alien Removal Act), H.R. 2671.

17. *U.S. v. Morrison*, 529 U.S. 598 (2000).

7. Good Neighbors and Good Citizens

1. Jeffrey S. Passel, "The Size and Characteristics of the Unauthorized Migrant Population in the U.S.: Estimates Based on the March 2005 Current Population Survey," Research Report (Washington, DC: Pew Hispanic Center, March 7, 2006), 5.

2. *American Public Opinion and Foreign Policy: Global Views 2004* (Chicago: Chicago Council on Foreign Relations, 2004), 12–13, 47–48.

3. John Higham, *Strangers in the Land: Patterns of American Nativism 1860–1925* (New York: Atheneum, 1975).

4. John Higham, "Another Look at Nativism," in *Send These to Me: Jews and Other Immigrants in Urban America* (New York: Atheneum, 1975), 103.

5. John Higham, "Instead of a Sequel, or, How I Lost My Subject," in *The Handbook of International Migration: The American Experience*, ed. Charles Hirschman, Philip Kasinitz, and Josh DeWind (New York: Russell Sage Foundation, 1999), 383–389.

6. Higham, "Another Look at Nativism," 106–108; see also Higham, "Ethnic Pluralism in Modern American Thought" and "Another American Dilemma," in his *Send These to Me*, 196–246.

7. See recent polling data in "America's Immigration Quandary: No Consensus on Immigration Problem or Proposed Fixes" (Washington, DC: Pew Hispanic Center, March 30, 2006), 13.

8. This point gets elaborated in Peter Skerry and Devin Fernandes, "Citizen Pain: Fixing the Immigration Debate," *New Republic*, May 8, 2006, 14–16.

9. Passel, "The Size and Characteristics of the Unauthorized Migrant Population in the U.S.," 2–3.

10. Jeffrey S. Passel, "Unauthorized Migrants: Numbers and Characteristics – Background Briefing Prepared for Task Force on Immigration and America's Future" (Washington, DC: Pew Hispanic Center, June 14, 2005), 11–13.

11. Seth Mydans, "Poll Finds Tide of Immigration Brings Hostility," *New York Times*, June 27, 1993, A1, A16.

12. "Demographic Profile of the Electorate: November 8, 1994," *Los Angeles Times* Election Poll.

13. Alan Wolfe, *One Nation, After All* (New York: Viking, 1998), 147.

14. Ronald Brownstein, "Bush Needs to Imitate Clinton to Solve Immigration," *Los Angeles Times*, July 23, 2001, A10.

15. Linda Chavez, "Legalizing Immigrants Just Makes Sense," *Chicago Sun-Times*, July 18, 2001, 47.

16. Cardinal Roger Mahony, "Immigrant Workers Deserve Legal Status and Respect," *Los Angeles Times*, June 8, 2000, 13.

17. Quoted in Edward Alden and Scott Heiser, "A Border War: Why America Is Split Over Its Rising Numbers of Illegal Immigrants," *Financial Times*, August 29, 2005, 11.

18. See John Bowe, "Nobodies: Does Slavery Exist in America," *New Yorker*, April 21 and 28, 2003, 106–133.

19. Passel, "Unauthorized Migrants: Numbers and Characteristics," 35.

20. Passel, "The Size and Characteristics of the Unauthorized Migrant Population in the U.S.," 5.

21. Derived from the numbers cited in Passel, "Unauthorized Migrants: Numbers and Characteristics," 35; and the Census Bureau's 2005 estimate of the total number of Hispanics in the United States – 42.7 million.

22. Ruth Milkman, "Immigrant Organizing and the New Labor Movement in Los Angeles," *Critical Sociology* 26, Nos. 1/2 (2000): 59.

23. Rob Paral, "The Potential for New Homeownership Among Undocumented Latino Immigrants," prepared for the National Association of Hispanic Real Estate Professionals, n.d.

24. Roberto Suro, "Survey of Mexican Immigrants – Part One: Attitudes About Immigration and Major Demographic Characteristics" (Washington, DC: Pew Hispanic Center, March 2, 2005), 10, 23.

25. Marti Dinerstein, "Giving Cover to Illegal Aliens: IRS Tax ID Numbers Subvert Immigration Law," Center for Immigration Studies Backgrounder (Washington, DC: Center for Immigration Studies, November 2002).

26. Passel, "The Size and Characteristics of the Unauthorized Migrant Population in the U.S.," 6–9.

27. "Modes of Entry for the Unauthorized Population," Fact Sheet (Washington, DC: Pew Hispanic Center, May 22, 2006), 1.

28. Douglas S. Massey and Nolan Malone, "Pathways to Legal Immigration," *Population Research and Policy Review* 21 (2002): 474.

29. For an instructive critique of this program, see Mark Krikorian, "Taking Chances: The Folly of the Visa Lottery," Center for Immigration Studies Backgrounder (Washington, DC: Center for Immigration Studies, July 2004).

30. Massey and Malone, "Pathways to Legal Immigration," 477–479, 484–486.

31. David A. Martin, "Twilight Statuses: A Closer Examination of the Unauthorized Population," Policy Brief (Washington, DC: Migration Policy Institute, June 2005).

32. Martin, "Twilight Statuses," 6.

33. Peter Skerry, field interview notes with the U.S. Border Patrol, February 13–27, 1998.

34. On the Catholic Church's position, see Donald Kerwin, "Immigration Reform and the Catholic Church," Migration Information Source (Washington, DC: Migration Policy Institute, May 1, 2006). Also see Roger Mahony, "Called by God to Help," *New York Times*, March 22, 2006, A19.

35. This is actually a very complicated issue. Like most law enforcement, immigration control is highly discretionary. For a now dated but still invaluable treatment of this question, see Edwin Harwood, *In Liberty's Shadow: Illegal Aliens and Immigration Law Enforcement* (Stanford, CA: Hoover Institution Press, 1986).

36. Stephen Losey, "When Alien Smugglers Go Free, Morale Suffers at Border Patrol," *FederalTimes.com*, June 7, 2006. This has long been a problem for immigration law enforcement; see George J. Weissinger, "Law Enforcement and the Immigration and Naturalization Service: Resolving an Apparent Contradiction," PhD dissertation (New York: New York University Press, 1982), 74–76.

37. Peter Skerry, field interview notes with the U.S. Border Patrol along the California-Mexico border, 1996–1998.

38. Miriam Jordan, "California Race Highlights Split on Immigration," *Wall Street Journal*, October 18, 2005, B1, B9.

39. *FOX News*/Opinion Dynamics Poll, April 5–6, 2006.

40. *Time*, January 27, 2006.

41. Richard Alba and Victor Nee, *Remaking the American Mainstream: Assimilation and Contemporary Immigration* (Cambridge, MA: Harvard University Press, 2003), 217–230.

42. See George Borjas and Lawrence Katz, "The Evolution of the Mexican-Born Workforce in the United States," NBER Working Paper No. 11281 (Cambridge, MA: National Bureau of Economic Research, 2005).

43. Here we agree with Stanley Renshon, who puts it well when he acknowledges among Americans today "the premature, but not unrealistic, concern of our potential evolution into a country in which separate psychological, cultural, and political loyalties trump a coherent national identity." See Stanley A. Renshon, *The 50% American: Immigration and National Identity in an Age of Terror* (Washington, DC: Georgetown University Press, 2005), 144.

44. Robert D. Putnam, *Bowling Alone: The Collapse and Revival of American Community* (New York: Simon and Schuster, 2000).

45. For an early and thoughtful analysis of this problem, see Todd A. Eisenstadt and Cathryn L. Thorup, *Caring Capacity Versus Carrying Capacity: Community Responses to Mexican Immigration in San Diego's North County* (La Jolla: Center for U.S.-Mexican Studies, University of California-San Diego, 1994).

46. Abel Valenzuela, Jr., Nik Theodore, Edwin Melendez, and Ana Luz, *On the Corner: Day Labor in the United States* (Los Angeles: Center for the Study of Urban Poverty, University of California-Los Angeles, January 2006), 14–16.

47. Valenzuela et al., *On the Corner*, 17.

48. Michael Jones-Correa, ed., *Governing American Cities: Inter-Ethnic Coalitions, Competition, and Conflict* (New York: Russell Sage Foundation, 2001); Patrick D. Joyce, *No Fire Next Time: Black–Korean Conflicts and the Future of America's Cities* (Ithaca, NY: Cornell University Press, 2003).

49. Peter A. Morrison and Ira S. Lowry, "A Riot of Color: The Demographic Setting," in *The Los Angeles Riots: Lessons for the Urban Future*, ed. Mark Baldassare (Boulder, CO: Westview Press, 1994), 38, 43.

50. See Renshon, *The 50% American*, 222–223.

51. Samuel P. Huntington, *Who Are We? The Challenges to America's National Identity* (New York: Simon and Schuster, 2004), 238.

52. See Representative Lamar Smith, as quoted on *Morning Edition*, National Public Radio, March 25, 1997; John Fonte, testimony given at U.S. Senate, Committee on the Judiciary, Subcommittee on Immigration, Hearing on Naturalization Requirements and the Rights and Privileges of Citizenship, October 22, 1996; John J. Miller, "The Naturalizers," *Policy Review* 78 (July–August 1996): 50, 52; John J. Miller, *The Unmaking of Americans: How Multiculturalism Has Undermined Americans' Assimilation Ethic* (New York: Free Press, 1998), 149; and Georgie Anne Geyer, *Americans No More: The Death of Citizenship* (New York: Atlantic Monthly Press, 1996), chapters 2–4. See also Peter Salins, *Assimilation, American-Style* (New York: Basic Books, 1997), 215; and Noah Pickus, *True Faith and Allegiance: Immigration and American Civic Nationalism* (Princeton, NJ: Princeton University Press, 2005), 175–178.

53. Higham, "Another American Dilemma," in *Send These to Me*, 243.

54. James C. Scott, *Seeing Like a State: How Certain Schemes to Improve the Human Condition Have Failed* (New Haven, CT, and London: Yale University Press, 1998).

55. A similar point is made in Krishna Guha, "Ethnic Communities Can Be Devout as Well as Good Citizens," *Financial Times*, July 16–17, 2005, 7.

56. For an exploration of these issues in the context of one suburban community, see Peter Skerry, "Immigration and Social Disorder," in *Uniting America: Restoring the Vital Center to American Democracy*, ed. Norton Garfinkle and Daniel Yankelovich (New Haven, CT: Yale University Press, 2006), 124–138.

57. Philip Selznick, *The Communitarian Persuasion* (Washington, DC: Woodrow Wilson Center Press, 2002), 103, 136–137; Philip Selznick, *The Moral Commonwealth: Social Theory and the Promise of Community* (Berkeley: University of California Press, 1992).

58. Selznick, *The Communitarian Persuasion*, 44.

59. Ibid., 20.

60. Ibid.,150.

61. Ibid., 42.

62. Edward Shils and Morris Janowitz, "Cohesion and Disintegration in the Wehrmacht in World War II," in *Center and Periphery: Essays in Macrosociology*, ed. Edward Shils (Chicago and London: The University of Chicago Press, 1975), 383. See also Morris Janowitz, *The Reconstruction of Patriotism: Education for Civic Consciousness* (Chicago and London: The University of Chicago Press, 1983).

63. A recent exploration of this dynamic in the context of the American Southwest can be found in Amy Bridges, *Morning Glories: Municipal Reform in the Southwest* (Princeton, NJ: Princeton University Press, 1997).

64. One treatment of this tendency can be found in Daniel J. Tichenor, *Dividing Lines: The Politics of Immigration Control in America* (Princeton, NJ: Princeton University Press, 2002), 75–85, 114–149.

65. Jean Bethke Elshtain, *Jane Addams and the Dream of American Democracy: A Life* (New York: Basic Books, 2002), 77.

66. Ibid., 168–173.

67. Jane Addams, *Twenty Years at Hull House* (New York: New American Library, 1981), 204.

68. Elshtain, *Jane Addams and the Dream of American Democracy*, 161–163.

69. For an informative and balanced analysis of the Americanization movement that contrasts it with the perspective developed by University of Chicago sociologists with whom Addams was in contact, see Janowitz, *The Reconstruction of Patriotism*, 85–94. See also Morris Janowitz, *Last Half-Century: Societal Change and Politics in America* (Chicago and London: The University of Chicago Press, 1978), 305–306, 453–454.

70. For an informative but critical analysis of Addams and her Progressive colleagues, see Rivka Shpak Lissak, *Pluralism and Progressives: Hull House and the New Immigrants, 1890–1919* (Chicago: University of Chicago Press, 1989), especially 157–181.

71. Addams, *Twenty Years at Hull House*, 42.

72. Addams, *Twenty Years at Hull House*, 41–42; see also Elshtain, *Jane Addams and the Dream of American Democracy*, 52–53.

73. James Q. Wilson, *Varieties of Police Behavior: The Management of Law and Order in Eight Communities* (Cambridge, MA: Harvard University Press), 16.

74. George L. Kelling and James Q. Wilson, "Broken Windows: The Police and Neighborhood Safety," *The Atlantic* 249 (March 1982): 3, 29–38.

75. George L. Kelling and Catherine M. Coles, *Fixing Broken Windows: Restoring Order and Reducing Crime in Our Communities* (New York: The Free Press, 1996).

76. We acknowledge that there is another possible inference about immigration to be drawn from Kelling and Wilson's work. After all, their approach to crime also meant convincing law enforcement professionals to pay more attention to the minor offenses that they traditionally disdained as "social work." Given the ambiguity surrounding illegal immigration that we have emphasized here, one might conclude that Kelling and Wilson's perspective points to waging a campaign to eliminate that ambiguity and persuading law enforcement and the public alike that illegal immigration is an offense worthy of law enforcement's attention. A relevant analogy would be the transformation in public attitudes toward drunken driving wrought by Mothers Against Drunk Driving. Nevertheless, it is our judgment that the ambiguous status of illegal immigration is much more deeply rooted in contemporary American life and not likely to be changed in this way.

77. On the intention of Mexican illegal immigrants not to settle permanently and to return home, see Leo R. Chavez, *Shadowed Lives: Undocumented Immigrants in American Society*, 2nd ed. (Fort Worth, TX: Harcourt Brace College Publishers, 1998). See also Massey and Malone, "Pathways to Legal Immigration."

78. Peter Skerry, "Citizenship Begins at Home: A New Approach to the Civic Integration of Immigrants," *The Responsive Community* (Winter 2003/2004), 30.

79. Little Hoover Commission, *We the People: Helping Newcomers Become Californians* (Sacramento, CA: Little Hoover Commission, June 2002), 34–35, 50–54.

80. *We the People*, 47.

81. A similar point is made in Renshon, *The 50% American*, 179–181.

82. Skerry, "Citizenship Begins at Home," 28.

8. Alien Rights, Citizen Rights, and the Politics of Restriction

1. Daniel J. Tichenor, *Dividing Lines: The Politics of Immigration Control in America* (Princeton, NJ: Princeton University Press, 2002), 8.

2. Milton D. Morris, *Immigration: The Beleaguered Bureaucracy* (Washington, DC: Brookings Institution, 1985), 24–25.

3. Tichenor, *Dividing Lines*, 87–113; Desmond King, *Making Americans: Immigration, Race, and the Origins of the Diverse Democracy* (Cambridge, MA: Harvard University Press, 2000), 199–236.

4. Morris, *Immigration*, 88–89, 110–121; Committee on Government Oper ations, "The Immigration and Naturalization Service: Overwhelmed and Unprepared for the Future," House Report 103–216, Second Report by the Committee on Government Operations (Washington, DC: Congressional Budget Office, 1993).

5. Jim Rutenberg, "G.O.P. Draws Line in Border," *New York Times*, May 26, 2006, A1.

6. Tichenor, *Dividing Lines*, 275–278; American Bar Association Commission on Immigration, "American Justice Through Immigrants' Eyes," available at http://www.abanet.org/publicserv/immigration/Due_Process.html.

7. Peter Brimelow, *Alien Nation: Common Sense About America's Immigration Disaster* (New York: Random House, 1995), 9–10, 264.

8. Audrey Singer, "Welfare Reform and Immigrants: A Policy Review" (2004), 26, available at http://www.brook.edu/dybdocroot/urban/pubs/200405_singer.pdf.

9. See bill at http://www.fas.org/irp/crs/96–499.htm.

10. In fact, PRWORA originally made even many immigrants present at the time of its enactment ineligible for Social Security Income (SSI) and food stamps, but Congress restored eligibility to most preenactment immigrants via the 1997 Balanced Budget Act, the 1998 Agricultural Research Extension and Education Act, and the Farm Security and Rural Investment Act of 2002. The states have chosen to provide TANF and Medicaid benefits to most preenactment immigrants (Singer, "Welfare Reform," 23, 27–28).

11. See summary at http://uscis.gov/graphics/shared/aboutus/statistics/LegisHist/act142.htm.

12. For example, see Michael Fix and Ron Haskins, "Welfare Benefits for Non-Citizens" (2002), available at http://www.brookings.edu/dybdocroot/es/wrb/publications/pb/pb15.htm; and Shawn Fremstad, "Recent Welfare Reform Research Findings: Implications for TANF Reauthorization and State TANF Policies" (2004), available at http://www.cbpp.org/1–30–04wel.htm.

13. Singer, "Welfare Reform," 29–30.

14. Available online at http://www.epic.org/privacy/terrorism/hr3162.html.

15. Available online at http://www.whitehouse.gov/news/releases/2001/11/20011113–27.html.

16. Human Rights Watch, "United States: Guantanamo Two Years On" (2004), available at http://hrw.org/english/docs/2004/01/09/usdom6917.htm.

17. James Risen and Eric Lichtblau, "Bush Lets U.S. Spy on Callers Without Courts," *New York Times*, December 16, 2005, A1; Leslie Cauley, "NSA Has Massive Database of Americans' Phone Calls," *USA Today*, May 11, 2006, available online at http://www.usatoday.com/news/washington/2006–05–10-nsa_x.htm.

18. Rachel L. Swarns and Christopher Drew, "Aftereffects: Immigrants; Fearful, Angry and Confused, Muslim Immigrants Register," *New York Times*, April 25, 2003, A1.

19. Suleman Din, "Terror City," *ColorLines* 7, No. 3 (2004), available online at http://www.arc.org/C_Lines/CLArchive/story7_2_02.html.

20. Maria Panaritis and Jane M. Von Bergen, "Unions Embracing Immigrants," *Philadelphia Inquirer*, September 30, 2003, available online at http://www.philly.com/mld/inquirer/news/local/6893203.htm.

21. Rutenberg, "G.O.P."

22. Neil A. Lewis, "U.S. Judge Halts War-Crime Trial at Guantánamo," *New York Times*, November 9, 2004, A1; Neil A. Lewis, "Federal Judge Deals Setback to Guantánamo Bay Detainees," *New York Times*, January 20, 2005, A20; Neil A. Lewis, "Judge Extends Legal Rights for Guantánamo Detainees," *New York Times*, February 1, 2005, A12.

23. Linda Greenhouse, "Justices to Rule on a Challenge to U.S. Tribunals," *New York Times*, November 8, 2005, A1.

24. Detainee Treatment Act of 2005, available online at http://jurist.law.pitt.edu/gazette/2005/12/detainee-treatment-act-of-2005-white.php.

25. Joel Brinkley and Eric Lichtblau, "U.S. Releases Saudi-American It Had Captured in Afghanistan," *New York Times*, October 12, 2004, A15.

26. Associated Press, "National Briefing/Washington: Hispanic Vote Grew for Bush," *New York Times*, December 22, 2004, A24.

27. Bill Mears, "Rehnquist Slams Congress Over Reducing Sentencing Discretion" (2004), available online at http://www.cnn.com/2004/LAW/01/01/rehnquist.judiciary/.

9. Borderline Madness

1. Peter Andreas, *Border Games: Policing the US-Mexico Divide* (Ithaca, NY: Cornell University Press, 2000).

2. Ibid.

3. Joseph Nevins, *Operation Gatekeeper: The Rise of the "Illegal Alien" and the Making of the U.S.-Mexico Boundary* (New York: Routledge, 2002).

4. See Timothy J. Dunn, *The Militarization of the U.S.-Mexico Border, 1978–1992: Low-Intensity Conflict Doctrine Comes Home* (Austin: Center for Mexican American Studies, University of Texas at Austin, 1996).

5. Nevins, *Operation Gatekeeper*.

6. Andreas, *Border Games*; Nevins, *Operation Gatekeeper*.

7. Andreas, *Border Games*.

8. Douglas S. Massey and René Zenteno, "A Validation of the Ethnosurvey: The Case of Mexico-U.S. Migration," *International Migration Review* 34 (2000): 765–792; Douglas S. Massey, Jorge Durand, and Nolan J. Malone, *Beyond Smoke and Mirrors: Immigration Policy and Global Economic Integration* (New York: Russell Sage Foundation, 2002).

9. Computed from MMP border-crossing histories using methods developed by Massey and Singer. See Douglas S. Massey and Audrey Singer, "New Estimates of Undocumented Mexican Migration and the Probability of Apprehension," *Demography* 32 (1995): 203–213.

10. Thomas J. Espenshade, "Undocumented Migration to the United States: Evidence from a Repeated Trials Model," in *Undocumented Migration to the United States: IRCA and the Experience of the 1980s*, ed. Frank D. Bean, Barry Edmonston, and Jeffrey S. Passel (Washington, DC: Brookings

Institution, 1990), 159 181; Audrey Singer and Douglas S. Massey, "The Social Process of Undocumented Border Crossing," *International Migration Review* 32 (1998): 561–592.

11. Massey et al., *Beyond Smoke and Mirrors*.

10. Immigrant Employment Gains and Native Losses, 2000–2004

1. Studies that have found a significant impact on native wages include George Borjas, "The Labor Demand Curve Is Downward Sloping: Reexamining the Impact of Immigration on the Labor Market," *Quarterly Journal of Economics* 118 (November 2003): 1335–1374; Steven Camarota, "The Effect of Immigrants on the Earnings of Low-Skilled Native Workers: Evidence from June 1991 Current Population Survey," *Social Science Quarterly* (June 1997): 417–431; Robert Topel, "Regional Labor Markets and the Determinants of Wage Inequality," *American Economic Review Papers and Proceedings* 43 (May 1994): 17–22; and Augustine J. Kposowa, "The Impact of Immigration on Unemployment and Earnings Among Racial Minorities in the United States," *Ethnic and Racial Studies* 18 (July 1995): 605–628. Studies that have found small or no impact on native wages include Joseph G. Altonji and David Card, "The Effects of Immigration on the Labor Market Outcomes of Less-Skilled Natives," in *Immigration, Trade, and the Labor Market*, ed. John M. Abowd and Richard B. Freeman (Chicago: University of Chicago Press, 1991); and David Card, "The Impact of the Mariel Boatlift on the Miami Labor Market," *Industrial and Labor Relations Review* 43 (1990): 245–257.

2. Andrew Sum, Paul Harrington, and Ishwar Khatiwada, "New Immigrants in the Labor Force and the Number of Employed New Immigrants in the U.S., 2000–2003," Center for Labor Market Studies, Northeastern University, Boston, November 2003; Andrew Sum, Neeta Fogg, Ishwar Khatiwada, and Sheila Palma, "Foreign Immigration and the Labor Force of the U.S.: The Contributions of New Foreign Immigration to the Growth of the Nation's Labor Force and Its Employed Population, 2000 to 2004," Center for Labor Market Studies, Northeastern University, Boston, July 2004; and Steven Camarota, "Immigration in a Time of Recession" (Washington, DC: Center for Immigration Studies, November 2003).

3. All figures in this study reflect the 2000-based population weights, which were put out by the Census Bureau after the 2000 census revealed that the nation's population was larger than previously thought. By using the new weights, we are able to make comparisons between the years 2000 and 2004. The March data, called the Annual Social and Economic Supplement, includes an extra-large sample of minorities and is considered one of the best sources for information on the foreign-born. The foreign-born are defined as persons living in the United States who were not U.S. citizens at birth.

4. The *CPS* shows that fewer than 200,000 of the 4 million increase in the number of natives not in the labor force was due to an increase in the number of mothers staying home with young children. In terms of college students, the *CPS* shows that the number of natives (18 to 64) not in the labor

force attending college increased by 750,000 between 2000 and 2004. Part of this increase reflects a growth in the overall size of the native college-attending population, but unemployment and non–labor-force participation also increased among college students. Had the labor force participation rate remained the same, the growth in the number of native college students would have accounted for 550,000 of the rise in non–labor-force participation since 2000. With regard to early retirement, the number of natives age 60 to 64 not in the labor force increased by only 330,000 between 2000 and 2004. In total, increases in the number of mothers with young children, college attendees, and early retirees account for only about 25 percent of the 4 million increase in natives not in the labor force.

5. It should be noted that each state in this analysis was treated as just one case, so a large state such as California did not unduly influence the results. As in Tables 10.5, 10.6, and 10.7, the results in Figure 10.3 are what we would expect to find if immigration harmed job opportunities for natives. However, the results from the state tables and Figure 10.3 should be interpreted with caution.

11. Economics of Immigration and the Course of the Debate since 1994

1. Attributed to Will Rogers. Some readers of this chapter have attributed it to Josh Billings.
2. Peter Brimelow, "Time To Rethink Immigration?" *National Review*, June 22, 1992, 30–46.
3. Peter Brimelow, *Alien Nation: Common Sense About America's Immigration Disaster* (New York: Random House, 1995).
4. See Reed Ueda, "Alien Nation: Natterings of a Neo-Nativist," *Wall Street Journal*, April 18, 1995.
5. For the best summary, see George J. Borjas's *Heaven's Door: Immigration Policy and the American Economy* (Princeton, NJ: Princeton University Press, 1999).
6. Charles MacKay, *Extraordinary Popular Delusions and the Madness of Crowds* (New York: Barnes and Noble, 1994).
7. George J. Borjas, "The Economic Benefits of Immigration," *Journal of Economic Perspectives* 9 (Spring 1995): 3–22.
8. Larry Neal and Paul Uselding, "Immigration, a Neglected Source of American Economic Growth: 1790 to 1912," *Oxford Economic Papers*, March 1972, 68–88.
9. Richard A. Easterlin, "Immigration: Economic and Social Characteristics," in *Harvard Encyclopedia of American Ethnic Groups*, ed. Stephan Thernstrom (Cambridge, MA: Belknap Press/Harvard University Press, 1980), 485.
10. Simon Kuznets, *Modern Economic Growth: Rate, Structure and Spread* (New Haven, CT: Yale University Press, 1966).
11. Claudia Goldin, "The Political Economy of Immigration Restriction in the United States, 1890–1921," NBER Working Paper No. 4345 (Cambridge, MA: National Bureau of Economic Research, 1993).

12. James P. Smith and Barry Edmonston, eds., *The New Americans: Economic, Demographic, and Fiscal Effects of Immigration* (Washington, DC: National Academy Press, 1997).

13. George J. Borjas, *Friends or Strangers: The Impact of Immigration on the U.S. Economy* (New York: Basic Books, 1990).

14. George J. Borjas, *Heaven's Door: Immigration Policy and the American Economy* (Princeton, NJ: Princeton University Press, 1999).

15. George J. Borjas, "The Labor Demand Curve Is Downward Sloping: Re-examining the Impact of Immigration on the Labor Market," *Quarterly Journal of Economics* 118 (November 2003): 1335–1374; see http://www.vdare.com/pb/borjas_bombshell.htm.

16. George J. Borjas, *Immigration in High-Skill Labor Markets: The Impact of Foreign Students on the Earnings of Doctorates* (March 2006). NBER Working Paper No. W12085. Available at SSRN, http://srn.com/abstract=888287.

17. Donald Davis and David Weinstein, "Technological Superiority and the Losses from Migration," NBER Working Paper No. 8971 (Cambridge, MA: National Bureau of Economic Research, 2002); see http://www.columbia.edu/~dew35/PDF/Migration.pdf.

12. Immigration and Future Population Change in America

1. The ratio of an earlier (by two years) medium series with and without migration was applied to the most recent Census Bureau projections. See Frederick W. Hollmann, Tammany J. Mulder, and Jeffrey E. Kallon, "Methodology and Assumptions for the Population Projections of the United States: 1999 to 2100" (Washington DC: Bureau of the Census, U.S. Department of Commerce, 2000).

2. The dependency ratio here is the ratio of the population 65+ to those 15–64 expressed as a percentage.

3. Min Zhou, "Contemporary Trends in Immigration to the United States: Gender, Labor-Market Incorporation, and Implications for Family Formation," *Migraciones Internacionales* 2 (2003): 77–95.

13. The Congressional Black Caucus and the Impact of Immigration

1. This chapter focuses on what the CBC does as a collective entity. Some individual CBC members such as Shelia Jackson-Lee (Texas) and Major Owens (New York) have become active sponsors of immigration bills protecting selected groups and expanding immigrant rights and categories.

2. Brian DeBose, "Blacks, Whites View Immigration Similarly, Poll Says Think U.S. Should Limit Number," *Washington Post*, November 17, 2005, A12; Jeff Diamond, "African American Attitudes Towards Immigration Policy," *Internal Migration Review* 32, No.2 (Summer 1998): 451–470; Gallup Poll News Service, "Gallup Poll Social Series Governance," field survey (September 12–15, 2005), Qn. 42.

3. Robert Weisberg, "Collective Versus Dyadic Representation in Congress," *American Political Science Review* 72 (1978): 535–547.

4. Hanna F. Pitkin, *The Concept of Representation* (Berkeley: University of California Press, 1967), 210.
5. Kathleen A. Bratton and Kerry L. Haynie, "Agenda Setting and Legislative Success in State Legislatures: The Effects of Gender and Race," *Journal of Politics* 61 (1999): 658–679; David T. Cannon, *Race, Redistricting, and Representation: The Unintended Consequences of Black Majority Districts* (Chicago: University of Chicago Press, 1999); Katherine Tate, *Black Faces in the Mirror: African Americans and Their Representatives in the U.S. Congress* (Princeton, NJ: Princeton University Press, 2004); Kenny Whitby, *The Color of Representation: Congressional Behavior and Black Interests* (Ann Arbor: University of Michigan Press, 1997).
6. Lawrence H. Fuchs, "The Reactions of Black Americans to Immigration," in *Immigration Reconsidered: History, Sociology, and Politics*, ed. V. Vans-McLaughlin (New York: Oxford University Press, 1990), 304; Diamond, "African American Attitudes," 460–462.
7. When nonelected black leaders such as Jesse L. Jackson, Sr., and Reverend Al Sharpton have weighed in on the issue, more often than not it has been to denounce racist statements or negative portrayals of blacks by the Mexican government and not to advance mutually beneficial policy proposals that take into consideration the needs of American workers who compete with immigrants for basic services and goods. See Cinnamon Stillwell, "Racism Rears Its Ugly Head in Mexico," *San Francisco Chronicle*, August 3, 2005, available at http://www.sfgate.com/cgi-bin/article.cgi?file=/gate/archive/2005/08/03cstillwell.DTL; and CNN.com, "Fox 'Regrets' Remarks About Blacks," May 17, 2005, available at http://www.cnn.com/2005/WORLD/americas/05/16/mexico.fox/.
8. Carol M. Swain, *Black Faces, Black Interests: The Representation of African Americans in Congress* (Cambridge, MA: Harvard University Press, 1993), 3–19.
9. Pitkin, *The Concept of Representation*, 210.
10. Congressional Black Caucus, "Congressman Jesse Jackson, Jr. to Deliver Weekly CBC 'Message To America,'" press release, May 5, 2006, available at http://www.congressionalblackcaucus.net/.
11. Ibid.
12. Peter Katel, "Do Illegal Workers Help or Hurt the Economy?" *Congressional Quarterly* 15, No. 17 (May 6, 2005), available at http://library2.cqpress.com/cqresearcher/document.php?id=cqresrre2005050600&type=hitl.
13. Between January 2005 and October 2006, 11 CBC members sponsored 28 bills, with the majority (13) coming from Shelia Jackson-Lee (Texas). For a description of all bills sponsored in the 109th Congress, see http://www.thomas.loc.gov/cgi-bin/thomas. This is a Library of Congress listing of 779 bills introduced since January 2005.
14. Lynette Clemetson, "Hispanics Now Nation's Largest Minority," *New York Times*, January 22, 2003, available at http://www.nytimes.com/2003/01/22/national/22CENS.html; Alejandro Portes, "From South of the Border: Hispanic Minorities in the United States," in *The Immigration Reader: America in a Multidisciplinary Perspective*, ed. David Jacobson (Washington, DC: Blackwell, 1998), 113–143.

15. Leo F. Estrada, "Making the Voting Rights Act Relevant to the New Demographics of America: A Response to Farrell and Johnson," 79 *North Carolina Law Review* 1283 (June 2001); Bernard Grofman and Lisa Handley, "Minority Population Proportion and Hispanic Congressional Success in the 1970s and 1980s," *American Politics Quarterly* 17 (October 1989): 436–445.

16. The new demographics establish a different playing field. When, for example, New Jersey experienced a vacancy in its U.S. Senate seat after its Democratic senator Jon Corzine became its governor-elect, Corzine nominated Representative Robert Menendez as the state's first Hispanic senator, even though the state has never had an African American senator. Given that there was only one black member of the U.S. Senate during the 109th Congress and two Hispanics, Corzine could have easily justified nominating black representative Donald Payne (D-NJ). The fact that he found it politically expedient to name a Hispanic senator points to the growing influence of Hispanics in the state.

17. Diamond, "African-American Attitudes," 451–470; Fuchs, "Reactions of Black Americans."

18. Douglas S. Massey, Jorge Durand, and Nolan J. Malone, *Beyond Smoke and Mirrors: Mexican Immigration in an Era of Economic Integration* (New York: Russell Sage Foundation, 2002); Hitty Calavita, "Gaps and Contradictions in U.S. Immigration Policy: An Analysis of Recent Reform Efforts," in Jacobson, *The Immigration Reader*, 92–107.

19. Rakesh Kochbar, "Latino Labor Report, 2004: More Jobs for Immigrants but at Lower Wages," Report of the Pew Hispanic Center, 18.

20. Steven A. Camarota, Testimony for U.S. House Committee on Education and the Workforce, November 16, 2005.

21. Ibid.

22. Ibid.

23. Katel, "Do Illegal Workers Help?"

24. George Borjas, Richard Freeman, and Lawrence Katz, "Searching for the Effect of Immigration on the Labor Market," *American Economic Association Papers and Proceedings* 44, No. 3 (May 1996): 246–251.

25. William H. Frey, "Immigration, Domestic Migration, and Demographic Balkanization in America: New Evidence for the 1990s," *Population and Development Review* No. 1 (December 22, 1996): 741–763.

26. William H. Frey, "Central City White Flight," *American Sociological Review* 44 (1979): 425–448.

27. Mary Brown, *Shapers of the Great Debate on Immigration* (Westport, CT: Greenwood Press, 1999).

28. George Borjas, "The Labor Demand Curve Is Downward Sloping: Reexamining the Impact of Immigration on the Labor Market," *Quarterly Journal of Economics* 41, No. 4 (November 2003): 1335–1374.

29. Hugh Graham, "Unintended Consequences: The Convergence of Affirmative Action and Immigration Policy," *American Behavioral Policy* 41 (April 1998): 901.

30. Ibid., 899.

31. Ibid., 910.

32. Jennifer Lee, *Civility in the City: Blacks, Jews, and Koreans in Urban America* (Cambridge, MA: Harvard University Press, 2002).

33. Borjas et al., "Effect of Immigration," 247.
34. Ibid., 250.
35. Frey, "Immigration, Migration, and Balkanization"; William H. Frey and Jonathan Tilove, "Immigrants in, Native Whites Out," *New York Times*, August 20, 1995, 44–45.
36. George Borjas, *Friends or Strangers* (New York: Basic Books, 1990).
37. Brown, *Great Debate*, 241.
38. Roy Beck, *The Case Against Immigration: The Moral, Economic, and Environmental Reasons for Reducing U.S. Immigration Back to Traditional Levels* (New York: Norton, 1996), 121.
39. Ibid., 138.
40. Kenneth Bredemeier, "Work Visas Swell Area's Tech Corps," *Washington Post*, December 1, 2000, E1.
41. William J. Wilson, *When Work Disappears: The World of the New Urban Poor* (New York: Knopf, 1996), 141.
42. Calavita, "Gaps and Contradictions," 95.
43. Camarota, Testimony for U.S. House (see note 18).
44. Congressional Black Caucus, "November Jobless Rate for African Americans a Miserable 10.6 Percent," press release, December 2, 2005, available at http://www.congressionalblackcaucus.net/.
45. Katherine S. Newman, *No Shame in My Game: The Working Poor in the Inner City* (New York: Alfred A. Knopf and the Russell Sage Foundation, 1999); Mary Waters, *Black Identities: West Indian Immigrants and American Realities* (New York: The Russell Sage Foundation and Harvard University Press, paperback edition, 2001).
46. Congressional Black Caucus, "November Jobless Rate."

14. Hispanic and Asian Immigrants

1. Martha Farnsworth Riche, "We're All Minorities Now," *American Demographics* 13, No. 10 (October 1991): 26.
2. For further discussion of the diversity within unity paradigm, refer to Amitai Etzioni, *The New Golden Rule*; Amitai Etzioni, "Diversity within Unity," in *21st Century Opportunities and Challenges: An Age of Destruction or an Age of Transformation*, ed. Howard F. Didsbury, Jr. (Bethesda, MD: World Future Society, 2003), 316–323; Amitai Etzioni, "In Defense of Diversity Within Unity," *The Responsive Community* 13, No. 2 (Spring 2003): 52–57; and www.communitariannetwork.org for the Diversity Within Unity platform and a list of those who have endorsed it.
3. Sheldon Hackney, former chairman of the National Endowment for the Humanities, suggested that "jazz [is] the ideal metaphor for America.... As befits a democratic society, it was created from the bottom up, is non-hierarchical in both its performance and appeal..." (Sheldon Hackney, "Organizing a National Conversation," *Chronicle of Higher Education*, April 20, 1994, A56). See also Roberto Suro, *Remembering the American Dream: Hispanic Immigration and National Policy* (New York: Twentieth Century Fund Press, 1994).

4. Personal communication with Raul Yzaguirre, National Council of La Raza.

5. Rosalie Pedalino Porter, *Forked Tongue: The Politics of Bilingual Education* (New York: Basic Books, 1990), 211 (table). Six states have English-only constitutional amendments, and 11 have statutes or resolutions to that effect.

6. Tamar Jacoby, "What It Means to Be American in the 21st Century," in *Reinventing the Melting Pot: The New Immigrants and What It Means to Be American*, ed. Tamar Jacoby (New York: Basic Books, 2004), 306.

7. In an effort to define the shared framework, Fuchs identifies three concepts as key to the foundation of "civic culture." The ability of people to self-govern responsibly through officials chosen by the polity and the right to equal participation in "public life" comprise two of the inherent ideals integral to the formation of the civic culture. But the third proves the most interesting in its implications for the DWU model. Fuchs writes, "... and third, that individuals who comport themselves as good citizens of the civic culture are free to differ from each other in religion and in other aspects of their private lives...," thus demonstrating that an acceptance of a certain amount of cultural diversity indeed exists as one of the values shared within the very framework. Lawrence H. Fuchs, *The American Kaleidoscope: Race, Ethnicity, and the Civic Culture* (Hanover, PA: Wesleyan University Press, 1990). Ravitch proves slightly more general in her assessment of those values implied within a shared framework or civic culture. But she, too, emphasizes the preeminence of both "tolerance and liberty," as well as "responsibilities of citizenship." See Diane Ravitch, "The Future of American Pluralism," in *The New Promise of American Life*, ed. Lamar Alexander and Chester E. Finn, Jr. (Indianapolis: Hudson Institute, 1995), 85.

8. As stated, various data have been published that scholars on both sides of the issue of Hispanic and Asian voter turnout utilize. Refer to the following publications for additional information about some of the studies on voter turnout for these groups: Carol A. Cassel, "Hispanic Turnout: Estimates from Validated Voting Data," *Political Research Quarterly* 55, No. 2 (June 2002); Rodolfo O. de la Garza, Louis DeSipio, and Martha Menchaca, eds., *Barrio Ballots: Latino Politics in the 1990 Elections* (Boulder, CO: Westview Press, 1994); Rodolfo O. de la Garza, Louis DeSipio, F. Chris Garcia, John Garcia, and Angelo Falcon, eds., *Latino Voices: Mexican, Puerto Rican, and Cuban Perspectives on American Politics* (Boulder, CO: Westview Press, 1992); Louis DeSipio and Harry Pachon, *New Americans by Choice: Political Perspectives of Latino Immigrants* (Boulder, CO: Westview Press, 1994).

9. Linda Chavez, *Out of the Barrio: Toward a New Politics of Hispanic Assimilation* (New York: Basic Books, 1991), 106, 134.

10. de la Garza et al., *Latino Voices*, 100–101.

11. Ibid., 102.

12. Ibid., 87–89.

13. Peter D. Salins, "The Assimilation Contract: Endangered but Still Holding," in Jacoby, *Melting Pot*, 107.

14. Nathan Glazer, "Assimilation Today," in Jacoby, *Melting Pot*, 70.

15. DeSipio and Pachon, *New Americans by Choice*, 93–96.
16. Rodolfo O. de la Garza, "Interests Not Passions: Mexican-American Attitudes Toward Mexico, Immigration from Mexico, and Other Issues Shaping U.S.-Mexican Relations," *International Migration Review* 32, No. 2 (Summer 1998): 406.
17. William J. Bennett, in John Leo, "Cash the Check, Bob," *U.S. News and World Report*, September 18, 1995, 43.
18. James Davidson Hunter, *Before the Shooting Begins: Searching for Democracy in America's Culture War* (New York: Free Press, 1994).
19. Etzioni, *Monochrome Society*, 18–19.
20. Peter Skerry, *Mexican Americans: The Ambivalent Minority* (New York: Free Press, 1993), 16–17.
21. Etzioni, *Monochrome Society*, 25.
22. Ibid., 27.
23. Ibid.
24. Porter, *Forked Tongue*, 214–216.
25. Ibid., 193–221.
26. Samuel P. Huntington, "Mexican Immigration and Hispanization," in *Who Are We? The Challenges to America's National Identity* (New York: Simon and Schuster, 2004), 221–256.
27. de la Garza et al., *Latino Voices*, 98.
28. Alejandro Portes and Richard Schauffler, "Language and the Second Generation: Bilingualism Yesterday and Today," in *The New Second Generation*, ed. Alejandro Portes (New York: Russell Sage Foundation, 1996), 28.
29. Etzioni, *New Golden Rule*.
30. Louis Hartz, *The Liberal Tradition in America: An Interpretation of American Political Thought Since the Revolution* (New York: Harcourt, Brace, 1955); J. G. A. Pocock, *The Machiavellian Moment: Florentine Political Thought and the Atlantic Political Tradition* (Princeton, NJ: Princeton University Press, 1975); Isaac Kramnick, *Republicanism and Bourgeois Radicalism: Political Ideology in Late Eighteenth Century England and America* (Ithaca, NY: Cornell University Press, 1990); Rogers M. Smith, "Beyond Tocqueville, Myrdal and Hartz: The Multiple Traditions in America," *American Political Science Review* 87, No. 3 (September 1993): 549–566.
31. Seymour Martin Lipset, *American Exceptionalism: A Double-Edged Sword* (New York: Norton, 1996).
32. For further discussion of the common good, refer to Amitai Etzioni, *The Common Good* (Cambridge: Polity Press, 2004).
33. Robert Bellah, *Habits of the Heart: Individualism and Commitment in American Life* (Berkeley: University of California Press, 1985).
34. The following works address in greater detail the repercussions of the excessive individualism manifested in the United States during the 1990s: Bellah, *Habits of the Heart*; Francis Fukuyama, *The Great Disruption: Human Nature and the Reconstitution of Social Order* (New York: Free Press, 1999); Mary Ann Glendon, *Rights Talk: The Impoverishment of Political Discourse* (New York: Free Press, 1991); Amitai Etzioni, *The Spirit of Community:*

Rights, Responsibilities, and the Communitarian Agenda (New York: Crown, 1993); Etzioni, *New Golden Rule*. Robert Putnam also followed this line of analysis and provided considerable data to support it in his *Bowling Alone: The Collapse and Revival of American Community* (New York: Simon and Schuster, 2000).

35. Amitai Etzioni, *My Brother's Keeper: A Memoir and a Message* (Lanham, MD: Rowman and Littlefield, 2003); Etzioni, *New Golden Rule*.

36. Francis Fukuyama, "Immigration," in Alexander and Finn, *The New Promise of American Life*, 105. For additional perspectives on how immigrants reinforce the American framework through the strength of their "traditional" values, refer to David Reimers, *Unwelcome Strangers: American Identity and the Turn Against Immigration* (New York: Columbia University Press, 1998), 114; and Raymond Rocco, "Citizenship, Culture, and Community: Restructuring in Southeast Los Angeles," in *Latino Cultural Citizenship: Claiming Identity, Space, and Rights*, ed. William V. Flores and Rina Benmayor (Boston: Beacon Press, 1997), 120.

37. Chavez, *Out of the Barrio*, 108. Note that, as I discussed in *The Monochrome Society*, I do not find acceptable the use of the word "whites" to distinguish between Hispanic and non-Hispanic Americans (refer to Chapter 1 of that volume).

38. Etzioni, *Monochrome Society*.

39. de la Garza et al., *Latino Voices*, 117.

40. DeSipio and Pachon, *New Americans by Choice*, 33–34.

41. Chavez, *Out of the Barrio*, 109.

42. Peggy Levitt, "Two Nations under God?: Latino Religious Life in the United States," in *Latinos Remaking America*, ed. Marcelo M. Suárez-Orozco and Mariela M. Páez (Berkeley: University of California Press, 2002), 150.

43. Ibid., 153–154.

44. Data extrapolated from figures in Population Projections Program, Population Division, Census Bureau, Projections of the Total Resident Population by 5-Year Age Groups, Race, and Hispanic Origin with Special Age Categories: Middle Series, 2050 to 2070; and Population Projections Program, Population Division, Census Bureau, Projections of the Total Resident Population by 5-Year Age Groups, Race, and Hispanic Origin with Special Age Categories: Middle Series, 2075 to 2100. Available at www.census.gov/population/projections/nation/summary/np-t4-h.txt.

45. Data extrapolated from figures in Population Projections Program, Population Division, Census Bureau, Projections of the Total Resident Population by 5-Year Age Groups, Race, and Hispanic Origin with Special Age Categories: Middle Series, 2050 to 2070; and Population Projections Program, Population Division, Census Bureau, Projections of the Total Resident Population by 5-Year Age Groups, Race, and Hispanic Origin with Special Age Categories: Middle Series, 2075 to 2100. Available at www.census.gov/population/projections/nation/summary/np-t4-h.txt.

46. The conclusions drawn in one study, the Latino National Political Survey, suggested optimism from Hispanics regarding their future.

15. Strange Bedfellows, Unintended Consequences

1. Jonathan Tilove and Joe Hallinan, "A Changing America: Patterns of Immigration Followed by White Flight," *Star-Ledger*, August 8, 1993, A1. A more complete version of the story appeared in the *Times-Picayune*, August 8, 1993, A8, under the headline "Immigrants Spur Latest White Flight."
2. Toni Morrison, "On the Backs of Blacks," *Time* magazine special issue, *The New Face of America*, December 2, 1993.
3. William H. Frey and Jonathan Tilove, "Immigrants In, Native Whites Out," *New York Times* magazine, August 20, 1995, 44–45.
4. Frank Sharry, letter to the editor, "Immigrants In, Native Whites Out," *New York Times* magazine, September 10, 1995, 14.
5. Frey and Tilove, "Immigrants In."
6. Census data.
7. Joel Millman, "Going Nativist: How the Press Paints a False Picture of the Effects of Immigration." *Columbia Journalism Review* (January/February 1999), 60ff.
8. Census data and "Population Projections by Race/Ethnicity, Gender and Age for California and Its Counties 2000–2050," California Department of Finance Demographic Research Unit (May 2004).
9. Joel Millman, *The Other Americans: How Immigrants Renew Our Country, Our Economy, and Our Values* (New York: Viking, 1997).
10. Ibid., 314.
11. Ibid., 52–53.
12. Stephen Steinberg, "Immigration, African Americans, and Race Discourse," *New Politics* 10, No. 3 (Summer 2005), 39.
13. Peter H. Schuck, "The New Immigration and the Old Civil Rights," *The American Prospect*, September 21, 1993.
14. Millman, *The Other Americans*, 74.
15. Ibid., 86.
16. "Mexican Leader Criticized for Comment on Blacks," *CNN.com*, May 15, 2005.
17. Ray Marshall, "Hunger on the Farm," *New York Times*, August 25, 1993, A15.
18. Steinberg, "Immigration."
19. Jonathan Tilove, "Affirmative Action Takes a Turn Away From Blacks," *Star-Ledger*, January 2, 1994.
20. "Taking America's Pulse: A Summary Report of The National Conference Survey of Inter-Group Relations" (New York: National Conference of Christians and Jews, 1994).
21. Tim Golden, "Oakland Scratches Plan to Teach Black English," *New York Times*, January 14, 1997, A10.
22. Tilove, "Affirmative Action."
23. Amitai Etzioni, *The Monochrome Society* (Princeton, NJ: Princeton University Press, 2001).
24. Jonathan Tilove, "Census More than Black and White: African-Americans Vying with Hispanics for No. 1 Status," *Times-Picayune*, March 8, 2001, A1.

25. Sonya Ross, "Clinton's Race Panel Disagree on Depth of Black–White Study," *Associated Press*, July 15, 1997.
26. "Gunnar Myrdal's American Dilemma: Do Whites Still Wish that Blacks Would Simply Go Away?" *Journal of Blacks in Higher Education* 42 (January 31, 2004): 71.
27. Jonathan Tilove, "Immigrants Spur Latest White Flight," *Times-Picayune*, August 8, 1993, A8.

16. The Free Economy and the Jacobin State

1. Phil Triadafopoulos, "Shifting Boundaries: Immigration, Citizenship, and the Politics of National Membership in Germany and Canada," PhD dissertation, New School for Social Research, 2004.
2. Christian Joppke, *Immigration and the Nation-State* (Oxford: Oxford University Press, 1999).
3. Matthew J. Gibney and Randall Hansen, "Deportation and the Liberal State: The Forcible Return of Asylum Seekers and Unlawful Migrants in Canada, Germany and the United Kingdom," UNHCR Online, February 2003. Available at http://www.unhcr.org/cgi-bin/texis/vtx/research/opendoc.pdf?tbl=RESEARCH&id=3e59de764#search=%22Deportation%20and%20the%20Liberal%20State%22.
4. Philip L. Martin, "U.S. Immigration," in *Immigration and Asylum from 1900 to the Present*, ed. Matthew J. Gibney and Randall Hansen (Santa Barbara, CA: ABC-CLIO, 2005), 634–645.
5. James F. Hollifield, "France: Republicanism and the Limits of Immigration Control," in *Controlling Immigration: A Global Perspective*, ed. Wayne A. Cornelius, Takeyuki Tsuda, Philip L. Martin, and James F. Hollifield (Stanford, CA: Stanford University Press, 2004), 183–214; Matthew J. Gibney and Randall Hansen, "Asylum Policy in the West: Past Trends and Future Possibilities," in *Poverty, International Migration and Asylum*, ed. George J. Borjas and Jeff Crisp (New York: Palgrave Macmillan, 2005), 70–96.
6. Zig Layton-Henry, "Britain: From Immigration Control to Immigration Management," in Cornelius et al., *Controlling Immigration*, 297–333.
7. Martin, "U.S. Immigration."
8. Rudd Koopmans, "Tradeoffs Between Equality and Difference – The Failure of Dutch Multiculturalism in Cross-National Perspective," paper for the conference "Immigrant Political Incorporation," Radcliffe Institute for Advanced Study, Harvard University, April 22–23, 2005.
9. Suzanne Model, E. P. Martens, Justus Veenman, and Roxane Silberman, "Immigrant Incorporation in France, England and the Netherlands," paper presented at the 50th annual meeting of RC 28, Libourne, France, May 13, 2000.
10. John Mollenkopf, "Assimilating Immigrants in Amsterdam: A Perspective from New York," *Netherlands Journal of Social Sciences* 36, No.2 (2000): 15–34; Robert C. Kloosterman, "Amsterdamned: The Rise of Unemployment in Amsterdam in the 1980s," *Urban Studies* 31, No.8 (1994): 1324–1344.

11. Heather Antecol, Peter Kuhn, and Stephen Trejo, "Assimilation via Prices or Quantities? Labor Market Institutions and Immigrant Earnings Growth in Australia, Canada and the United States," Working Paper Series, Economics Department, Claremont McKenna College, March 2004. Available at http://econ.claremontmckenna.edu/papers/2004–07.pdf.

12. Yasemin N. Soysal, *The Limits of Citizenship* (Chicago: University of Chicago Press, 1994).

13. Pew Research Center, *The Great Divide: How Westerners and Muslims View Each Other* (Washington, DC: The Pew Global Attitudes Project, 2006).

17. The Politics of Immigration and Citizenship in Europe

1. See, for example, Stephen Castles and Mark J. Miller, *The Age of Migration*, 3rd ed. (New York: Guilford Press, 2003).

2. The 14th Amendment states that "All persons born or naturalized in the United States and subject to the jurisdiction thereof are citizens of the United States and of the State wherein they reside." The one exception is for the children of foreign diplomats.

3. For example, many countries offer a form of *jus soli* (the granting of citizenship to the children of noncitizens who are born in that country), but most restrict it to legal immigrants and longer-term residents, with many specific variations in practice.

4. On September 29, 2005, the Subcommittee on Immigration, Border Security, and Claims of the U.S. House of Representatives held an Oversight Hearing on "Dual Citizenship, Birthright Citizenship, and the Meaning of Sovereignty," in which these long-standing American policies were put into question. For academic treatments along the same lines, see Stanley A. Renshon, *The 50% American: Immigration and National Identity in an Age of Terror* (Washington, DC: Georgetown University Press, 2005); and Samuel P. Huntington, *Who Are We? The Challenges to America's National Identity* (New York: Simon and Schuster, 2004).

5. Rogers Brubaker, *Citizenship and Nationhood in France and Germany* (Cambridge, MA: Harvard University Press, 1992), x.

6. Seyla Benhabib, "Transformation of Citizenship: The Case of Contemporary Europe," *Government and Opposition* 37, No. 4 (2002): 439–465, especially 449–453.

7. Brubaker, *Citizenship and Nationhood in France and Germany*, 21.

8. T. H. Marshall, *Citizenship and Social Class* (London: Cambridge University Press, 1950).

9. For a list of countries and regions that allow different forms of franchise for noncitizens, see T. Alexander Aleinikoff and Douglas Klusmeyer, *Citizenship Policies for an Age of Migration* (Washington, DC: Carnegie Endowment for International Peace, 2002), 48–49.

10. Saskia Sassen, *Losing Control? Sovereignty in an Age of Globalization* (New York: Columbia University Press, 1996), 95.

11. Yasemin Nuhoglu Soysal, *Limits of Citizenship: Migrants and Postnational Membership in Europe* (Chicago: University of Chicago Press, 1994).

12. Aleinikoff and Klusmeyer, *Citizenship Policies for an Age of Migration*, 67–68.

13. Ibid., 71–72.

14. For arguments and evidence about the positive effect of naturalization on immigrant integration, see Randall Hansen, "A European Citizenship or a Europe of Citizens? Third Country Nationals in the EU," *Journal of Ethnic and Migration Studies* 24, No. 4 (1998); and Aleinikoff and Klusmeyer, *Citizenship Policies for an Age of Migration*. For the origin of the term "denizen," see Tomas Hammar, *Democracy and the Nation-State: Aliens, Denizens and Citizens in a World of International Migration* (Aldershot: Avebury, 1990).

15. As one EU report put it, most pension systems will be facing an "unsustainable financial burden" within 10–15 years. See European Commission, "Proposal for a Joint Report by the Commission and the Council on Adequate and Sustainable Pensions" (2002), 11–12.

16. My use of the word "liberal" in this chapter is mainly with reference to the issue of citizenship policies, not to the various meanings and traditions associated with the concept of liberalism. In other words, the categories "liberal" and "restrictive" are essentially measures of the inclusiveness of each country's citizenship policies.

17. Note that this is quite different from whether countries allow their émigrés who naturalize elsewhere to maintain their original citizenship. This form of emigrant dual citizenship comes at little direct cost to the emigrant or sending country, and it often serves to maintain and promote stronger cultural and linguistic connections among people who reside permanently in another country. Immigrant dual citizenship, on the other hand, involves the integration of foreigners as naturalized citizens who plan to live, work, and settle permanently in the host or receiving country. This distinction is very important, particularly for the historical countries of emigration – Germany, Greece, Ireland, Italy, the Netherlands, Portugal, Spain, and the United Kingdom – all of which have allowed and even encouraged their ethnic descendants or diaspora to maintain their earlier citizenship but only some of which have extended that option to immigrants within their borders. Immigrant dual citizenship clearly carries a much higher standard.

18. Although in most cases a country's law matches its administrative practices fairly closely, I have attempted to stay true to the latter – based on secondary literature on the countries – when coding for each of these criteria because this represents how the policy is actually carried out in practice. The only noticeable discrepancy in this regard occurs with the Netherlands, as I have explained.

19. I intentionally use the label "1980s," rather than an arbitrary cut-off date, in order to account for any changes that may have occurred at any time during that decade. In a sense, therefore, the effective cut-off date for this time period is 1990.

20. To summarize briefly: *jus soli* is coded as either 0 (not allowed) or 2 (allowed); residency requirements for naturalization are coded as 0 (at least 10 years), 1 (6–9 years), and 2 (5 years or less); and acceptance of dual citizenship for immigrants is coded as either 0 (naturalized citizens must relinquish their

prior citizenship) or 2 (naturalized immigrants can retain their previous citizenship). For a more detailed justification of this coding procedure, as well as the scoring of the individual components for each country, see Marc Morjé Howard, "Variation in Dual Citizenship Policies in the Countries of the EU," *International Migration Review* 39, No. 3 (2005): 697–720.

21. For historical overviews of all 15 EU countries, see the excellent chapters in Randall Hansen and Patrick Weil, eds., *Towards a European Nationality: Citizenship, Immigration, and Nationality Law in the EU* (New York: Palgrave, 2001).

22. For a more complete explanation of the historical variation on citizenship policies, along with a figure showing how the 15 "older" EU countries map out on these factors, see Howard, "Comparative Citizenship," especially 446–448.

23. Italy is an unusual case in that it became more liberal on one factor but more restrictive on another, with no overall change to its aggregate score. It began to accept dual citizenship starting in 1992, but this was balanced by the lengthening of the residency requirement for non-EU citizens from 5 to 10 years.

24. Note that while the official policy of the Netherlands still does not allow for dual citizenship, numerous exceptions were established over the course of the 1990s, resulting in a very liberal dual-citizenship policy in practice. See Maarten P. Vink, "The Limited Europeanization of Domestic Citizenship Policy: Evidence from the Netherlands," *Journal of Common Market Studies* 39, No. 5 (2001).

25. That said, despite the initial objectives of the incoming Schröder government in 1998, dual citizenship is still not permitted for immigrants, and in fact the children of long-term legal foreign residents must choose either their parents' or German citizenship by the age of 23. In other words, the change was significant, but it was still partial in comparison with the original proposal. See Simon Green, "Beyond Ethnoculturalism? German Citizenship in the New Millennium," *German Politics* 9, No. 3 (2000): 105–124.

26. This latter point is strongly reinforced if one incorporates the policies of the 10 recent "accession" countries, which have quite restrictive citizenship policies. For a comparison of the accession countries and the EU-15, see Howard, "Variation in Dual Citizenship Policies."

27. As Christian Joppke has argued, proponents of the "convergence" thesis have exaggerated the extent to which liberal countries have imposed restrictions, but the general trend among the restrictive countries has certainly been in the direction of liberalization. See Joppke, "How Immigration Is Changing Citizenship: A Comparative View," *Ethnic and Racial Studies* 22, No. 4 (1999).

28. Sassen, *Losing Control?* and Saskia Sassen, "The de facto Transnationalizing of Immigration Policy," in *Challenge to the Nation-State*, ed. Christian Joppke (Oxford: Oxford University Press, 1998).

29. Alan Butt Philip, "European Union Immigration Policy: Phantom, Fantasy, or Fact," *West European Politics* 17, No. 2 (1994): 168–191.

30. Soysal, *Limits of Citizenship.*

31. Gary P. Freeman, "Migration Policy and Politics in the Receiving States," *International Migration Review* 26, No. 4 (1992): 1144–1167.

32. Christian Joppke, "Why Liberal States Accept Unwanted Immigration," *World Politics* 50, No. 2 (1998): 266–293.
33. Although there is of course some variation across countries, the striking finding in these surveys is that large numbers of people across the EU are quite hostile to immigrants. See European Monitoring Centre on Racism and Xenophobia, *Attitudes Towards Minority Groups in the European Union: A Special Analysis of the Eurobarometer 2000 Survey* (Vienna: European Monitoring Centre, 2001); and *European Social Survey* (2002), available at www.europeansocialsurvey.org.
34. Space limitations prevent me from showing these data, but there is absolutely no relationship between any of these factors and citizenship liberalization.
35. Christian Joppke, "Citizenship Between De- and Re-ethnicization," *European Journal of Sociology* 44, No. 3 (2003): 429–458.
36. It should be pointed out, however, that while the new law is certainly more restrictive than it was previously, Ireland still grants *jus soli* and in fact is still more liberal than most other countries, such as Germany, which have lengthier residency requirements for the parents of children born in the host country and sometimes include employment requirements that many poorer immigrants lack.
37. The same phenomenon has occurred repeatedly in Switzerland – including, most recently, in September 2004 – where voters have consistently rejected referenda that would liberalize the extremely restrictive Swiss citizenship law. And it should be added that Germany was close to passing a major liberalization (including full dual citizenship for immigrants) in 1998–1999, but this proposal was shelved after the opposition Christian Democrats resorted to an extremely successful petition campaign against dual citizenship that garnered five million signatures in a matter of weeks and succeeded in forcing the compromise law that took effect in 2000. See Green, "Beyond Ethnoculturalism?"
38. Of course, I have not addressed the important issue of what explains variation in the strength or weakness of Far Right movements, but not only does this question go beyond the scope of an analysis of the causes of variation and change in citizenship policies, it has also not yet been satisfactorily answered by specialists on this topic. For a powerful critique of this literature, along with a very convincing argument – based on the contrasting case studies of Germany and Austria – that focuses on public debates and the extent to which elites from all political parties and persuasions exclude and categorically reject the claims and strategies of the Far Right, see David Art, *The Politics of the Nazi Past in Germany and Austria* (Cambridge: Cambridge University Press, 2005).
39. For a more focused argument along these lines, see Marc Morjé Howard, "Can Populism Be Suppressed in a Democracy? Austria, Germany, and the European Union," *East European Politics and Societies* 15, No. 1 (2001): 27–30.

Index